THE FRIGHT OF REAL TEARS

THE FRIGHT OF REAL TEARS

Krzysztof Kieślowski between Theory and Post-Theory

Slavoj Žižek

bfi Publishing

First published in 2001 by the
British Film Institute
21 Stephen Street, London W1P 2LN

Reprinted 2001

The British Film Institute promotes greater understanding of, and access to, film and moving image culture in the UK.

Cover design: Paul Wright/Cube

Set in Italian Garamond by Fakenham Photosetting, Norfolk
Printed in England by St Edmundsbury Press, Bury St Edmunds, Suffolk

British Library Cataloguing-in-Publication Data
A catalogue record for this book is available from the British Library
ISBN 0 85170 754 8 pbk
ISBN 0 85170 755 6 hbk

Contents

Preface

This book grew out of a series of lectures that Slavoj Žižek delivered at London's National Film Theatre in the summer of 1998. My invitation to give these lectures had a very precise purpose. I wanted Slavoj to address the weaknesses and insularity of film studies as they had developed in the university sector over the previous two decades. The lectures were intended to mark the end of a cycle of work in which at every level from primary school to graduate studies, the BFI had attempted to place the study of the moving image at the centre of a revived and revised traditional curriculum. This had been the then newly-appointed director of the BFI Wilf Stevenson's aim in setting up a research division in 1989 and inviting me to head it.*

Most of the initiatives that followed took years of planning and preparation. I decided, however, that there was a speedy way of beginning the process of bringing thinking about cinema back into the intellectual mainstream and that was to invite as visiting fellows a series of thinkers who were centrally concerned with film but were not specialised film scholars; thinkers who kept closer to the contemporary form of our culture in which the image is encountered at every turn but in the most complicated of juxtapositions. Cornel West was the first visitor and he was followed by John Berger, Fredric Jameson, Marina Warner and bell hooks. In each of these cases the reason for the invitation was to bring to the Institute someone who was passionately engaged with film, but who placed it in the widest possible intellectual and cultural context. Žižek was the perfect final lecturer in this series because he had the closest professional contact with university film studies and I was thus able to ask him to address directly the problems of the narrowness and sterility of the university discipline that had promised so much a generation before.

If the creation of a separate discipline of film studies has enabled the carrying out of vital and important historical work, film theory itself has become less interesting within its new university home. It was Žižek himself in the early 90s who showed how film theory could be genuinely developed instead of banally rehashed or obtusely opposed. He is a thinker who understands absolutely that French theory of the 60s cannot be understood outside the intellectual context of the German philosophical tradition and, most importantly, Hegel and Heidegger. He is himself an intellectual who naturally inhabits the broad currents of European thought from which Lacan's paradoxical account of subjectivity came. In addition Žižek is absolutely immersed in the cinema – someone who understands films not as structures, which could illustrate this or that theoretical claim, but as living effective forms that themselves lucidly sketch out the structures of desire and lack that psychoanalysis theorises in less vivid terms. The priority that Žižek affords to the film text is wittily encapsulated in the title of one of his best-known works: *Everything You Always Wanted to Know about Lacan (But Were Afraid to Ask Hitchcock)*.

To give a full introduction to the range of Žižek's thinking and writing would require a book in itself but in giving an account of the initial context of this book it is impossible not to say a word about the extraordinary experience of hearing Žižek lecture. When as a young researcher I was investigating the Puritanism of the Civil War period, I never quite understood how a congregation could be so enthralled by a Puritan divine's three-hour sermon that, on its conclusion, they would beg and entreat the minister to continue. To hear Slavoj speak is to understand this reaction with ease. I have never seen anyone so obviously enthralled by the movement of thought, so determined to follow the logic of any concept or text through to its bitter or sweet end and to take his audience with him to that conclusion.

Žižek's work, and this book is as good and ambitious as anything he has done, could be taken as the exemplar for a project of renewing the study of cinema by intensifying its theoretical ambition. For those followers of fashion who look for a retreat from Marx and Freud, a hideous mimicking of the threadbare nonsense of the 'third way', this book will be a grave disappointment. This book intervenes in one of the most contemporary intellectual debates – concerning 'Post-Theory' and cognitivism – but it does so without ever abandoning questions of class struggle and the unconscious. Žižek's engagement with Post-Theory lays bare both its obvious fallacies and its more hidden vanities. He then goes on, via extended readings of Kieślowski's films, to offer a dazzling alternative that sacrifices neither the particularities of individual texts nor the nuances of broad philosophical argument. Like all of his work *The Fright of Real Tears* combines polemic and rigour, wit and insight. It makes clear that there can be no fundamental analysis of film which is not theoretically informed – but that theory must always revive itself in a real love of the cinema.

Colin MacCabe
Professor of English, Universities of Pittsburgh and Exeter
Head of Research, British Film Institute, 1989–98

* The most important element of this work was a research programme on literacy and the media conducted with King's College London. This programme was abandoned by the BFI when it was 'restructured' in the wake of New Labour's 1997 election victory. Also abandoned was the Master's programme directed by Laura Mulvey and the London Consortium, a taught Ph.D which linked the Institute with the Tate Gallery, the Architectural Association and Birkbeck College. Although all these initiatives continue in different forms, they no longer inform the work of the Institute. That was presumably the aim of Labour's anti-intellectual policy. For an overall account of the situation which saw many longserving members of staff, myself included, leave the Institute, see John Caughie and Simon Frith, 'The film institute and the rising tide: an interview with Colin MacCabe', *Screen* vol. 41 no. 1, Spring 2000, 51–66.

Introduction:
The Strange Case of the Missing Lacanians

If this book had been published twenty-five years ago, in the heyday of 'structuralist Marxism', its subtitle, undoubtedly, would have been 'On Class Struggle in Cinema'.

Let me begin by stating the obvious, with what in France they call *une verité de la Palice*: to put it in good old Maoist terms, the principal contradiction of today's cinema studies is the one between the deconstructionist/feminist/post-Marxist/psychoanalytic/sociocritical/cultural studies etc. approach, ironically nicknamed 'Theory' (which, of course, is far from a unified field – the above chain is more a series of Wittgensteinian 'family resemblances') by its opponents, and the so-called 'Post-Theory', the cognitivist and/or historicist reaction to it. Here, however, we immediately encounter a paradox. Although Post-Theorists acknowledge the inner differences in the field of Theory (say, between the early *Screen* focus on interpellation, Gaze, suture, and the later more historicist-culturalist feminist orientation), they nonetheless emphasise a common Lacanian element as central. They even acknowledge that the only unity of their own project is negative, that of excluding (Lacanian) psychoanalysis – David Bordwell and Noel Carroll made it clear, in their introduction to the *Post-Theory* volume, that '[t]he unifying principle in this book is that all the research included exemplifies the possibility of scholarship that is not reliant upon the psychoanalytic framework that dominates film academia.'[1] So who *are* these Lacanians? Post-Theorists like to emphasise that writers of Theory refer to mythical entities like the (capitalised) Gaze, entities to which no empirical, observable facts (like actual cinema viewers and their behaviour) correspond – one of the essays in the *Post-Theory* volume actually has the Sherlock Holmesian title 'Psychoanalytic Film Theory and the Problem of the Missing Spectator'.[2] In the same vein, I would like to claim that, in the global field designated by Post-Theorists as that of Theory, we are dealing with a no less mysterious 'case of the missing Lacanians': except for Joan Copjec, myself and some of my Slovene colleagues, I know of no cinema theorist who effectively accepts Lacan as his or her ultimate background. The authors usually referred to as Lacanians (from Laura Mulvey to Kaja Silverman) as a rule 'engage with' Lacan: they appropriate some Lacanian concepts as the best description of the universe of patriarchal domination, while emphasising that Lacan remained a phallogocentrist who uncritically accepted this universe as the only imaginable framework of our socio-symbolic existence. So, as a Lacanian, I seem to be caught in an unexpected double-bind: I am, as it were, being deprived of what I never possessed, made responsible for something others generated as Lacanian film theory. My response to this is, of course: what if one should finally give Lacan himself a chance? So, to continue in a Maoist vein, I am tempted to determine the opposition between the ambiguous reference to Lacan that has predominated in cinema studies and those who fully endorse Lacan as the second, non-antagonistic contradiction of cinema studies, to be resolved through discussion and self-criticism.

My second *lapalissade* is that these struggles point towards a global and much more far-reaching crisis in cultural studies. What looms in the background is a whole set of dilemmas, from the purely epistemological to politico-ideological ones: do cultural studies provide an adequate instrument to counteract global capitalism, or are they simply the ultimate expression of its cultural logic? Will cognitive scientists and other representatives of the so-called 'Third Culture' succeed in replacing cultural critics as the new model of 'public intellectuals'? That is to say, the antagonism between Theory and Post-Theory is a particular case of the global battle for intellectual hegemony and visibility between the exponents of post-modern/deconstructionist cultural studies and, on the other hand, cognitivists and popularisers of hard sciences, a battle which caught the attention of a wide public first through the so-called de Man affair (where the opponents endeavoured to prove the proto-Fascist irrationalist tendencies of deconstruction) and then through the Sokal–*Social Text* affair.

Such 'affairs' or 'scandals' should be taken much more seriously than is usually the case – they are part of a long tradition, consubstantial with philosophy itself. Did Socrates not cause a scandal which involved all – male, adult, free – citizens? Was this not the reason why he was condemned to death? Among later scandals one should mention at least the *Atheismusstreit* in Weimar in 1802, when Fichte, the German Idealist, had to resign his post because of his ethical teaching, which equated God with the ideal moral order of freedom and autonomy towards which humanity should strive (Goethe, the eternal conformist, interceded, imploring Fichte to compromise, and then raised his hands in despair at Fichte's stubborn attitude). So when some philosopher causes a scandal in the city, in his community, one should be wary of quickly dismissing it as a cheap affair of publicity that has nothing whatsoever to do with the inner truth of philosophising per se – as if the proper attitude of a philosopher were to sit alone in the pose of Rodin's thinker (who, if one were to complete the statue in a post-modern way, should undoubtedly be revealed to sit on a toilet). A much more serious thing is at stake: to put it in Hegelian terms, a properly *philosophical* scandal erupts when some philosophy effectively disturbs the very substance of the communal being, what Lacan referred to as the 'big Other', the shared implicit set of beliefs and norms that regulate our interaction.

The deception of 'scandals' is not so much that they are superficial public events, but that they *displace* the true dimension of the conflict. Let us take the two great 'scientific' scandals of the last two centuries: Darwin and Freud. The 'scandal' of Darwin's discovery is not the notion that humanity emerged from the animal kingdom through the natural process of evolution; rather, it resides in the more uncanny notion that evolution is not a gradual progressive movement, but a radically contingent emergence of new species with no objective measure which would allow us to prioritise them. In a similar vein, what is really 'scandalous' about the Freudian revolution is not the assertion of the central role of sexuality in human life, but, on the contrary, the assertion of the structurally *excessive and/or failed* character of human sexuality as opposed to animal mating.

And this holds more than ever for the most recent 'philosophical' scandal, the so-called Sloterdijk affair, which exploded in Germany in 1999, when a majority in the liberal media accused Peter Sloterdijk, the author who first became known twenty years ago with his *Critique of Cynical Reason*, of promoting the renewed Nazi agenda of genetic breeding to create a superior race. Whatever one thinks of Sloterdijk, what he actually did was expose the inability of the predominant left–liberal ethical stance (best embodied in Habermas's ethics of communicative action) to cope with the new challenges posed by the digitalisation of our daily lives and by the prospect of biogenetic interventions into the 'substance' of the human individual. Ultimately, all this traditional stance can offer are variations on the motif of limits not to be violated (in total accord with the Catholic Church's reaction): how far are we allowed to go? Where should we stop? In short, this stance is reactive and protective: it accepts the inherited notion of 'humanity', and then goes on to tackle the question: what limits should we impose on new technologies so that the essence of 'humanity' will not be threatened? The real question to be addressed is exactly the opposite one: how do the new technologies compel us to redefine this very standard inherited notion of 'humanity'? Is a person whose genome is exposed to technological manipulation still fully 'human', and if yes, in what does his/her freedom reside? The true site of the scandal is thus again displaced: the need to rethink the very notion of what is human.

And, at a different level, the same goes for the so-called Sokal–*Social Text* affair. What was actually at stake in it? When Alan Sokal's essay for *Social Text* was revealed to be a parody, my first thought was: would it not be even simpler for a Lacanian to write an inverted parody, i.e. to imitate convincingly the standard scientistic commonsense critical rejection of post-modern deconstructionism? Then, after reading the book Alan Sokal co-wrote with Jean Brichmont, *Impostures intellectuelles,*[3] in which the two authors propose a detailed 'serious' denunciation of the way selected 'post-modern' authors (from Lacan to Baudrillard) refer to 'hard' sciences, especially mathematics and physics, it suddenly struck me that this book, although meant to be taken seriously by its authors, already *is* this parody (does its characterisation of opponents not as a rule amount to a caricaturalised version of what post-modern Theory is?). And the same goes for the large majority of the Post-Theory attacks on Theory: does what they describe as Theory, or what they attribute to Theory, not read as a comically simplified caricature of Lacan, Althusser et al.? Can one really take seriously Noel Carroll's description of Gaze theorists? Nonetheless, there is, for precisely this reason, a positive function of Post-Theory for Theorists: Theory often does degenerate into jargon. Thus what we get in Post-Theory by way of a description of a Theory is not simply a misunderstanding or misreading. It confronts us with a certain deconstructionist 'post-modern' ideology that accompanies Theory proper as its indelible shadow. In doing this, Post-Theory compels us to define in precise terms where we stand, and to draw – in an unabashedly Platonic way – a line of separation between Theory proper and its jargonistic imitation.

On 26 January 1999, Cardinal Medina Estevez presented to the public on behalf of the Vatican the new version of the Catholic Church's manual on exorcism, *De Exorcismis et supplicationibus quibusdam* (in Latin, but soon to be translated in modern languages). The interest of this volume resides in its reference to Freud: it emphasises the need to distinguish between authentic possession by the Devil (when its victim fluently and inexplicably speaks unknown languages, violates physical laws, etc.) and phenomena that are merely expressions of the human mind taking a pathological turn – and in order to distinguish between the two, psychoanalysis can be of help. So when someone claims to be possessed by the Devil, one should first send him to an analyst to exclude the possibility that we are dealing with a mere subjective delusion. A similar constraining of the scope of psychoanalysis is often at work in so-called 'applied psychoanalysis' – psychoanalysis can explain a lot, like the psychic background of a work of art, but not its essence ... This attitude is the falsest of them all, worse than any cognitivist outright rejection of psychoanalysis, which at least has the merit of pushing us to confront our own platitudes.

Some months before writing this, at an art round table, I was asked to comment on a painting I had seen there for the first time. I did not have *any* idea about it, so I engaged in a total bluff, which went something like this: the frame of the painting in front of us is not its true frame; there is another, invisible, frame, implied by the structure of the painting, which frames our perception of the painting, and these two frames do not overlap – there is an invisible gap separating the two. The pivotal content of the painting is not rendered in its visible part, but is located in this dislocation of the two frames, in the gap that separates them. Are we, today, in our post-modern madness, still able to discern the traces of this gap? Perhaps more than the reading of a painting hinges on it; perhaps the decisive dimension of humanity will be lost when we lose the capacity to discern this gap ... To my surprise, this brief intervention was a huge success, and many following participants referred to the dimension in-between-the-two-frames, elevating it into a term. This very success made me sad, really sad. What I encountered here was not only the efficiency of a bluff, but a much more radical apathy at the very heart of today's cultural studies.

A little over 200 years ago, at the zenith of early modernity, Immanuel Kant grounded the greatest revolution in the history of philosophy in a shocking experience of the so-called antinomies of pure reason: with regard to the most fundamental questions of our existence, our reasoning unavoidably gets caught in a series of antinomies – the two opposed, mutually exclusive conclusions (there is God and there is no God; there is a free will and there is no free will) can both be demonstrated. For Kant, as is well known, the way out of this epistemological shock was through practical reason: when I am engaged in an ethical act, I resolve the antinomy in practice and display my free will.

Today, however, our experience confronts us with a different set of antinomies. But, these antinomies have lost their ability to shock us: the two opposed poles are simply left to coexist. Already in the 20s, the epistemological crisis generated by quantum mechanics was not really resolved: the predominant attitude of today's quantum physicists is: 'Who cares about ontological questions concerning the reality of observed phenomena, the main thing is that the quantum formulae function!' And the same goes for the Freudian unconscious and other epistemological shocks: they are simply accepted and neutralised, and business goes on as usual. The personification of the contemporary subject is perhaps the Indian computer programmer who, during the day, excels in his expertise, while in the evening, upon returning home, lights a candle to the local Hindu divinity and respects the sacredness of the cow. What we encounter here is a certain radical split: we have the objectivised language of experts and scientists that can no longer be translated into the common language accessible to everyone, but is present in it in the mode of fetishised formulae that no one really understands, but which shape our artistic and popular imaginary (Black Hole, Big Bang, Superstrings, Quantum Oscillation). The gap between scientific insight and common sense is unbridgeable, and it is this very gap which elevates scientists into the popular cult-figures of the 'subjects supposed to know' (the Stephen Hawking phenomenon). The strict obverse of this scientific objectivity is the way in which, in cultural matters, we are confronted with the multitude of life-styles which cannot be translated into each other: all we can do is secure the conditions for their tolerant coexistence in a multicultural society.

The present book approaches these deadlocks at three levels. Through critical dialogue with cognitivist/historicist Post-Theory as well as with standard deconstructionist cinema theory, the first part endeavours to demonstrate that the reading of Lacan operative in the 70s and 80s was a reductive one – there is 'another Lacan' reference to whom can contribute to the revitalisation of the cinema theory (and of critical thought in general) today. This general approach is followed by an interpretation of the film-maker the very mention of whom triggers an immense aesthetico-ideological controversy: Krzysztof Kieślowski. Against the standard 'post-modernist' as well as the now fashionable 'post-secular' obscurantist readings, I endeavour to demonstrate how his work, the site of antagonistic ideological tensions, of the 'class struggle in art', can be redeemed by a Lacanian approach. The second part analyses the fundamental motifs that run through Kieślowski's entire opus, while the third part proposes a detailed reading of his three main achievements: the *Decalogue* series (1988); *The Double Life of Véronique* (1991); the *Colours* (1993–4) trilogy.

Kieślowski definitely belongs to *Mitteleuropa*; if one is to look for the identity of this spectral entity, dismissed by many either as a purely geographic notion or as the product of reactionary nostalgia, one of the keys to it is a series of strange cultural phenomena from the turn-of-the-century novels of Karl May to the Irish folk-rock band The Kelly Family. Karl May's adventure novels (the most popular ones take place in an imagined American West, with the narrator Old Shatterhand – May himself in disguise – and the Apache chief Winnetou as their main heroes) were immensely popular throughout the entire twentieth century; in the mid-90s, the popularity of The Kelly Family's kitschy, family-values idealised 'Irish' songs surpassed that of all of the main Anglo-American bands, with a key proviso: in both cases, *the success was geographically limited to the precise confines of 'Central Europe'*: Germany, Austria, Poland, the Czech Republic, Hungary, Croatia and Slovenia. If nothing else, this shared image of the Other (of the imagined American West or Ireland) demonstrates that there *is* something to the notion of 'Central Europe' as a common cultural-ideological space. Does this mean, however, that, in order to understand Kieślowski properly, we should locate him in the unique historical context of the disintegration of Middle European real socialism – in short, that only somebody well attuned to the life-world of Poland in the 80s (ultimately: only a Pole) can 'really understand' Kieślowski?

The first thing that strikes the eye of a viewer aware of the historical circumstances in which *Decalogue* – the series of ten one-hour TV films, arguably Kieślowski's masterpiece – was shot, is the total absence of any reference to politics: although the series was shot in the most turbulent period of post-World War II Polish history (the state of emergency imposed by General Jaruzelski's *coup d'état* in order to curb Solidarity), one cannot but admire Kieślowski's heroic ascetism, his resistance to scoring easy points by spicing up the story with dissident thrills. Of course, it is not only legitimate, but also necessary, to inquire into the concrete social conditions within which Kieślowski accomplished the turn from socio-political concerns to more global ethico-religious ones: the fundamental lesson of dialectics is that universality as such emerges, is articulated 'for itself', only within a set of particular conditions. (All great historical assertions of *universal* values, from Ancient Roman Stoicism to modern human rights, are firmly embedded in a *concrete* social constellation.) However, one should avoid here the historicist trap: this unique circumstance does not account for the 'truth' and universal scope of the analysed phenomenon. It is precisely against such hasty historicisers that one should refer to Marx's famous observation apropos of Homer: it is easy to explain how Homer's poetry emerged from early Greek society; what is much more difficult to explain is its universal appeal, i.e. why it continues to exert its charm even today. And, *mutatis mutandis*, the same goes for Kieślowski: it is easy to identify his 'roots' in the unique moment of Polish socialism in decay; it is much more difficult to explain the universal appeal of his work, the way his films touch the nerves of people who have no idea whatsoever about the specific circumstances of Poland in the 80s.

Kieślowski is often (mis)perceived as a director whose work is falsified the moment one translates its content into the terms of a (social, religious, psychoanalytic) interpretation – one should simply immerse oneself in it and enjoy it intuitively, not talk about it, not apply to it the terms which irreparably reify its true content ... Such a resistance to Theory is often shared by the artists who feel hurt or misunderstood by the theoretical explanations of their work, and who insist on the distinction between *doing* something and *describing* it, talking *about* it: the critic's or theorist's discourse about the anxiety or pleasure discernible in a work of art just talks about them, it does not directly *render* them, and in this sense it is deeply *irrelevant* to the work itself. However, in all fairness, one should bear in mind that the same distinction holds also for Theory itself: in philosophy, it is one thing to talk about, to report on, say, the history of the notion of subject (accompanied by all the proper bibliographical footnotes), even to supplement it with comparative critical remarks; it is quite another thing to work in theory, to elaborate the notion of 'subject' itself.[4] The aim of this book is to do the same apropos of Kieślowski: not to talk *about* his work, but to refer to his work in order to accomplish the *work* of Theory. In its very ruthless 'use' of its artistic pretext, such a procedure is much more faithful to the interpreted work than any superficial respect for the work's unfathomable autonomy.

Part One

THE UNIVERSAL: SUTURE REVISITED

Chapter One
Universality and its Exception

If I were to quote one name which is emblematic of the present-day state of cinema theory, it is Ben Brewster, well known in the 60s as a hardline theorist, member of the editorial board of *Screen*, the English translator of Althusser's texts on ideology and Interpellation which formed the very basis of Theory, who later turned into a 'pure' cinema historian, focusing on early cinema prior to 1917 – that is to say, significantly, prior to the October Revolution, as if to emphasise the will to obliterate the trauma of the failed leftist involvement in Theory.[1] It is effectively this incredible coincidence – the year of the October Revolution was also the year when 'classical' film-making was consolidated into a unified aesthetic practice – that, perhaps, provides the key to the impact of a lot of Post-Theory: the enthusiastic professionalism of Post-Theory is often sustained by a stance of profound political resignation, by a will to obliterate the traces and disappointments of political engagement. Restricting oneself to pre-1917 cinema involves a kind of fetishistic disavowal, an expression of the will to halt one's view just prior to hitting the traumatic spot that discloses the Other's castration, like Freud's fetishist who, in his attachment to feet, stops his gaze just prior to perceiving the feminine genitalia. The exclusive preoccupation with pre-1917 cinema is thus, in its very formalist and/or historicist disavowal of political engagement, a gesture of ultimate *fidelity* to Revolution, like the brass-band players in *Brassed Off* (1996) who continue to play even when they lose their jobs, their attachment to 'pure', depoliticised music expressing their fidelity to the lost political cause. The problem is that, with standard Post-Theory's turn to academic professionalism, this inherent traumatic disavowal of – and fidelity to – Revolution gets lost: unlike Ben Brewster, they simply go the 'full monty' in getting rid of the last vestiges of an engaged leftist attitude.

For the cognitivist Post-Theorists, the demise of Theory is experienced as a relief from a nightmarish burden: finally, we are no longer terrorised by Grand Theoretical notions, we are free to approach a particular problem without having to possess an articulate TOE (Theory Of Everything) . . . Although Post-Theorists can sometimes alert us to the element of state dogma in Theory, this sense of 'being released from the nightmarish burden of Theory' is false, since it relies on a kind of retroactive undoing of the traumatic past: the price paid for it is that (Post-)Theory starts to behave as if there were no Marx, Freud, semiotic theory of ideology, i.e. as if we can magically return to some kind of naiveté before things like the unconscious, the overdetermination of our lives by the decentred symbolic processes, and so forth became part of our theoretical awareness. Furthermore, is (deconstructionist) Theory really a new version of the TOE? We should be very precise on this point. Post-Theorists basically reproach Theory with two opposite, mutually exclusive deficiencies: on the one hand, Theory is a new version of the global TOE (against which one should assert *theories* (in the plural): modest, mid-level, empirically verifiable research programmes); on the other hand, Theory involves a cognitive suspension characteristic of historicist relativism: Theorists no longer ask the basic questions like 'What is the nature of cinematic perception?', they simply tend to reduce such questions to the historicist reflection upon the conditions in which certain notions emerged as the result of historically specific power relations. The paradoxical result is that cultural studies share with Post-Theory a rejection of the big metaphysical TOE, although from a different standpoint (not mid-level empirically tested knowledge, but historical relativism and local knowledge).

Does this mean, however, that the only alternative to these two positions, i.e. to mid-level empirical research and cultural studies historical relativism, is the old-fashioned metaphysical TOE? Here, a proper *dialectical* approach offers a way out of the predicament. The key feature of this approach concerns the paradoxical relationship between universality and its constitutive exception. Post-Theorists often claim to pursue a dialectical path; this claim, at least, should be flatly rejected. What Post-Theorists mean by a 'dialectical approach' is simply the notion of cognition as the gradual progress of our always limited knowledge through the testing of specific hypotheses. For example, when Noel Carroll claims that 'the fundamental framework for film theory is dialectical', and emphasises 'the need for film theorizing to become more conscious of its dialectical responsibilities', his notion of 'dialectics' involves two interconnected theses: firstly, theories are always defended through a dialogue with opposing theories, by demonstrating that they succeed where alternative theories fail, i.e. that they do a better job answering the questions posed by competing views; secondly, this process is unending, so that no theory can claim to provide the ultimate standpoint – instead of one big theory critically dismissing all the others, one should endorse a modest view of endless competitive struggle.[2] Well, if this is dialectics, then Karl Popper, the most aggressive and dismissive critic of Hegel, was the greatest dialectician of them all!

What separates dialectics proper from its cognitivist version is the way the subject's position of enunciation is included, inscribed, into the process: the cognitivist speaks from the safe position of the excluded observer who knows the relativity and limitation of all human knowledge, including his own. What, exactly, does this mean? There are different modes of saying, 'I'm lying'. When I say, 'The theory (which I am deploying) is just an impotent mental construct, while real life persists outside,' or engage in similar modes of referring to the wealth of pre-theoretical experience, the apparent modesty of such statements harbours the arrogant position of enunciation of the subject who assumes the capacity to compare a theory with 'real life'. When, in a similar vein, I present my intervention in a debate as a 'modest contribution', I again imply the arrogant position of enunciation from which I can afford such a deprecating self-designation. For this very reason, the only proper way to counter such statements is to take them more literally than they were meant: 'Actually, what you're saying *is* just a modest contribution!', or, to paraphrase Freud, 'Why are you saying that you're only giving a modest opinion, when what you're giving is only a modest opinion?' The crucial point is: which position of enunciation is involved in the statement 'What I am saying now is a lie'? If this position is safely exempted from the content, the statement is a lie; if the subject is himself/herself included in the content, admitting the falsity of his/her very position of enunciation – and such is the case in what Hegel, in his *Phenomenology of Spirit*, calls *despairing* (*Verzweiflung*) as opposed to the simple *doubt* (*Zweifel*) – we have the effect of truth. Hegel is thus far from simply varying the old Pascalean motif according to which man's greatness resides in the fact that he is a mere particle of dust, but a particle that *knows* itself as such: once I know that, in my objective being, I am just a particle of dust, I sooner or later have to concede that my subjectivity is *not even that* . . .

Consequently, when Post-Theory insists on clear theoretical classifications and gradual generalisations based on careful empirical research, one should bear in mind that this apparently modest position involves a much more immoderate position of enunciation of the Post-Theorist himself/herself as the observer exempted from the object of his/her study.

This immoderate aspect is clearly discernible apropos of the status of *universality*. The prototypical procedure of Post-Theorists is, say, Jerrold Levinson's with regard to music (enumerating its seven principal functions)[3] or Bordwell's to shot/reverse shot procedure (accounted for by a series of levels from direct physiological reactions through contingent universals to culturally specified, codified procedures).[4] In arguing for his 'problem-solution model' of explaining the predominance of certain stylistic procedures, Bordwell comments on the longevity of the 'classic' continuity established in the 1910s:

> If we cannot imagine a widely accessible filmmaking practice that does not utilize this set of norms, it may be because it has proved itself well suited to telling moderately complicated stories in ways that are comprehensible to audiences around the world.[5]

This claim nonetheless begs a series of questions: is there a neutral notion of a (moderately complicated) story? Is not modern (post-Renaissance) Western culture characterised by its own specific notion of narrative (which is why, say, Chinese or Japanese novels often strike us Western readers as 'dull' and 'confused')? And is there a neutral, global notion of what is 'comprehensible'? The status of narrative in cinema is much more fragile than it may appear: suffice it to recall the recent crisis of narrative, where we witness a kind of unexpected return to the early 'cinema of attractions' – big blockbusters have to rely more and more on the wild rhythm of spectacular special effects, and the only narrative which seems still to be able to sustain the viewer's interest is, significantly, that of the conspiracy theory. (Although Cameron's *Titanic* [1997] is praised as the return to the good old pre-deconstructionist romantic narrative, it can also be seen as the ultimate proof of narrative failure: one way to read the film is that the iceberg strikes in order to save us from unavoidable narrative deadlock – imagine what a boring film *Titanic* would be if it just continued as a love story between Jack and Rose).[6]

The same goes for Bordwell's other popular trans-cultural universal, the function of 'directing and guiding the spectator's attention': does the fact that a non-Western (or even a medieval Western) painting can appear to us extremely confusing not indicate that there are no simple trans-cultural functions of guiding attention? In short, while the problem-solution model of historical research can undoubtedly lead to a lot of precise and enlightening insights, one should nonetheless insist that the procedures of posing problems and finding solutions to them always and by definition occur within a certain ideological context that determines which problems are crucial and which solutions acceptable. It is, to put it in the simplest possible terms, like the old reproach that spoons in Chinese restaurants are clumsy: are our standard Western spoons not far more appropriate if we want to finish our soup as quickly and effortlessly as possible? If we answer 'yes' to this question, do we not attribute to the Chinese a rather strange sort of stupidity?

So while Bordwell and other Post-Theorists like to distinguish trans-cultural universal features (part of our evolutionary heritage and the psychic structure of human beings) from features that are specific to particular cultures and periods – i.e. to operate with a simple pyramid from natural or other trans-cultural universal features to more and more specific characteristics that depend on localised contexts – the elementary counter-argument to it is that the very relationship between trans-cultural universals and culture-specific features is not an ahistorical constant, but historically overdetermined: *the very notion of a trans-cultural universal means different things in different cultures*. The procedure of comparing different cultures and isolating or identifying their common features is never a neutral procedure, but presupposes some specific viewpoint – say, while one can claim that all cultures recognise some kind of difference between subjective imagination and reality – things as they exist out there – this assertion still begs the question of what 'objective reality' means in different cultures: when a European says that 'ghosts don't exist in reality' and when a Native American says that he communicates with them and that they therefore do exist in reality, does 'reality' mean the same thing for them? Is not our notion of 'really existing' (which relies on the opposition between *is* and *ought*, between *being* and *values*) specific to modernity?

To take a further example from Bordwell himself,[7] while depth of field has of course been operative from the early 'cinema of attractions' through the elaborate theatrical settings of around 1910 and the Eisensteinian or Wellesian wide-angle contrast between the aggressively protruding foreground figure and the distorted background, up to different versions in today's cinema, this (abstractly) 'same' procedure is not simply 'the same', since it is each time 'trans-functionalised', included in a different, historically specific totality. The key point is that it is misleading to conceive of these concrete figurations of depth of field as subspecies of the universal genus: the totality which accounts for their specific meaning is the 'mediated' totality of each historical epoch of cinematic style, the way depth of field is located in the articulated whole of stylistic procedures. Suffice it to recall how a simple fact of soundtrack can totally change the situation of the visual depth of field, allowing the director to focus the attention of the spectator by vocal information; or how, in the famous shot from Wyler's *Little Foxes* (1941), a minus dialectically reverts into a plus, i.e. the very blurred, out-of-focus background, instead of signalling the relative unimportance of what goes on there, is the place where, tantalisingly inaccessible to the spectator's clear view, the crucial event – the fatal heart attack – takes place.

Orson Welles goes even further than Wyler in this direction. We all remember Bazin's famous analysis of the long take of the kitchen table from *The Magnificent Ambersons* (1941), in which George prattles while voraciously eating his cake, with Fanny silently sitting at his side. The real emotional focus of the shot (Fanny's silent breakdown) stands out against the 'pretext action', George's incessant double oral activity of eating and talking – an exemplary case of how the viewer must scan the screen and locate the true focus of the action by to some extent ignoring the lure of the centre of activity.[8] This scene could have also been shot in the vein of the famous lines from Proust's *Un amour de Swann* which describe the catastrophic effects Odette's prattle about her love life has on Swann by limiting itself to Odette and rendering only the way she herself perceives the effect of her words on Swann. Let us imagine the same scene from *Ambersons* as a subjective shot from Fanny's perspective, focusing on George's insensitive, voracious eating and prattle: at some point, some small change (a slight trembling of the camera or George casting a perplexed cast at it, i.e. at Fanny) should give us a clue indicating that his words have had a catastrophic effect on the person from whose point of view we observe the score.

The suppressed final scene of *The Magnificent Ambersons* would probably have been Welles's ultimate masterpiece, bringing this effect to an unbearably powerful extreme. Eugene (Joseph Cotten) goes to visit Fanny (Agnes Moorehead), who lives bitter and alone in a cheap boarding house. Eugene speaks to her in elated terms about the reconciliation between George and Lucy, and how, in a deeper spiritual sense, this new couple also redeems through repetition the failed love between him and Isabel, George's mother. However, the key feature is that there is no proper dialogue between Eugene and Fanny, who loves him: immersed in his spiritual hectoring, Eugene is totally blind to Fanny's utter despair and bitterness and her sense of lost life:

> As filmed, Agnes Moorehead's participation in the exchange was so minimal that the scene became virtually a monologue for Eugene punctuated and punctured with dissonant elements – the creaking of Fanny's rocking chair and the distant playing on a phonograph record of a comic vaudeville patter.[9]

We can imagine the scene shot in long takes of Eugene, unable to perceive the cruel, devastating effect of his words – this despair being signalled to us spectators only through the disturbing background sounds ... Everything is here: the official redemptive 'happy ending' that is denounced in its own terms as male obsession erasing the true victim from the picture.

What we are dealing with here is the Hegelian 'concrete universality', which is not the result of gradual empirical generalisation or the patient search for common features, but – what? Let us take the case of cross-cutting. Bordwell demonstrates how this procedure asserted its predominance after a period of trial-and-error oscillation when it coexisted with the alternative procedure of showing first, in a long take, the entire course of action from the outside, and then, in another long take, the same action from the inside. Although temporality overlapped here, i.e. although we were shown twice what went on at the same diegetic 'real' time, the procedure was accepted as 'natural'. For example, there are two versions of an early film about firemen saving a family from their house on fire: one version is done in (what is now considered) the standard cross-cutting manner, while the other first shows in a long take the suffering family in the house, and then in another long take from outside the burning house the efforts of the firemen to break in and take them out.[10]

From this standpoint, Griffith's *Intolerance* (1916) is of special interest, insofar as it not only contains the standard example of cross-cutting conveying the last-minute rescue, but, in a kind of *redoubled* cross-cutting, goes to the opposite excess and practises cross-cutting not only inside its main narrative line, but between four different narrative lines – Griffith called this procedure a 'cinematic fugue'. That is to say, *Intolerance* endeavours to make its points about the catastrophic consequences of intolerance in four episodes, usually referred to as 'The Modern Story' (the story of a low-class family, in which the young father is wrongly condemned to death and the mother deprived of the child as being unfit to raise him); 'The Judean Story' (three episodes from Christ's life, culminating in the Crucifixion); 'The French Story' (a Huguenot French family falls victim to the Catholic intrigues during the St Bartholomew's Day Massacre); and 'The Babylonian Story' (the fall of the good King Belshazzar when Babylon is attacked by the evil Persians and the Babylonian enemies of the King). These four episodes, covering sacred, ancient, medieval and modern times, are not presented one after another, but in a parallel interchange (another example of this is Coppola's *The Godfather, Part II* [1974], which interchanges the prequel and the sequel to *The Godfather* [1972]), so that, towards the end, the three past catastrophes (the Crucifixion, the fall of Babylon, St Bartholomew's Day Massacre) are shown in interchange with the present-day last-minute rescue. Significantly, only the present events end happily, with the husband reunited with his wife. We have thus an intricate dramaturgy of a present-day happy outcome played against the fantasmatic background of three mythical and/or historical past catastrophic outcomes – the procedure practised in the same years at a 'higher' artistic level in modernism (from Stravinsky's *Sacre du printemps* to Joyce's *Ulysses*) is here given a specific twist, since the actual present-day real-life events deny, i.e. *melodramatically* invert, the tragic patterns on which they rely.

What makes Griffith's cross-cutting of such interest is the way this procedure, although universally applied to create tension by showing alternately the two codependent courses of action, is in his work obviously anchored in a very specific situation that serves as its paradigmatic case: that of the so-called last-minute chase, in which a saviour comes to the rescue of the victim under siege at the very last moment. Suffice it to mention four examples, which are also the climactic points of the four films in question. First, of course, the legendary sequence from *The Birth of a Nation* (1915), in which the Ku Klux Klan riders come to the rescue of the white family in a lone cottage besieged by the mob of liberated black slaves; then, in *Intolerance,* a wife and a policeman in a car racing to reach the prison in time to prevent the husband's hanging (he was wrongly condemned to death and the wife has just obtained the Governor's pardon after the true culprit was arrested); then, in *Way Down East* (1920), perhaps the most spectacular one, the desperate endeavour of the lover who jumps from one unstable melting ice floe to another to save his beloved (Lilian Gish) who, lying half unconscious on another ice floe, is being carried by a fast current towards a deadly waterfall; finally, in *Orphans of the Storm* (1922), Danton with his military escort riding like mad through the streets of Paris in order to prevent the unjust killing of the heroine who is already tied to the guillotine. Of course, this anchoring of cross-cutting in the last-minute-rescue scenario does not forever seal the fate of cross-cutting. Cross-cutting functions as a 'floating signifier': although generated in this concrete, fantasmatic scenario, it cut itself off and was reappropriated for a series of other paradigms which are in no way grounded in the last-minute-rescue scenario. Is, for example, cross-cutting not appropriate to emphasise class distinction – say, to present the same event (a dance, a social gathering, a seduction scene) alternatively in its upper-class and in its lower-class version? A dialectical history of cross-cutting, presenting this notion in its 'concrete universality', would consist precisely in the deployment of the successive forms of particular fantasmatic scenarios which hegemonised this universal procedure.

The libidinal economy underlying the last-minute-rescue matrix relies on the fetishistic split of *je sais bien, mais quand même* ... : although we know very well that the rescuer will arrive just in time to save the victim, we nonetheless feel extreme tension, as if the possibility that the catastrophic outcome will realise itself is a serious one. (*Superman* [1978] contains an ironic-reflexive redoubling of this code: our expectation is disappointed: he *does* come too late to save his beloved Lois, who suffocates in her car under the avalanche of mud; however, in order to undo the catastrophe and thus prevent the disintegration of the entire cinematic code, he has to do – and he can do it, since he is Superman – the impossible: he turns time backwards to just before the deadly avalanche and this time arrives at the scene of catastrophe early enough to save Lois.) The procedure of last-minute rescue is thus a paradigmatic case of what is usually referred to as narrative closure: the hero can by definition *never* arrive too late to save the innocent victims under siege, i.e. the danger of his coming too late can be evoked only insofar as we are sure in advance that it will not be realised. It is in violating this rule, much more than in its 'politically correct', anti-capitalist and multiculturalist approach to the colonisation of the American West, that resides the subversive sting of Cimino's underrated masterpiece *Heaven's Gate* (1980). In its climactic scene, the hero (Kris Kristofferson) *does* arrive too late, after the settlers under siege by the company's mercenaries, including his lover, have already been slaughtered.[11] Therein resides the obvious *ideological* investment of last-minute-chase sequences and, consequently, also of cross-cutting whose paradigmatic case is a last-minute-chase sequence. (A more detailed analysis would have to identify as the underlying theme of the last-minute-chase sequence that of death and sexuality: the rescuer has to arrive in time to prevent the death of the innocent victims and/or to prevent their rape. No wonder that the paradigmatic Griffithian place which awaits rescuers is a lone home cottage: the underlying scenario of the last-minute rescue is that of a miraculous external force saving our home from the threat of our aggressive enemies. It is even possible to establish here a link with Tarkovsky: isn't the home cottage under threat and awaiting a rescuer Griffith's version of Tarkovsky's famous wooden datcha? It is well known that Griffith modelled these cottages after his family house in Kentucky.)[12]

In philosophy proper, it is with regard to this key feature that, perhaps, Derrida's outstanding reading of Hegel in his *Glas* misses the point.[13] Derrida focuses on the inconsistency of Hegel's reading of *Antigone*: although Hegel claims that Antigone defends family and its rights against state power, her privileging of the attachment to her brother explodes the family framework. (In her famous problematic statement, she claims that all other losses – of her parents, husband and children – could be endured; the only truly irreplaceable loss is that of a brother.) What emerges here, in the very midst of family, is an excessive attachment that cannot be contained within the framework of family 'mediations'. Derrida's operation, of course, is here double: not only does he emphasise the excess of Antigone's attachment with regard to the 'closed' economy of the family, at the same time, he proposes the family as the underlying matrix of the entire Hegelian system which, ultimately, always turns out to be *une affaire de famille*, a movement of sublating/incorporating every otherness into the 'familiar' network.

The problem with this reading is simply its *iterability*: upon a close inspection, it soon becomes clear that *every* determinate figure of the dialectical process engenders a strictly homologous excess that explodes 'familiar' closure (are phrenology, the terror of absolute negativity, etc., in phenomenology, not the names of the same excess?). So when Derrida proposes the family network and its excess as the underlying matrix of the entire process, one should counter this thesis not by rejecting it, but by multiplying it: *each and every* determinate figure of the dialectical process can, in its turn, be elevated into the matrix of the entire process. (Again, to stay within phenomenology, there is a whole series of attempts to do exactly this, starting with Jean Wahl's privileging of the 'unhappy consciousness' way back in the 20s, and Alexandre Kojeve's privileging of the struggle for life and death of the (future) Lord and Bondsman in the 30s.)

This, then, is the Hegelian 'concrete universality': at every stage of the dialectical process, the concrete figure 'colours' the totality of the process, i.e. the universal frame of the process becomes part of (or, rather, drawn into) the particular content.[14] To put it in Ernesto Laclau's terms, at every stage its particular content is not only a subspecies of the universality of the total process: it 'hegemonises' this very universality, the 'dialectical process' is nothing but the name for this permanent shift of the particular content which 'hegemonises' the universality.

For a long time Germans perceived themselves as an aberrant ('delayed') nation, becoming a 'normal' nation only today, after the reunification in 1990 (i.e. at the very moment when national sovereignty became obsolescent in the face of advancing globalisation and new, supra-national politico-economic formations like the European Union). However, in a properly dialectical approach, the question 'Which nation is fully normal (in Hegelese: fully fits the notion of Nation)?' should be reversed into: 'Is nation itself something normal, an obvious form of communal life, or a monstrous exception, a modern aberration?' In such a dialectical reversal – what Hegel called the double, self-relating negation – the gap that separates every particular nation from its ideal notion is reflected into this notion itself, as its inherent, internal split and hindrance.

Universality thus relates in a different way to its different species: a Russian is still a 'typical Russian', while what is 'typical' of an American is rather that he does *not* consider himself 'typical' at all, but perceives himself as an eccentric individual – it is typical for an American 'individualist' to perceive himself as atypical . . . Or, with regard to cuisine: each country has its own particular cuisine, but there are cities whose particular cuisine is the modified version of other particular cuisines (a New Yorker eats pizzas and Chinese food, etc.). Underlying it is, of course, the process of the modern 'reflexivisation' of cuisine, where the choice between (artificially recreated and transformed) traditions, not tradition itself, becomes the rule, so that sticking to one's own particular traditional cuisine, far from functioning as the zero-level or starting point, is considered the most eccentric choice.

When Bordwell discusses the gradual establishment of the standard Hollywood narrative code, he himself provides some good examples of this dialectic: Griffith did not 'invent' cross-cutting, close-ups, shot/counter-shot, etc.; these procedures were already there in the pre-narrative 'cinema of attractions', where they served other purposes. What Griffith and others did was to 'transfunctionalise' (or, as Gould would have put it, not so much to adapt as to 'exapt') these procedures, to put them in the service of the psychologically realist narrative line. (For example, in the early 'cinema of attractions', a close-up served the purpose of focusing the viewer's attention to the key element of the global tableau, without involving a narrative dynamic.)[15] New historicists in cinema theory like to emphasise the diversity of problem-solving trial and error procedures and inventions: the history of cinema was not a gradual pseudo-Hegelian unfolding of its essence, but a bric-a-brac of overdetermined solutions that could easily also have turned in a different direction; invaluable as these precise insights are, they should nonetheless be supplemented with the proper *conceptual* analysis. Or, to put it in (anti-Hegelian) Althusserian terms, one should make the step from the empirical multitude to *articulation*, to the concrete totality within which particular solutions work (or fail to work). Recall Ernesto Laclau's analysis of Fascism: any of the elements that constitute the Fascist ideology (anti-establishment populism; anti-democratic authoritarian ethics of self-sacrifice; fierce nationalism; economic corporatism; anti-Semitism) can also be incorporated into a different, non-Fascist, edifice, i.e. the presence of any or all of these elements does not guarantee that we are dealing with Fascism – what makes Fascism Fascism is a specific *articulation* of (some of) these elements into a distinctly flavoured 'Fascist' ideological field.[16]

Is, however, the end-point of this argument not a kind of redoubled historicism, in which the very universality is caught in the process of its historical specification? At this point, one should accomplish the crucial step forward which only brings us to the proper dialectical procedure, practised by Hegel as well as in Freud's great case studies, the procedure which can be best described as a direct jump from the singular to the universal, by-passing the mid-level of particularity so dear to Post-Theorists:

> In its dialectic of a clinical case, psychoanalysis is a field in which the singular and the universal coincide without passing through the particular. This is not common in philosophy, with the exception, perhaps, of certain Hegelian moments.[17]

When Freud deals with a case of claustrophobia, he always starts the search for some *singular* traumatic experience which is at the root of this phobia: the fear of closed spaces in general is grounded in an experience of . . . here

Freud's procedure is to be distinguished from the Jungian search for archetypes: the root is not a paradigmatic universal traumatic experience (say, the fear of being enclosed in mother's womb), but some singular experience which, perhaps, is linked to a closed space in a wholly contingent, external way – say, what if I witnessed some traumatic scene (that could have taken place also elsewhere) *in a closed space*? Even more stunning is the opposite case, when, in his case analyses, Freud as a rule makes a direct jump from the close dissection of a singular case (like that of the Wolfman or of the fantasy 'A child is being beaten') to the universal assertion of what 'fantasy (masochism, etc.) "as such" is'.

From the standpoint of Post-Theory, of course, this short-circuit immediately gives rise to a host of critical questions: how can Freud be so sure that he has picked a truly representative example? Should we at least not compare this case with a representative sample of other, different, cases, and so verify the universality of the concept in question? The dialectical counter-argument to it is that such careful empirical generalisation never brings us to a true universality. Why not? Because all particular examples of a certain universality do not entertain the same relationship towards their universality: each of them struggles with this universality, displaces it in a specific way, and the great art of dialectical analysis consists in being able to pick out the exceptional singular case which allows us to formulate the universality 'as such'. In the same way in which Marx articulated the universal logic of the historical development of humanity on the basis of his analysis of capitalism as the excessive (imbalanced) system of production (for Marx, capitalism is a contingent, monstrous formation whose very 'normal' state is a permanent dislocation, a kind of 'freak of history', a social system caught in the superego vicious circle of incessant expansion – yet precisely as such, it is the 'truth' of all preceding 'normal' history), Freud was able to formulate the universal logic of the Oedipal mode of socialisation through the identification with paternal Law precisely because he lived in exceptional times in which Oedipus was already in a state of crisis.

Of course, today's cognitive semantics no longer advocate the simplistic logic of empirical generalisation, of the classification into genera through identifying common features; rather, it emphasises how terms that designate species display a kind of 'radial' structure of intricate family resemblances, without any unambiguous feature unifying all the members of a species (see precisely the difficulties in elaborating a definition of *noir* that would effectively comprise all films we 'intuitively' perceive as *noir*).[18] However, this is not yet what a properly dialectical notion of the Universal amounts to. Where, then, is universality 'as such'? That is to say, if all individual cases of the species are just so many failed attempts to actualise the universal notion, where do we locate this notion 'as such'? *In the exception*. According to Steven Pinker, our linguistic capacity results from the interaction of two agencies: the general rules we tend to apply to all cases and the ability to memorise particular idiosyncratic cases. In this way, he endeavours to account for the mistakes young children make with the past tense: since they haven't yet learned/memorised the exceptions, they tend to apply the rule automatically – for example, a child will often say *bleeded* instead of *bled*; gradually, he or she will then learn the exception, the irregular verbs.[19] However, from the structural standpoint, something is missing in this account: it is not sufficient to explain the exceptions from the simple external interaction between rules and idiosyncratic, externally/contingently determined cases. What one should ask is *why does the domain of rules itself need exceptions*, i.e. why is the exception *structurally necessary*, why would the domain of rules collapse without its founding exceptions?

The basic rule of dialectics is thus: whenever we are offered a simple enumeration of subspecies of a universal species, we should always look for the exception to the series. For example, it is my conjecture that the key to Hitchcock's entire opus is the film which is integral and at the same time an exception, i.e. whose benevolent natural-cycle life-rhythm underpinning obviously violates the basic out-of-joint, 'derailed' tenor of his universe, *The Trouble With Harry* (1954). (And is not Alfred Hitchcock in such a position of exception with regard to the standard Hollywood narrative? Is he not the very embodiment of the Hollywood 'as such' precisely insofar as he occupies the place of exception with regard to it?)

This exception ultimately coincides with the founding gesture of a universality. Among E. S. Gardner's Perry Mason novels, *The Case of the Perjured Parrot*, published in 1939, is famous for involving the unique case of a double denouement (Mason is not satisfied with his own global explanation of the crime, and repeats it, reinterpreting the clues and pinning the crime down on another culprit). There is nonetheless something mechanical about this double denouement: it lacks inherent narrative logic. However, in the very first Perry Mason novel, *The Case of the Velvet Claws* from 1934, we also find a kind of double denouement that is much more interesting in its implications for the generic formula of the standard whodunit.

Mason's client is a prototypical hysterical and deceptive *femme fatale*, changing her attitude instantly from self-pitying crying to disdainful smile, lying to her lawyer all the way and even, in order to conceal the fact that it was she herself who shot her husband, claiming that she heard Mason himself violently arguing with her husband just before she heard the gunshot, thus effectively involving Mason himself in the plot. These, of course, are features of the hardboiled universe, as is the final violent confrontation in which Mason breaks his client down and makes her confess the crime (reminding us of the last pages of *The Maltese Falcon* in which Sam Spade confronts and breaks down the hysterically evil Brigid O'Shaughnessy), and, consequently, of the fact that the very task for which the client hires the detective turns out to be a lure destined to involve him in another crime.

Given these hardboiled elements, how does Gardner nonetheless reassert the standard whodunit, logic-and-deduction formula to which he belongs? He adds another turn of the screw to the plot: although his client breaks down and confesses the murder, Mason, persistent in his fidelity to her as a client, proves that she only *thought* she killed her husband: she shot at him and then escaped, not knowing that she had missed him; immediately afterwards, the husband's nephew grabbed the gun and shot him, convinced that the murder would be ascribed to the wife . . . This second denouement, *following* the *femme fatale*'s admission of guilt and the breakdown of her hysterical masks, is Gardner's way to reassert the logic-and-deduction formula: no, the *femme fatale* is not guilty, even if she thinks she is; there is another plot behind her apparent guilt, and, furthermore, the detective/investigator himself is not emotionally involved with her, but retains his unconditional fidelity to her as a client precisely insofar as he brutally rejects her erotic advances.

So, in this precise sense, Gardner's Perry Mason novels cannot be *directly* inscribed into the logic-and-deduction canon as opposed to the hardboiled universe: in Mason's novels, the logic-and-deduction universe loses its immediacy, it is already 'mediated' by the *noir*, hardboiled universe that historically follows it, i.e. the Mason novels reassert the logic-and-deduction formula not simply against, but *within* the hardboiled universe – and, as we have just seen, traces of this distantiation from the hardboiled universe are inscribed into the very paradoxical narrative structure of the *first* Perry Mason novel. So the beginning is not yet 'typical': only after this distantiation, this inherent overcoming of the *noir* universe rules, can Gardner's logic-and-deduction formula start to function 'normally', in the endless series of 'formulaic' novels. (Another version of such reflective distancing is the first Sherlock Holmes literary appearance, *A Study in Scarlet*, whose second part, told in flashback, is a passionate melodrama of love, forced marriage and revenge – as if the distance from the main form of popular literature against which Conan Doyle wanted to establish his canon had to be inscribed into the very first appearance of the new canon. The paradox is thus again that the beginning is not and cannot be 'typical': it is exceptional, since it has to bear the marks of the violent gesture of distantiation through which it establishes itself. Only the first repetition – the *second* story – can be 'typical'.)

The same goes for philosophical concepts themselves. Jeremy Bentham deployed the unique notion of 'self-icon', i.e. the notion that a thing is its own best sign (like in the Lewis Carroll joke about Englishmen using ever larger maps, until they finally settled on using England itself as *its own map*). He also uses this argument in favour of real punishment: although the whole point of punishment is to dissuade people, i.e. although the crucial dimension of a punishment resides in the effect it has on potential future criminals, the way it appears to them, reality is *its own best appearance*. On the other hand, it is well known that he wanted his body, not his painting or statue, to be stuffed and displayed after his death as his monument. In this case, it is not enough to say that he was consistent in applying the principle of self-icon to his own body, so that, after his death, his own real body would continue to serve as its best sign. One should go a step further and claim that the singular example of his body is *the* example which directly sustains the universal notion of self-icon, the example on account of which this notion was invented: the problem that bothered him was how to mark his presence after his death, and the solution to this problem was the notion of self-icon.

Chapter Two
Back to the Suture

Until now, however, we have only proposed a series of variations and exemplifications of the dialectical tension between the universal and the particular. Why do it in a book about cinema? There is a notion which played a crucial role in the heyday of Theory, the notion which, perhaps, condenses everything Theory was about in cinema studies, and is, consequently, the main target of the Post-Theoreticist criticism – the notion of *suture*, which concerns precisely the gap between the Universal and the Particular: it is this gap that is ultimately 'sutured'. The time of suture seems to have irrevocably passed: in the present-day cultural studies version of Theory, the term barely occurs; however, rather than accepting this disappearance as a fact, one is tempted to read it as an indication of the decline of cinema studies.

The concept of 'suture' has a long history. It was elevated from a casual word that occurs once in Lacan into a concept by Jacques-Alain Miller, in his first and seminal short article, an intervention at Jacques Lacan's seminar of 24 February 1965. Here, it designates the relationship between the signifying structure and the subject of the signifier.[20] Then, in the late 60s, it was taken over by Jean-Pierre Oudart.[21] It was only later, when it was again taken over and elaborated by the English *Screen* theorists, that it became a major concept in cinema theory and opened up to wider discussion. Finally, years later, it again lost its specific mooring in cinema studies and turned into a part of the deconstructionist jargon, functioning as a vague notion rather than a strict concept, as synonymous with 'closure': 'suture' signalled that the gap, the opening, of a structure was obliterated, enabling the structure to (mis)perceive itself as a self-enclosed totality of representation.

What, then, is suture? Let me begin with Ernesto Laclau's concept of *hegemony*, which provides an exemplary matrix of the relationship between universality, historical contingency and the limit of an impossible Real – one should always keep in mind that we are dealing here with a distinct concept whose specificity is often missed (or reduced to some proto-Gramscian vague generality) by those who refer to it. The key feature of the concept of hegemony resides in the contingent connection between intrasocial differences (elements *within* the social space) and the limit that separates society itself from non-society (chaos, utter decadence, dissolution of all social links) – the limit between the social and its exteriority, the non-social, can only articulate itself in the guise of a difference (by mapping itself on to a difference) between the elements of social space. In other words, although radical antagonism can only be represented in a distorted way, through the particular differences internal to the system, it *has* to be represented, which means that the signifying structure has to include its own absence: the very opposition between the symbolic order and its absence has to be inscribed *within* this order, and 'suture' designates the point of this inscription.

Reappropriated by cinema theory, the elementary logic of suture consists of three steps.[22]

Firstly, the spectator is confronted with a shot, finds pleasure in it in an immediate, imaginary way, and is absorbed by it.

Then, this full immersion is undermined by the awareness of the frame as such: what I see is only a part, and I do not master what I see. I am in a passive position, the show is run by the Absent One (or, rather, Other) who manipulates images behind my back.

What then follows is a complementary shot which renders the place from which the Absent One is looking, allocating this place to its fictional owner, one of the protagonists. In short, one passes thereby from imaginary to symbolic, to a sign: the second shot does not simply follow the first one, it is *signified* by it.

So, in order to suture the decentring gap, the shot which I perceived as objective is, in the next shot, reinscribed/reappropriated as the point-of-view shot of a person within the diegetic space. In Lacanian terms, the second shot represents (within the diegetic space of representation) the absent subject for/of the first shot. When the second shot replaces the first one, the 'absent one' is transferred from the level of enunciation to the level of diegetic fiction.

We can see clearly now the homology between suture in cinema and the logic of hegemony: in both cases, external difference is mapped onto the inside. In suture, the difference between image and its absence/void is mapped onto the intra-pictural difference between the two shots. Of course, such suturing procedure is rather rare in its pure form described above; numerous analyses have provided examples of other, more complex forms of this elementary matrix, as well as examples which bear witness to the system of suture falling apart, no longer successfully sustaining the appearance of seamless continuity (in Bresson, Godard, Hitchcock, etc.).[23] What one should bear in mind is the fundamental ideological operation that is involved here: the threatening intrusion of the decentring Other, the Absent Cause, is 'sutured'. The trickery thus resides in the fact that the gap that separates two totally different levels – that of the enunciated content (the narrative fiction) and that of the decentred process of its enunciation – is flattened: enunciation is reduced to one in the series of elements that constitute the enunciated fiction, i.e. the element which functions as the stand-in for the Absent Cause of the process appears as one of the elements within this process. It is as if we have a Moebius strip, but deceptively rendered as one continuous surface. In Hegelese, the elementary matrix of suture functions as the 'concrete universality': as the particular element out of which one can generate through variations all the others, although this element is very rarely encountered in its purity.

A more fundamental reproach to the standard notion of suture is that the elementary matrix of classical Hollywood narrative cinema is rather the opposite one: it's not that, ideally, each objective shot has to be reinscribed as the subjective (point-of-view) shot allocated to a certain protagonist within the space of the narrative fiction; it's rather that each subjective (point-of-view) shot has to be firmly allocated to some subject *within* diegetic reality, who is presented in an objective shot, so that the standard procedure is rather that of first seeing the protagonist (in an objective shot) and *then*, in a complementary shot, seeing what this protagonist sees in a point-of-view shot.[24] In short, the ultimate threat is not that of an objective shot which will not be 'subjectivised', allocated to some protagonist within the space of diegetic fiction, but that of a *point-of-view shot* which will not be clearly allocated as the point of view of some protagonist, and which will thus evoke the spectre of a free-floating Gaze without a determinate subject to whom it belongs. So what one should do here is to apply to suture Chion's logic of *la voix acous-*

matique: of the Gaze of an impossible subjectivity which *cannot* be located within the diegetic space.[25]

In its criticism of the 'Gaze', Post-Theory relies on the commonsense notion of the spectator (the subject who perceives cinematic reality on the screen, equipped with his emotional and cognitive predispositions, etc.), and, within this simple opposition between the subject and the object of cinematic perception, there is, of course, no place for the Gaze as the point from which the viewed object itself 'returns the Gaze' and regards us, the spectators. No wonder, then, that Post-Theorists speak of the 'missing Gaze', complaining that the Freudian-Lacanian Gaze is a mythical entity nowhere found in the actuality of the spectator's experience. That is to say, crucial for the Lacanian notion of Gaze is that it involves the reversal of the relationship between subject and object: as Lacan puts it in his *Seminar XI*, there is an antinomy between the eye and the Gaze, i.e. the Gaze is on the side of the object, it stands for the blind spot in the field of the visible from which the picture itself photo-graphs the spectator.[26] Does not Adorno's aphorism, 'The splinter in your eye is the best magnifying glass' – undoubtedly a mocking reference to the famous Bible passage about the detractor who sees the splinter in his neighbour's eye, yet does not see the beam in his own – render in a precise way the function of the Lacanian *objet petit a*, the blind spot without which nothing would be really visible? Or, as Lacan put it in his *Seminar I*, whose uncanny evocation of the paradigmatic shot of *Rear Window* is sustained by the fact that it was held in the same year that Hitchcock's film was shot (1954):

> I can feel myself under the gaze of someone whose eyes I do not see, not even discern. All that is necessary is for something to signify to me that there may be others there. This window, if it gets a bit dark, and if I have reasons for thinking that there is someone behind it, is straight-away a gaze.[27]

Is this notion of the Gaze not perfectly rendered by the exemplary Hitchcockian scene in which the subject is approaching some uncanny, threatening object, usually a house? In this scene, the objective shot of the person approaching the uncanny Thing (rendering the subject *not* in a direct frontal view, i.e. from the point of view of the Thing itself, but from aside) alternates with the point-of-view shot of the person fascinated by the Thing. Here we encounter the antinomy between the eye and the Gaze at its purest: the subject's eye sees the house, but the house – the object – seems somehow to return the Gaze ... No wonder, then, that the Post-Theorists speak of the 'missing Gaze', complaining that the Freudian-Lacanian Gaze is a mythical entity nowhere found in the actuality of the spectator's experience: this Gaze effectively *is* missing, its status being purely fantasmatic. This elementary Hitchcockian procedure already reads as a kind of uncanny inversion of the elementary suture procedure: it is the 'suturing' of the gap opened up by a point-of-view shot which fails.

Hitchcock is at his most uncanny and disturbing when he engages us *directly* with the point of view of this external fantasmatic Gaze. One of the standard horror movie procedures is the 'resignification' of the objective into the subjective shot (what the spectator first perceives as an

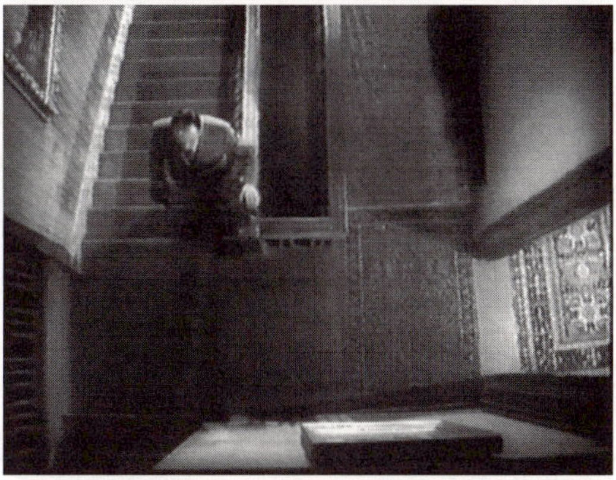

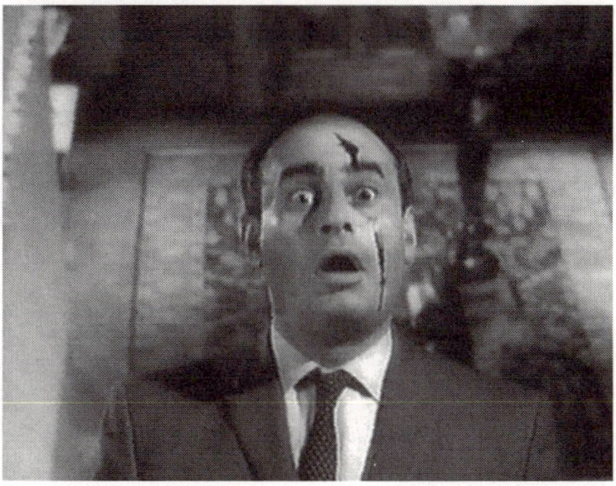

objective shot – say, of a house with a family at dinner – is all of a sudden, by means of codified markers like the slight trembling of the camera, the 'subjectivised' soundtrack, etc., revealed as the subjective shot of a murderer stalking his potential victim). However, this procedure is to be supplemented with another reversal, when, in the middle of a shot unambiguously marked as subjective, the spectator is all of a sudden compelled to acknowledge that *there is no possible subject within the space of diegetic reality who can occupy the point of view of this shot*. So we are not dealing here with the simple reversal of a subjective into an objective shot, but in constructing a place of *impossible* subjectivity, a subjectivity which taints the very objectivity with a flavour of unspeakable, monstrous evil. An entire heretic theology is discernible here, secretly identifying the Creator Himself as the Devil (which was already the thesis of the Cathar heresy in twelfth-century France). The exemplary cases of this impossible subjectivity are the 'subjective' shot from the standpoint of the murderous Thing itself upon the transfixed face of the dying detective Arbogast in *Psycho* (1960) and, in *The Birds* (1963), the famous God's-view shot of the burning Bodega Bay, which is then, with the entry into the frame of the birds, resignified, subjectivised into the point of view of the evil aggressors themselves.

We can see, now, how this Hitchcockian procedure undermines the standard procedure of suture. Firstly, already the elementary Hitchcockian exchange between the objective shot of a person approaching the Thing

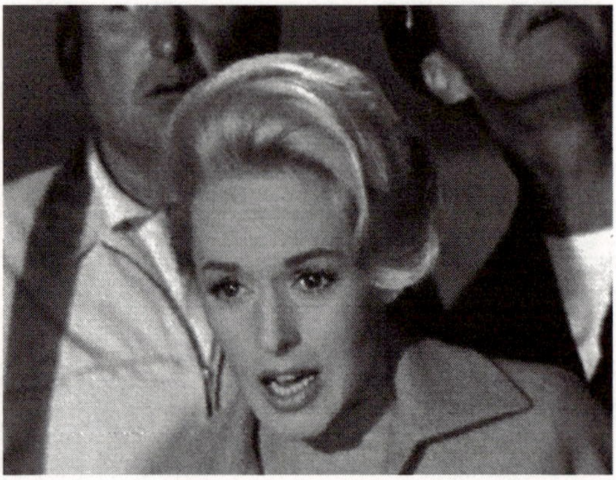

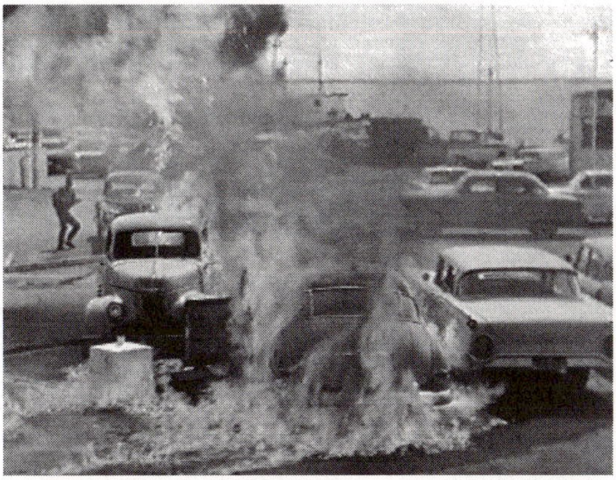

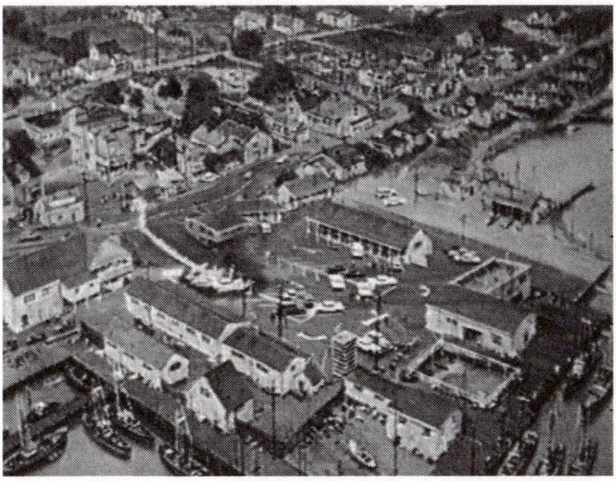

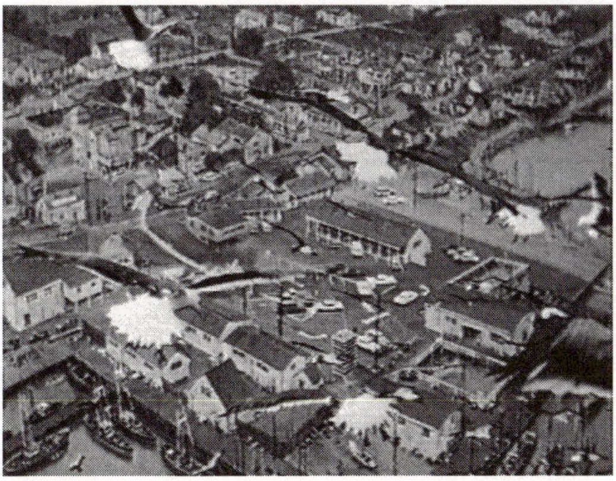

and the point-of-view shot of this Thing fails to produce the 'suturing' effect of appeasement: the tension remains unresolved. Then, it is as if this tension is released and simultaneously explodes, gets out of control, by being raised to a higher potency, i.e. by being accelerated into another, much more radical, duality: the shift from the objective 'God's-view' shot into its uncanny subjectivisation. *Another* subjectivity intervenes here, which is no longer the standard diegetic subjectivity of a protagonist of the fiction, but the impossible/traumatic subjectivity of the Thing itself. (Recall how, in both the above-mentioned examples from Hitchcock, the entrance of this impossible subjectivity is preceded by the elementary Hitchcockian exchange between the objective shot of a person approaching the Thing and the point-of-view shot of this Thing.)

Another Hitchcockian procedure of subverting his standard exchange of subjective and objective shots is the sudden intrusion into it of a violent element – a blot of the Real – from aside, which disturbs this smooth exchange. The ultimate example, of course, is the famous scene, from *The Birds*, analysed in detail by Raymond Bellour, of Melanie crossing the bay to Mitch's house: when, on her way back, she is approaching the wharf, a single bird enters the frame as a blot and hits her head.[28] Is the same matrix not discernible also in *Topaz* (1969), in one of its discarded endings, when, at the most tense moment of the duel between the hero and the Russian spy Granville, a hidden KGB sharp-shooter shoots Granville and thus disturbs the symmetry of the duel?

There is yet another subversion of the standard procedure of suture, which turns around the Hitchcockian subjectivisation of an objective shot: the unexpected objectivisation of what first appears to be a subjective shot. In a lot of scenes in Kieślowski's *Blind Chance*, the point of view initially seems to be subjective – from Witek's eyes – but the camera then reveals him within the frame.[29] The same procedure also occurs in many of Antonioni's films, starting with his first one, *Cronaca di un amore* (1950). During an illicit meeting a couple (a rich man's wife and the man who used to be and is now again her lover) look down an elevator shaft; then follows a cut to a shot looking down the shaft that, of course, seems to be a subjective shot from the couple's point of view; however, as the elevator starts to rise and the camera tilts up, we discover that the camera is in fact positioned across the shaft from the couple, who are now, without a cut, seen in long shot. We thought we were seeing through their eyes and, within the same shot, we find ourselves seeing them across the shaft from a considerable distance.[30] The uncanny poetic effect of these shots resides in the fact that it appears as if the subject somehow *enters his/her own picture* – as Lacan put it, not only is the picture in my eye, but I am also in the picture.[31]

What, then, happens when the exchange of subjective and objective shots fails to produce the suturing effect? Here enters the function of *interface*. Recall the stage of Kane's electoral rally in *Citizen Kane* (1941): behind the figure of Kane, there is a gigantic poster with his photo, as if the 'real' Kane is redoubled by his spectral shadow. Do we not encounter this procedure in almost every large political reunion and concert today? While the speaker or singer is barely perceptible in the large hall or stadium where the event takes place, there is, above him or her, a gigantic video screen on which even the most remote spectator can see the face of the performer and attach the image to the (amplified) voice. This arrangement is not as obvious as it may seem: the uncanny point is that the performer (politician, actor, singer), in his or her very 'real' gestures and words, already takes into account the fact that he or she is projected on to the video screen which intermediates between him/her and the public performance; the event is thus simultaneously 'direct', 'live' (people do pay enormous amounts of money to see Pavarotti 'live', although one's eyes are practically all the time turned towards the screen) and technologically reproduced, with the image usually even worse than on a home TV screen ... The question, 'Which of the two is more real?' is thus by no means superfluous: it is the very screen image which in a way guarantees that the spectator is effectively witnessing a 'real' event.

Kieślowski was the great master of making the spectator perceive this dimension of interface in an ordinary scene – a part of drab reality all of a sudden starts to function as the 'door of perception', the screen through which another, purely fantasmatic dimension becomes perceptible. What distinguishes Kieślowski is that, in his films, these magic moments of interface are not staged by means of standard Gothic elements (apparitions in the fog, magic mirrors), but as part of an ordinary, everyday reality. In *Decalogue* 6, for example, the brief scene in the post office when Maria, the

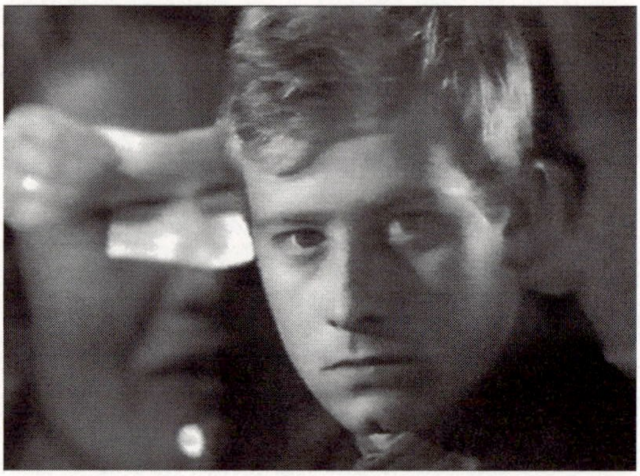

film's heroine, complains about the money orders is shot in such a way that, several times, we see a person in close-up face-to-face and, behind him or her, on a glass partition dividing the clerks from the customers, a larger-than-life reflection of the face of another person with whom the person we see directly is engaged in a conversation. By means of this simple procedure, the spectral dimension is rendered present in the middle of an utterly plain scene (customers complaining about bad service in a drab East European post office).

Leaving aside a series of similar shots from Hitchcock's *Frenzy* (1972) up to Jonathan Demme's *The Silence of the Lambs* (1991) – while Clarice visits Hannibal Lecter in the prison, we see her in (diegetic) reality, looking into the camera, while Lecter is seen as a spectre reflected on the glass pane across from Clarice[32] – suffice it to mention the more elaborate case which occurs in Syberberg's *Parsifal* (1982): the substitution of the male by the female Parsifal. While the (tenor) singing goes on, the Parsifal-boy gradually withdraws into the background and is replaced by the Parsifal-girl: the voice is passed as a torch from one body to another. This substitution occurs at the very point when Parsifal tears himself away from the mother, becomes 'human' and feels compassion – at this point, as if humanity is no longer allowed, he is transformed into a cold, asexual woman:

> Parsifal One, the boy, has torn himself away from his mother's kiss; he begins to take on substance and humanity. But then Parsifal Two, the girl, arrives, places herself alongside him, and takes up 'singing' earnestly where he left

> off, while Parsifal One fades out. With the latter, while his youth seemed a bit improbable as the source of the manly and vigorous tenor voice he carried, we could still believe that it was he. With Parsifal Two, the body knows it is only a temporary housing; it no longer hopes to fuse with the voice. From this comes its sadness, behind the cold and determined mask of Karen Krick. She must get through the score, accomplish what has been written.[33]

It is crucial that this replacement takes place against the background of the Thing (Wagner's gigantic death-mask). The scene is thus composed of three elements: the (diegetic) subject (or, rather, *two* of them); the spectral Thing in the background; and the voice, *objet petit a*, the remainder of the mute Thing. In the terms of figure and background, this Thing is the figure of the background itself, the background *as* figure.[34] So what *is* this Thing, if not the embodiment of that which remains the same in

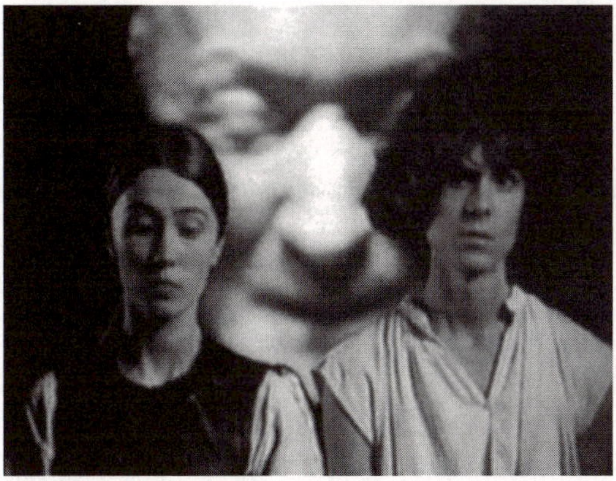

the 'passing of the torch (voice)' from one (masculine) to another (feminine) subject – namely *this voice itself*? This accounts for the spectral/ethereal character of the Thing: it is not an object which emits a voice, but an object which gives body to the impossible object-voice. (Another embodiment of the impossible object-voice is the alien intruder from science-fiction horror movies, usually a worm- or squid-like entity that penetrates a human body and takes possession of it from within.) The 'live' body is transformed into a puppet dominated by the voice – therein resides the meaning of the playback in *Parsifal*, of actors following the prerecorded voice:

> In playback, the body confesses to being the puppet brought to life by the voice. In Parsifal, everything begins with the puppet (think of the Prelude, and the awakening of the Flower-Girls).[35]

This scene from *Parsifal* also enables us to answer Kaja Silverman's critical claim that the *acousmetre*, the threatening, all-powerful, free-floating voice which cannot be attached to any diegetic personality, is inherently masculine, i.e. the male voice of the master controlling the hysterical woman.[36] Apart from the exceptions which immediately come to one's mind (and of which Silverman is well aware, from Mankiewicz's *Letter to Three Wives* [1949], in which the seductive *femme fatale* who sends the letter to the three wives is seen only briefly from behind, never in her face, while her voice introduces and comments on the story, up to Hitchcock's *Psycho*, in which the acousmatic voice in search of its body is the mother's voice), one is tempted to claim that the underlying fundamental matrix of the *acousmetre* is the paradox of *a woman speaking with the male voice*: the ultimate scene of the unmasking of the mystery of the acousmatic voice is the scene of revealing a woman as the source of the masculine voice (like Parsifal after his repudiation of Kundry in Syberberg's film version of the opera), in contrast to the standard homophobic cliché of a gay as a male person who speaks with a high-pitched feminine voice.[37]

Another earlier German film, Veit Harlan's *Opfergang* (1942–4), elevates this reflexive logic of suture to a second degree. It's a turn-of-the-century story of Albrecht, a Hamburg high-society adventurer who, upon returning home from a trip to the Far East, marries his cold, blonde, beautiful cousin Octavia, and then becomes fatally attracted to Aels, a rich Norwegian girl living in a nearby palace villa. Aels is full of life energy – she likes to ride a horse, swim and shoot a bow, and has a child from a previous relationship – but is mysteriously ill; the shadow of death is hanging over her. Although Octavia has one outburst of paranoiac curiosity, she tolerates her husband's passion with the patience of a saint. Towards the film's end, both Aels and Albrecht get infected by typhus; they both lie in their beds, Albrecht in a hospital, Aels at home, thinking of each other. Due to her weakness, typhus proves fatal to Aels; the only thing that keeps her alive is the regular appearance of Albrecht on the path in front of her window, when he stops his horse there for a minute and waves at her. Albrecht is soon also constrained to his hospital bed and thus unable to perform this life-saving ritual; Octavia learns about it from the doctor who takes care of both Albrecht and Aels, and she herself performs the ritual for a couple of days, thus prolonging Aels's life: each day, dressed up as Albert, she rides a horse past Aels's villa, stops there at the usual place and waves at her. When the doctor tells Albrecht of this sacrifice of his faithful wife, he discovers his full love for her. What then follows is the ultimate fantasmatic scene: first we see Albrecht lying in his bed, looking in the right direction, his inner voice saying: 'Aels, I have to do something that will hurt you very much.' Then follows a cut to Aels lying in her bed, looking left, as if they are in a kind of extra-sensory communication, who answers him: 'I know it all. But where are you, my love? Are you disappearing?' Cut to the shot of the view from her room to the path beyond the wooden fence, on which she sees Albrecht-Octavia on a horse, and then no one. What then follows is the supremely condensed 'suturing' shot/counter-shot: on the right side of the screen, we get the close-up of the dying Aels, and, on the left side, the American shot of Albrecht, these two appearances communicating. (This shot effectively resembles the final scene of mirages appearing to Julie in Kieślowski's *Blue*: in both cases, cuts are supplanted by mirages floating like islands against the blurred blue background.) Albrecht tells Aels the big secret that he really loves Octavia and that he is here to bid her farewell; after a mysterious exchange about what is real and what a mere phantasmagoric appearance (a kind of reflexive comment on what we see), Aels wishes him the best of luck in his marriage; then, Albrecht's image disappears, so that we see just a slightly blurred image of her as an island of light on the right side of the screen, surrounded by blue darkness. This image gets gradually more and more blurred – she dies. In the ensuing last scene of the film, Albrecht and Octavia ride alongside each other on the sea coast, observing the red rose on the sand moved by waves that stands for the dead Aels, who is identified with the immense sea.

The opposition of the two women, Octavia and Aels, is more complex than it may appear: each of them stands for a certain kind of death (and life). Octavia stands for the ethereal-anaemic life of social conventions – a role she plays with full identification, leading up to her ultimate saintly sacrifice for her husband; in this sense, she stands for death, for the stifling of the impulse to fully live one's life, beyond social conventions. However, precisely as such, she is the survivor, in contrast to Aels, who stands for a different death: not the death of the pallid saintly convention, but the death that comes with living out one's passions without constraints (recall the unexplained small son she has from her past). It is as if there is something lethal in such a full immersion into life – no wonder that Aels is from the very beginning presented as someone over whom the shadow of death lurks. This death is not simply the end of life, but an immersion into the eternally returning pulsation of Life itself, symbolised by the sea waves: in her death, Aels is transfigured into the cosmic, impersonal life-substance. The structure is here that of a double sacrifice: at one level, Aels stands for the untamed wilderness of the life energy that has to be sacrificed so that the 'normal' couple of Albrecht and Octavia can be reconstituted – the last shot of the film is the red rose in the sand moved by waves, the index of the third thing, sacrificed, untamed female sexuality (and it is as if part of this sexual energy passes on to Octavia who – for the first time in the film – is now also seen riding). At another level, of course, the sacrifice is that of Octavia, who accomplishes the supreme act of sustaining, through her masquerade, the illusion of her husband's fidelity to his mistress that keeps *her* alive. *This* is the supreme 'male chauvinist' fantasy: that of the mistress and wife, each sacrificing herself for each other, the wife accepting the husband's passion for the mistress and the mistress erasing herself out of the picture to enable the reunion of the husband and the wife ... In a pseudo-Hegelian dialectical twist, the wife wins her husband back precisely by accepting his illegitimate passion for another woman, and by even taking upon herself his desire, by acting as him in order to help her.

Paradoxically, if Harlan is to be believed in his autobiography,[38] the source for this pathetic finale is none other than Goebbels himself! In Rudolf Binding's story on which *Opfergang* is based,[39] it is the *husband* (Albrecht) who dies, and Aels is called 'Joie', a vivacious English girl with no pre-existing mortal illness. Both Albrecht and Joie also suffer from typhus. However, in the story, only Albrecht dies, and, in the last moment of his life, he tells Octavia of how Joie's only little joy that allowed her to cling to life was his regular daily appearances in front of her villa. It is *after*

Albrecht's death that Octavia continues to perform this ritual of dressing up as Albrecht – these four days are crucial for Joie's recovery. When Joie recovers, the doctor tells her that Albrecht died four days ago; shocked, Joie answers him that she saw Albrecht each evening performing his ritual. While the doctor dismisses this as her hallucination, Joie all of a sudden understands what has happened. Here are the last two paragraphs of the story:

> From this moment on, Joie's pain was somehow subdued through the act whose greatness totally filled her and engendered in her a beautiful disposition.
>
> And then Joie felt something like a duty to recover, and obtained the peace and ability to overcome her illness, so that the sacrifice of a noble lady would not be accomplished in vain.[40]

Goebbels opposed this ending, evoking the demoralising influence such a story about adultery in which the husband dies, might have upon the thousands of soldiers on the front who would see the film; in response to this criticism, Harlan turned Joie into Aels and made her fatally sick, so that she, not the husband, dies, thus totally changing the meaning of his wife's 'sacrifice' of impersonating him in his mistress's eyes. In the story, Octavia's sacrifice is a pure gesture of respect for her husband's love, not a witty manoeuvre destined to regain her husband's love. In this precise sense, the film 'pathologises' Octavia's sacrificial gesture, reducing a pure, 'disinterested' ethical act to a 'pathological' feminine subterfuge.

A more detailed analysis would have to add at least two elements: firstly, the unique, almost Hitchcockian, scene in which we see, for a brief moment, the cold, mechanically evil aspect of Octavia's saintliness. When she observes from her window Aels going out on some errand, she surreptitiously follows her with a manic determination and a fixed stare, reminding us of the standard Hollywood cliché of the mad woman blindly following her murderous compulsion. The other venture would have been to correlate *Opfergang* with Harlan's 'apolitical' films that were shot between the two historical dramas with explicit political connotations, *The Great King* (1942; a biography of Friedrich the Great) and *Kolberg* (1945): namely, *The Golden City* (1942) and *Immensee* (1943).

In *The Golden City*, the heroine (played by Harlan's wife Kristina Soederbaum, as in the other two films) ends her life by a sacrifice, drowning herself in the swamp after she is rejected by her family because of her illegitimate pregnancy; since, after her death, the swamp is dried out and turned into a fertile field, her sacrificial suicide can be seen as providing fertility to the land. In *Immensee*, a kind of mirror-inversion of *Opfergang*, Soederbaum plays a woman who is divided between two men: she is passionately in love with a young composer who, although he returns her love, leaves her to pursue his career abroad; left alone, she marries an ordinary man also deeply in love with her. After a couple of years, the composer returns on a Summer holiday and asks her to join him in the big city; her husband loves her so much that, sensing her unhappiness in the marriage, he gives her the freedom to leave him for the composer.[41] This gesture of unconditional devotion wins her over: she rediscovers her love for her husband and stays with him, painfully learning that he is the stronger of the two. The trick, of course, is that the very freedom of choice her husband gives her makes the choice a forced one, putting her under unbearable ethical pressure: while it is easy to leave a violently jealous husband, it is much more difficult to leave the husband who gives you the freedom to leave him – this freedom is the very form of appearance of the absolute coercion to freely make the right choice. The husband is thus strictly equivalent to Octavia in *Opfergang*: the angelic being of unconditional devotion whose acceptance of his/her partner's love for another wins him/her back. When, after long years, her husband dies, her great love, now a world-renowned composer, returns to her town for a concert: even now, she rejects his offer – although she continues to love him, she remains faithful to her dead husband ... The ultimate lesson of *Immensee* thus adds a kind of perverted twist to the psychoanalytical, ethical maxim 'do not compromise your desire': once you have compromised your desire by choosing conventional marriage over the risk of passionate love, you should stick to this choice even when the obstacle is no longer here – in other words, if you have already compromised your desire, then do not compromise again on the compromise itself, but stick to it whatever the cost. The parallel with the literary tradition of the ethical gesture of renunciation, which persists when the obstacle is no longer here also (from *Princesse de Clèves* to *The Portrait of a Lady*), cannot but strike the eye: to put it in somewhat ironic terms, the heroine of *Immensee* is a kind of 'Portrait of a Nazi Lady'.[42]

One should provide here a detailed analysis of the scene of Aels's death in *Opfergang*: what, exactly, is 'fantasy' and what (diegetic) 'reality' in it? At one level, of course, the appearance of Albrecht to the dying Aels is *her* hallucination. It has to happen for a reason that is more paradoxical than it may appear: *so that she can die*. Without the caring but sobering message that Albrecht really loves his wife, Aels would have been condemned to live forever as a kind of contemporary Wagnerian hero unable to find release in death; in a paradigmatic feminine fantasy, the awareness that her disappearance will render possible the constitution of a perfect couple, she gracefully withdraws from life, erasing herself from the picture. Read this way, the 'suturing' shot of the dying Aels and Albrecht appearing to her in

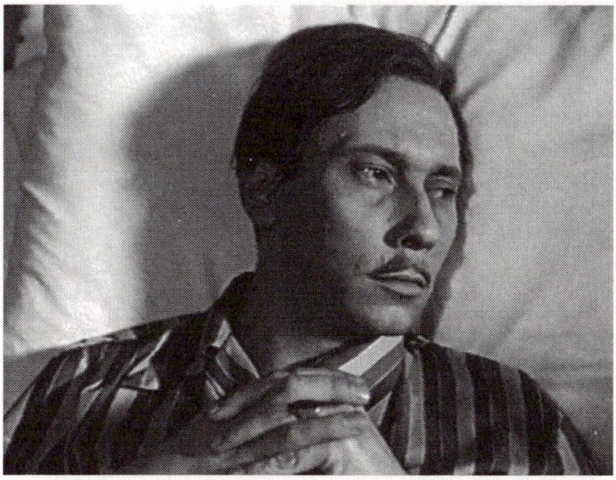

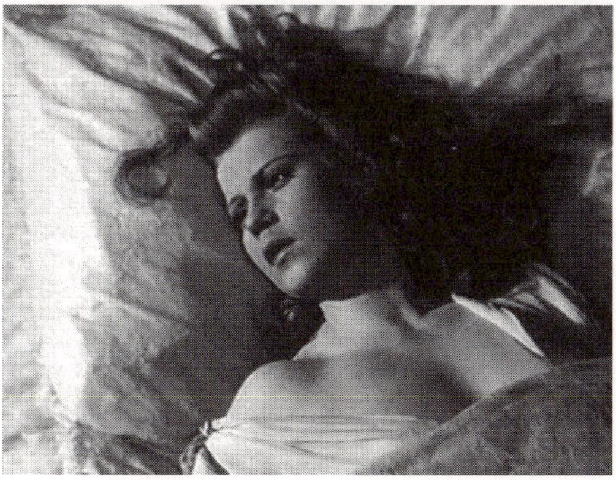

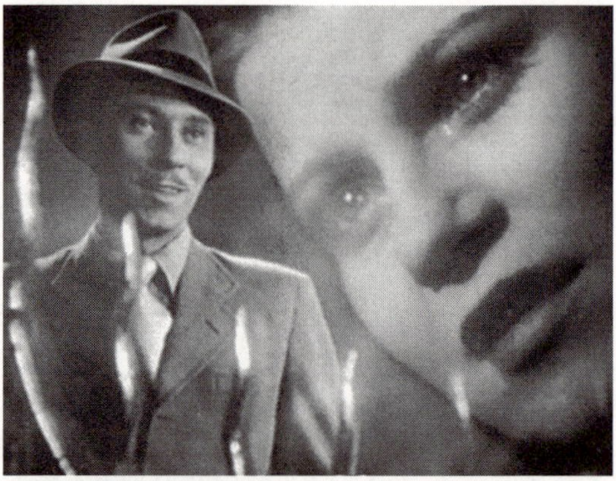

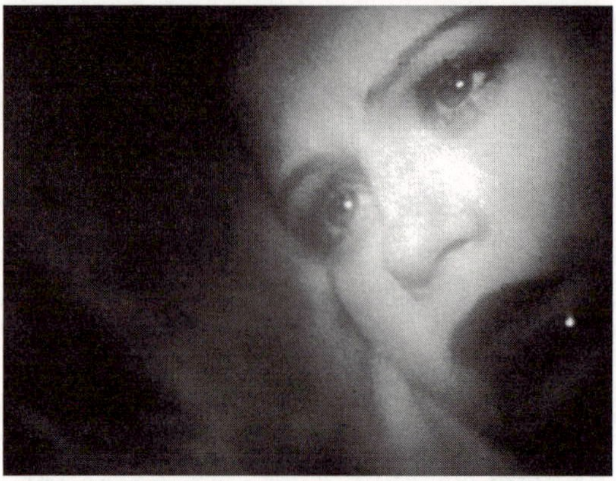

her final hallucination is the montage of the 'real' Aels and the 'hallucinated' Albrecht. At a different level, however, one should *simultaneously* claim that this *entire* shot, i.e. Aels *and* Albrecht, is *Albrecht*'s hallucination, so that we are already passing from (diegetic) reality to hallucination when we pass from Albrecht in his hospital bed to Aels in her bed: 'Aels in her bed hallucinating Albrecht' is *in its entirety* Albrecht's own hallucination, enabling him to rescue his marriage by fantasising Aels's forgiving withdrawal from his life after he tells her the bitter truth. The two fantasies are thus interwoven in a kind of spatial warp, and this impossible fantasy of the double sacrifice provides the only consequent solution to the male problem of being divided between a loving wife and a loving mistress – it provides the formula for getting out of the deadlock without betraying anyone. But, again, crucial for this solution to work is the ambiguous status of the 'suturing' shot that condenses shot and counter-shot: the actual subject of the fantasy (Albrecht) hallucinates about what? About *his own* appearance in the hallucination of the dying Aels.[43]

In the final moment of this hallucination, we see Aels alone, deprived of her hallucinatory support, reduced to a hallucinated bright island in the enveloping darkness of the screen – after the hallucination is deprived of its suturing counter-shot, of the hallucination *within* hallucination, it can only withdraw and disappear itself. This shot is 'doubly inscribed': it is at the same time the subject (Aels) deprived of her hallucinatory suturing supplement *and* the hallucinatory supplement (Albrecht's image of the dying Aels) standing alone. Shot and counter-shot are here not only combined within the same shot – it is *one and the same* image which is *at the same time* the shot (of the hallucinating Aels) and the counter-shot (what appears as a counter-shot to Albrecht in his hospital bed). This, perhaps, is the supreme case of what Michel Chion, in his analysis of Lang's *The Testament of Dr Mabuse* (1933), called the 'mirage of the absolute reverse shot'.[44] The ultimate lesson of this intricate staging is that the bitter truth (marriage will survive, Aels has to accept her death) can only be formulated in the guise of a hallucination within a hallucination. And, perhaps, here enters the fact that Veit Harlan was *the* Nazi director, author of the two key propaganda classics, *The Jew Suess* (1940) and *Kolberg*: does the same formal feature not hold also for Nazi ideology? In it, the truth can appear only as a hallucination within the hallucination, as the way the Nazi subject hallucinates Jews hallucinating.

Is not the same effect – not of achieving the illusion of reality, but, on the contrary, of introducing the dimension of spectral magic into drab reality itself – discernible in the wonderful long take of Joan Crawford facing the slowly passing train in *Possessed* (1931)? After saying goodbye to her boyfriend, an ordinary small-town guy, after arranging for him to bring some ice-cream to the family dinner, Crawford has to stop before the railway line as a train passes slowly through the small town. What one should take note of here is the extreme proximity of the background of the shot (the passing train) to the girl who observes it; the light also changes almost mysteriously – before, it was still daylight, while now she sees the train as if in darkness, which contrasts with the framed view of the wealthy life going on inside the train (a cook preparing an exquisite meal, a couple dancing). This very proximity and the change to darkness gives the scene the appearance of a cinema image, as if she found herself in a cinema, a spectator confronted with scenes of the life she longs for, scenes which are close, but nonetheless simultaneously somewhat ethereal, spectral, threatening to dissolve at any moment. And then a true miracle occurs. When the train stops for a brief moment, a kind, elderly gentleman is standing on the observation platform immediately in front of the girl, reaching out his hand, which is holding a drink. He creates a bridge between the fantasmatic reality of the train and the everyday reality of the girl; he engages in a friendly conversation with her – a magical moment when a dream seems to intervene into our daily reality ... The pleasing effect of this last shot resides in the way everyday reality itself – the scene of a train passing by an ordinary working girl – acquires the magic dimension of the poor girl encountering her dream; on account of its proximity and flatness, the play of foreground and background is not used here to produce the effect of reality, but, quite the opposite, to introduce a dream-like spectrality into everyday reality.

Perhaps, the supreme case of this magic momentary emergence of an interface is found in *The Double Life of Véronique*: when Véronique is sitting on a train next to a window, her perturbed state presaging her impending heart attack is signalled by the barely perceptible distortions of what we see through the train window due to the uneven glass surface.[45] This scene first renders visible her perturbed subjectivity (that is to say, subjectivity as such, since – as pointed out by Deleuze[46] – subjectivity as such is correlative to a fold, to a protracted or curved stain in the Real) in the guise of its 'objective correlative', the slightly distorted view of the countryside through the window-frame, i.e. the anamorphic stain which disfigures the clear view; then, Véronique takes into her hand the magic glass ball and, after shaking it, focuses her gaze on it: the relationship between the anamorphic stain and reality is now reversed, the subject perceives clearly the 'magic' interior of the ball, while 'reality' around it dissolves into a formless smear. This ball, of course, is the Lacanian *objet petit a*, the objectal stand-in for the subject.

A parallel imposes itself here between *Véronique* and *Citizen Kane*: does this magic ball which attracts Véronique's gaze not play the same structural role as the famous glass ball with the snowy house which exerts its fascination on Kane? The above-mentioned scene from *Véronique* has its precise correlate in a scene towards the end of *Citizen Kane* in which Kane, furious after his second wife has just left him, gives way to an outburst of childish rage and starts to smash objects in his wife's bedroom, so that the room soon loses its clear contours and changes into a fuzzy havoc. All of a sudden, he focuses on a small object, the glass ball, and gently takes it into his hand; after the entire scene around him has been transformed into mayhem, he seems to stick to this little object as his last link to reality ... The definition of 'maturity' is that the subject is ready to renounce his/her magic glass ball, i.e. the object which vouches for the fantasmatic, incestuous link – Kane's problem was that he was not able to do it while alive, so that the moment he let the glass ball fall from his hand was the moment of his death. A 'normal', 'mature' subject is able to 'tarry with the negative', as Hegel would have put it, to survive his own death (cutting off his links with the incestuous glass ball). In short, the problem with Kane was not that for all of his adult life he was in search of the lost incestuous object, trying to recapture it; the problem was rather the exact opposite: *he never really lost this object*, he stuck to it to the end and thus remained 'immature', a mixture of grandiosity, larger than life omnipotence and childish rage preventing him from accomplishing integration into his environment. The 'pathological' link to this object is responsible for the continuous gap between Kane and his social environs (or, in cinematic terms, between his figure and its background) which appears as simultaneously less real than Kane – a kind of fantasmatic, ethereal illusion – and more real than him, i.e. the obstacle which again and again frustrates his stubborn will. In this precise sense, the wide-lens effect of accentuating the gap between the subject in close-up and his background materialises the constitutive flaw of Wellesian subjectivity.

Among the interface effects which abound in Kieślowski's films, suffice it to mention two more complex examples. Firstly, the big red publicity poster of Valentine in *Red*, the middle term of its three variations (to begin with we see Valentine in 'reality' as the photographer makes this shot; then comes the poster itself; finally, in the very last shot of the film, we see Valentine in exactly the same profile, as the frozen image on a TV screen) – an exemplary case of what Deleuze called the cylindric stasis of compressed time. Secondly, the (deservedly) famous close-up shot of Julie's eye from the beginning of *Blue*, which immediately follows the car accident: the eye covers almost the whole screen, while the external reality (the doctor approaching Julie) is seen only as a reflection in the eye. Is this not the ultimate (reversal of the) shot which contains its own counter-shot? It is no longer (diegetic) reality which contains its suture-spectre; it is reality *itself* which is reduced to a spectre appearing *within* the eye's frame.

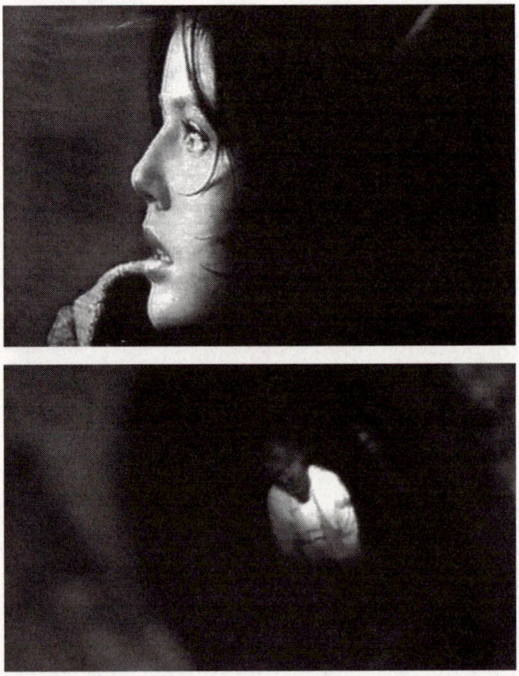

Interface thus operates at a more radical level than the standard suture procedure: it takes place when suturing no longer works – at this point, the interface-screen field enters as the direct stand-in for the 'absent one' (in the case of Syberberg's *Parsifal*, the gigantic spectral apparition of Wagner's head is such a stand-in for Wagner himself as the 'absent one', the master composer). As our brief example of the post-office scene from *Decalogue* 6 demonstrated, interface could appear as a simple condensation of shot and reverse-shot within the same shot; but it's not only that, since it adds to the included reverse-shot a *spectral* dimension, evoking the idea that there is no cosmos, that our universe is not in itself fully ontologically constituted, and that, in order to maintain an appearance of consistency, an interface-artificial moment must suture-stitch it (a kind of stage-prop that fills in the gap, like the painted background that closes off reality). And is Velásquez's *Las Meninas,* to which Oudart himself refers in his seminal essay on suture, not an exemplary case of such a condensation of shot and counter-shot into a single shot?[47]

Yet another supreme example of this meta-suturing function of the interface is found in David Lynch's *The Lost Highway* (1996), in a scene in Andy's house, when Pete observes the large screen on which the same pornographic scene is repetitively projected, showing Alice penetrated (anally?) from behind, with a face displaying pleasure-in-pain; at this

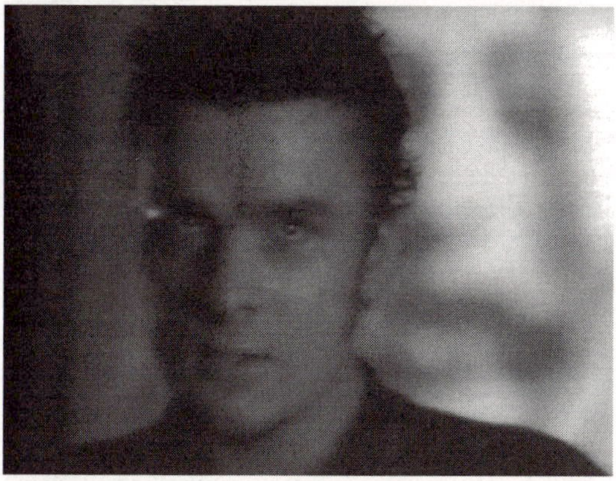

moment, the 'real' Alice comes towards him down the stairs ... This confrontation of the real Alice with her interface fantasmatic double produces the effect of 'This is not Alice', like that of 'This is not a pipe' in the famous Magritte painting – the scene in which a real person is shown side by side with the ultimate image of what she is in the fantasy for the male Other, i.e., in this case, enjoying being buggered by a large, anonymous black man ('A woman is being buggered' functions here somehow like Freud's 'A child is being beaten'). Andy's house is the last in the series of hellish places in Lynch's films, places in which one encounters the final (not truth but) fantasmatic lie (the other two best known are the Red Lodge in *Twin Peaks* [1990–91] and Frank's apartment in *Blue Velvet* [1986]). This site is that of the fundamental fantasy staging the primordial scene of *jouissance*, and the whole problem is how to 'traverse' it, acquire a distance towards it.[48] This side-by-side confrontation of the real person with her fantasmatic image seems to condense the overall structure of the film, which posits side-by-side the aseptic, drab everyday reality and the fantasmatic real of nightmarish *jouissance*. (The musical accompaniment is here also crucial: that of the German 'totalitarian' punk band Rammstein rendering a universe of the utmost *jouissance* sustained by the obscene superego injunction.)[49]

This shift from standard suture to the interface effect can be perfectly rendered in Lacanian terms: suture follows the logic of signifying representation (the second shot represents the absent subject – $\$$ – for the first shot), while the interface effect occurs when this signifying representation fails. At this point, when the gap can no longer be filled by an additional signifier, it is filled by a spectral *object*, in a shot which, in the guise of the spectral screen, includes its own counter-shot. In other words, when, in the exchange of shots and counter-shots, a shot occurs to which there is no counter-shot, the only way to fill this gap is by producing a shot which contains its own counter-shot. Here, then, we pass from S_1-S_2 to $\$$ *a*: a signifier cannot include the other signifier within itself (this would entail the impossible paradox of the signifier which signifies itself); it is only the *objet petit a* which can be directly included in the picture. Consequently, when a shot includes its own counter-shot, the two shots are no longer related as the two signifiers of a signifying dyad; the first shot now stands for the signifying chain as such, while the spectral counter-shot sutures it, providing the fantasmatic supplement that fills its hole.

Chapter Three
The Short-Circuit

Suture is usually conceived of as the mode in which the exterior is inscribed in the interior, thus 'suturing' the field, producing the effect of self-enclosure with no need for an exterior, effacing the traces of its own production: traces of the production process, its gaps, its mechanisms, are obliterated, so that the product can appear as a naturalised, organic whole (the same as with identification, which is not simply full emotional immersion in the quasi-reality of the story, but a much more complex split process). Suture is thus somewhat like the basic matrix of Alistair Maclean's adventure thrillers from the 50s and 60s (*The Guns of Navarone*, *Ice Station Zebra*, *Where Eagles Dare*): a group of dedicated commandos on a dangerous mission all of a sudden discovers that there must be an enemy agent among them, i.e. that their Otherness (the enemy) is inscribed *within* their group. However, the much more crucial aspect is the obverse one: not only 'no interior without exterior', *but also 'no exterior without interior'*. Therein resides the lesson of Kant's transcendental idealism: in order to appear as a consistent whole, external reality has to be 'sutured' by a subjective element, an artificial supplement that has to be added to it in order to generate the effect of reality, like the painted background that confers on a scene the illusion of 'reality'. And interface takes place at this level: it is the internal element that sustains the consistency of the 'external reality' itself, the artificial screen that confers the effect of reality on what we see. This is the *objet petit a* for Lacan: the subjective element constitutive of objective-external reality.

The matrix of an external site of production that inscribes itself into the domain of illusions it generates has thus to be supplemented: this matrix simply does not account for the emergence of the *subject*. According to standard (cinematic) suture theory, the 'subject' is the illusory stand-in, within the domain of the constituted-generated, for its absent cause, for its production process: 'subject' is the imaginary agent which, while dwelling inside the space of the constituted phenomena, is (mis)perceived as their generator. This, however, is not what the Lacanian 'barred subject' is about: the Lacanian subject can be conceptualised only when we take into account how the very externality of the generative process ex-sists only insofar as the stand-in of the constituted domain is present in it.

When, in Prokofiev's ballet *Romeo and Juliet*, Romeo finds Juliet dead, his dance renders his desperate effort to resuscitate her. Here, the action in a sense takes place at two levels, not only at the level of what the dance renders, but also at the level of the dance itself. The fact that the dancing Romeo is dragging around the dead corpse of Juliet, who is suspended like a dead squid out of water, can also be read as his desperate effort to return this immobile body to the state of *dance* itself, to restore its capacity to magically sublate the inertia of gravity and float freely in the air, so that his dance is in a way a reflexive dance, a dance aimed at the very (dis)ability to dance of the dead partner. The designated external content (Romeo's lament of the dead Juliet) is sustained by the self-reference to the form itself. We can see, now, why the notion of suture cannot function within Post-Theory. Post-Theory insists on multiple relatively independent levels. For example, one can examine the perception of films as a cognitive-psychological process, one can examine the narrative structuring of fiction cinema, one can examine ideological biases involved in the narrative line and visual presentations, one can examine cinema as an economic process . . . Of course, there may be intersections and overdeterminations between these levels (say, the narrative line can bear witness to a clear ideological bias), but they are a secondary phenomenon which should be proven in a detailed analysis, not asserted in a hasty generalisation.

In contrast to this approach, one should define suture as the structurally necessary *short-circuit* between different levels (style, narrative, the economic conditions of the studio system of production, etc.). However, suture must be distinguished from the otherwise very productive and interesting new historicist probing into the contingent, particular set of conditions (say, the economic limitations of cinema production) which gave birth to some well-known stylistic innovation. The best example here, perhaps, is Val Lewton's stylistic revolution in horror: the world of his *Cat People*

(1943) and *The Seventh Victim* (1943) simply belongs to a different universe when compared with the world of, say, *Frankenstein* or *Dracula* – and, as we know, Lewton's procedure of only hinting at the presence of evil in everyday reality in the guise of dark shadows or strange sounds, never directly showing it, was propelled by the financial limitations of B-productions.[50] In a homologous way, the greatest post-World War II revolution in opera staging, that of Bayreuth in the early 50s, which replaced bombastic stage costumes with bare stage and singers dressed only in pseudo-Greek tunics, the main effects being achieved by strong lighting, was an inventive solution occasioned by financial crisis: Bayreuth was practically broke, so they couldn't afford rich staging and costumes, but, through a stroke of luck the Siemens company offered them strong searchlights for free.

However, such explanations, insightful and interesting as they are, do not yet belong to Theory proper: they do not yet undermine (or, to use the old-fashioned term, 'deconstruct') the notion of the inherent evolution of stylistic procedures, i.e. the standard formalist narrative of the autonomous growth of artistic styles. These external conditions leave the internal logic intact, in the same way in which, if a scientist tells me that my passionate love is effectively conditioned by neuronal or biochemical processes, this knowledge in no way undermines or affects my passionate (self-)experience. Even if we go a step further and endeavour to discern global correspondences between different levels of the phenomenon of cinema (how a certain narrative structure relies on a certain set of ideological presuppositions and finds its optimal expression in a determinate set of formal procedures of montage, framing of shots, etc., like the standard notion that classic Hollywood involves the ideology of American individualism, linear narrative closure, the well-known shot/reverse-shot procedure, etc.), we do not yet reach the level of Theory proper.

What, then, is still missing? The notion of reflexivity might be of some help here: to put it succinctly, 'suture' means that *external* difference is always an *internal* one, that the external limitation of a field of phenomena always reflects itself within this field, as its inherent impossibility to fully become itself. To take a tragic example from philosophy: Étienne Balibar demonstrated convincingly how Louis Althusser's last theoretical writings not only 'deconstruct', but systematically endeavour to destroy his previous 'standard', theoretical propositions, how they are sustained by a kind of philosophical death-drive, by a will to obliterate, to undo, one's previous achievements (like the notion of Marx's epistemological cut).[51] However, if we account for this 'will to self-obliteration' in the simple terms of the unfortunate effects in his late work of a personal pathology, i.e. of the destructive twist which finally found its outlet in the murderous assault on his wife, we *miss the point*: true as it may be at the level of biographical facts, this external causality is of no interest whatsoever, if we do not succeed in interpreting it as a shock which set in motion some inherent tension already at work within Althusser's philosophical edifice. In other words, Althusser's self-destructive twist ultimately had to be accounted for in the terms of his philosophy itself. Or, to take the elementary example of sexual difference: in a patriarchal society, the external limit/opposition that divides women from men also functions as the inherent obstacle which prevents women from fully realising their potential.

We can see how, in this precise sense, suture is the exact opposite of the illusory, self-enclosed totality that successfully erases the decentred traces of its production process: suture means that, precisely, such self-enclosure is *a priori* impossible, that the excluded externality always leaves its traces within – or, to put it in standard Freudian terms, that there is no repression (from the scene of phenomenal self-experience) without the return of the repressed. In terms of cinema, this means that one cannot simply distinguish different levels – say, the narrative line from the formal procedures of shot/counter-shot, tracking and crane shots, etc. It is also not yet sufficient (for an account to count as true Theory) to try to establish structural correspondences between different levels and to determine how certain narrative modes entail or at least privilege certain formal procedures. We only attain the level of true Theory when, in a unique short-circuit, we conceive of a certain formal procedure not as expressing a certain aspect of the (narrative) content, but as marking/signalling the part of the content that is excluded from the explicit narrative line, so that – therein resides the proper theoretical point – *if we want to reconstruct 'all' of the narrative content, we must reach beyond the explicit narrative content as such, and include some formal features which act as the stand-in for the 'repressed' aspect of the content.*

To take a well-known elementary example from the analysis of melodramas: the emotional excess that cannot express itself directly in the narrative line finds its outlet in the ridiculously sentimental musical accompaniment or in other formal features. Exemplary here is the way Claude Berri's *Jean de Florette* and *Manon des Sources* (both 1986) displace Marcel Pagnol's original film (and his own later novelisation of it) on which they are based. That is to say, Pagnol's original retains the traces of the 'authentic' French provincial community life in which people's acts follow old, quasi-pagan religious patterns, while Berri's films fail in their effort to recapture the spirit of the closed pre-modern community. However, unexpectedly, the inherent obverse of Pagnol's universe is the theatricality of the action and the element of ironic distance and comicality, while Berri's films, while shot more 'realistically', put emphasis on destiny (the musical leitmotif of the films is based on Verdi's *La forza del destino*), and on the melodramatic excess whose hystericality often borders on the ridiculous (like the scene in which, after the rain passes his field, the desperate Jean cries and shouts at Heaven).[52] So, paradoxically, the closed, ritualised premodern community implies theatrical comicality and irony, while the modern 'realistic' rendering involves fate and melodramatic excess ... In this respect, Berri's two films are to be opposed to Lars von Trier's *Breaking the Waves* (1996): in both cases, we are dealing with the tension between form and content; however, in *Breaking the Waves*, the excess is located in the content (the subdued pseudo-documentary form makes palpable the excessive content), while in Berri, the excess in the form obfuscates and thus renders palpable the flaw in content, the impossibility today of realising the pure classical tragedy of destiny.

This is what Lacan aims at in his persistent reference to torus and other variations of the Moebius-strip-like structures in which the relationship between inside and outside is inverted: if we want to grasp the minimal structure of subjectivity, the clear-cut opposition between inner subjective experience and outer objective reality is not sufficient – there is an excess on both sides. On the one hand, we should accept the lesson of Kant's transcendental idealism: out of the confused multitude of impressions, 'objective reality' emerges through the intervention of the subject's transcendental act. In other words, Kant does not deny the distinction between the multitude of subjective impressions and objective reality; his point is merely that this very distinction results from the intervention of a *subjective* gesture of transcendental constitution. In a homologous way, Lacan's 'master-signifier' is the 'subjective' signifying feature which sustains the very 'objective' symbolic structure: if we abstract from the objective symbolic order this subjective excess, the very objectivity of this order disintegrates.

Lacan's claim that the 'imaginary' number (the square root of −1) is the 'meaning of phallus', its signified, is often referred to as the outstanding example of Lacan's intellectual imposture – so what does he mean by it? The paradox of the square root of −1 is that it is an 'impossible' number whose value cannot ever be positivised, but which nonetheless 'functions' – what has this to do with phallus? Precisely insofar as it is the signifier of the impossible fulness of meaning, phallus is a 'signifier without signified' – the 'minus 1', the supplementary feature which sticks out from the series of 'normal' signifiers, the element in which excess and lack coincide. The impossible fulness at the level of meaning (of the signified) is sustained by the void (the castrating dimension) at the level of the signifier – we encounter the 'meaning of phallus' when, apropos of some notion, we enthusiastically feel that 'this is *it*, the true thing, the true meaning', although we are never able to explicate *what*, precisely, this meaning *is*. In a political discourse, for example, the master-signifier of 'Nation' is this kind of empty signifier which stands for the impossible fulness of meaning. When you ask a member of the Nation to define in what the identity of his Nation consists, his ultimate answer will always be, 'I cannot say it, you must feel it, it is *it*, that which our lives are really about.'

In recent years, two new labels have become established in the fruit juice (and also ice-cream) market: 'forest fruit' and 'multi-vitamin'. Both are associated with a clearly identified flavour, but the point is that the connection between the label and what it designates is ultimately contingent, i.e. the label cannot be directly grounded in its designated content. A different combination of forest fruits would produce a different flavour, and it would be possible to generate the same flavour in an artificial way (with the same, of course, going also for 'multi-vitamin' juice), so that one can easily imagine a child who, after getting an authentic, home-made forest fruit juice, complains: 'That's not what I want! I want the *true* forest fruit juice!' It is all too easy to dismiss this as an example of the way fixed designations function within commodity fetishism: what they render visible is a gap and a concomitant determination of the signified by the signifier that pertains to language 'as such': there is always a gap between what a word actually means (in our case, the flavour recognised as 'multi-vitamin') and what would have been its meaning if it were to function literally (any juice rich with a multitude of vitamins).[53]

The way the cognitivist stance so dear to Post-Theory disavows this gap and thereby the symbolic order itself, is best formulated by John Searle: 'There are brute, blind neurophysiological processes, and there is consciousness, but there is nothing else.'[54] All you need is the process of mental representation and some form of rational agency – no need for some unfathomable third agency like the unconscious. At its most elementary, this unconscious level is, of course, the non-psychological symbolic order itself (the Lacanian big Other, the order of symbolic fictions, what Karl Popper called the Third World, neither that of psychological self-experience nor that of material reality), with its unique structure of symbolic *potentiality*. In a desperate suicidal situation, the subject can 'cheat' and thus save himself in adopting the very decision to kill himself as a fiction which allows him to survive: 'OK, the pressure is too much, I'll kill myself – not now, but one of these days, so it's decided, let's go on with business as usual.' The suicidal decision is here in a way totally sincere – only as such can it have the effect – of what? Of, precisely, endlessly *postponing* the suicide: why should I bother to do it, when I have already decided that I really intend to do it? This is the primordial lie, the *proton pseudos*, of the symbolic order. This potentiality provides the key for Kieślowski's virtualisation of reality: what he stages are the multiple potential scenarios which enable the subject to postpone the true – suicidal – act.

Plato's *Kratylos* (433–432BC) articulates the key change of the register from the Imaginary to the Symbolic, i.e. from the imaginary resemblance to the unary feature (*le trait unaire*) to which the object is reduced in its symbol. After reaching the dead end of resemblance (if the sign of Kratylos fully resembles Kratylos, we have no longer Kratylos and his sign, but simply two Kratylos), Socrates asserts that there should, obviously, be a 'different sort of suitability' for the image and for the sign (name): what is crucial in a proper sign (name) is not the full resemblance to the designated object, but only the fact that the name contains the 'characteristic feature' of the object. Here we encounter the constitutive 'violence' of the symbolic order: the name 'murders' the designated object by reducing it to a 'unary feature'. This is not a deficiency of the name, but its positive force of reducing the object to its essence: we enter the symbolic space proper when we are no longer within the field of *mimesis*, of the (im)perfect reproduction of resemblance – in the symbolic space, the very gap of the name with regard to the object splits the object from within, introducing the distance between the object in its brute reality and the object's essential dimension.

Against this background, one is tempted to reread Hitchcock's great trilogy *Vertigo* (1958), *North by Northwest* (1959) and *Psycho* – each film of which focuses on the question of identity: is Judy Madeleine? is Thornhill Kaplan? is Norman Mother?[55] In *Vertigo*, Judy *resembles* Madeleine; we are dealing here with the imaginary dimension: Judy is neither 'really' Madeleine (the true Madeleine was murdered), nor is she symbolically Madeleine, since she lacks what Plato would have called Madeleine's 'characteristic feature'. In *North by Northwest*, Thornhill is Kaplan at the level of *symbolic* identification: although he neither resembles Kaplan nor is he 'really' Kaplan (since there is no Kaplan), he is stuck on to the signifier 'Kaplan'. In *Psycho*, Norman Bates 'is' his own mother neither at the symbolic level nor in the Imaginary: although he speaks like his mother and dresses up like her, the proper imaginary and symbolic dimension are precisely missing here – he psychotically recreates the scene of his mother being alive in the Real of his hallucination.

One can also put it in the terms of Charles Sanders Peirce's triad of indexical, iconic and symbolic signs: Norman is indexically linked to Mother (like smoke to fire, part of the shared real situation); Judy is iconically Madeleine (she perfectly resembles her); Thornhill is symbolically Kaplan.[56] The Marx brothers' classic formula, 'Chicolini here may talk like an idiot, and look like an idiot, but don't let that fool you. He really is an idiot' perfectly renders the standard double deception (one feigns to feign) in which we all, 'normal' speaking subjects, participate, insofar as we dwell within the symbolic space. In order to designate a psychotic, one should simplify the formula into: 'This man acts and talks, but this should not deceive you – he is an idiot!' That is to say, the normal appearance of participating in communal life is just a fake, a superficial imitation, beneath which there lurks an idiot immersed into his solipsistic *jouissance*. In contrast to this, the hysterical formula would have been: 'This woman acts and talks, but this should not deceive you – she *is*!' All the talk and acting-out of the hysterical subject is here to deceive us with regard to what she is, with regard to the fantasmatic core of her being.

This structure of symbolic potentiality opens up and sustains the space for the multitude of reflexive phenomena, from alternative narrativisations to the intriguing procedure of films of a certain genre which implicitly refer to the codes of another genre, like the sequence of Jews departing from Egypt to their promised land in de Mille's *The Ten Commandments* (1923/56): this sequence rather obviously refers to the standard Western scene of a wagon train of settlers starting their trail towards the West – all the details are there, mothers gathering their children who run around, the merry shouts of enthusiastic young men, etc. This invisible Western code is indispensable if we are to account for the efficiency of the sequence.[57]

The mental experiment in Frank Capra's *It's a Wonderful Life* (1947) by means of which the hero visits his town and sees how it would look in the case of his own absence provides a more complex case of 'alternative history'; it is staged to make him accept his past life as effectively 'his own'. All his life till that fateful Christmas evening, the hero had been living in the expectation of another life, of leaving the town and going elsewhere – he had lived his actual life in a permanent state of suspension, as if 'this were not yet *it*', like the hero of Henry James's story awaiting all his life the jump of the 'Beast in the Jungle', the special event to come. How, on a closer look, is this full acceptance achieved? It is here that the allegorical dimension of the film – the reference of its content to cinema history, to the difference between cinema genres – becomes operative: the nightmare image of what the town would have turned into in the case of the hero's absence is clearly modelled on *film noir*, so that the mental experiment with alternative history is a cinematic one, i.e. one passes into another genre – the hero is the ultimate guarantee and bulwark against the *noir* universe. This reference to *noir* has to be mobilised in order to secure the ideological operation of the film, i.e. to make the hero (and the spectator) renounce his striving for Otherness and fully accept the obtuseness of (the ideological perception of) small-town everyday American life.

Here we encounter the ambiguity of Frank Capra's populism:[58] it is presented as a return from an artificial slapstick or musical universe to 'little real people', yet these real people, even if victims of economic depression, are thoroughly fictitious in their naive goodness and subtle stupidity.[59] However, this 'unbelievable' character of the ordinary people's naive goodness is calculated: spectators *know* that 'real people' are not like that, that they are mean and embittered – what Capra counts on is that they *want to believe* that they are like that. So Capra directly mobilises the split between belief and knowledge: the spectator of his films is not naive, he or she *knows* that people are not like that, that there are no idyllic large families like the one in *You Can't Take It With You* (1938), or towns like the one in *It's a Wonderful Life* – however, this very knowledge permits him or her to indulge in the fantasy of imagining such a community. Capra doesn't believe, he believes in belief itself . . . Here enters, in a surprising way, sexual difference: the ultimate enemy of the naive Capraesque hero is the emancipated screwball heroine – embittered, manipulative (exemplified by Barbara Stanwyck or Jean Arthur in the role of a cynical journalist), whose story is the story of how she abandons her cynical stance and accepts the naive honesty of the hero (Gary Cooper, James Stewart). We are thus again dealing with the genre cross-reference: Capra's films are only readable through their mediation with the sophisticated cynicism of the screwball comedy.

The underlying principle and support of this thesis of the relative autonomy of the symbolic order is that, in each field of meaning, if this field is to be 'totalised', there has to be an additional/excessive signifier which, as it were, gives a positive figure to that which cannot be properly included into this field, somewhat like Spinoza's well-known criticism of the traditional personalised notion of God: at the point at which our positive knowledge of the causal links fails, we supplement this lack with the idea of 'God', which, instead of providing a precise idea of a cause, just fills in the lack of this idea. In short: in order to produce the effect of self-enclosure, one must add to the series an excessive element which 'sutures' it precisely insofar as it does not belong to the series, but sticks out as an exception, like the proverbial 'filler' in classificatory systems, a category which poses as one among the species of a genus, although it is effectively just a negative container, a catch-all for everything that does not fit the species articulated from the inherent principle of the genus. In traditional Marxism the unfortunate concept of the 'Asiatic mode of production' played a somewhat similar role: this concept functioned as a kind of container for the inassimilable rest, i.e. it was not effectively defined by a set of positive determinations, but Marxists put into it that which did not fit any of the other modes of production, so that we find in it ancient China, Egypt, etc. So, far from being himself engaged in an intellectual imposture, what Lacan does with his theory of the 'meaning of phallus' is to provide a kind of elementary account of the very structure of symbolic 'imposture', of turning ignorance into a positive asset – phallus as signifier is for Lacan fundamentally a semblance. On the other hand, what Lacan calls *objet petit a* is the exact opposite of the phallic master-signifier: not the subjective supplement which sustains the objective order, but the objective supplement which sustains subjectivity in its contrast to the subjectless objective order. The *objet petit a* is that 'bone in the throat', that disturbing stain which forever blurs our picture of reality, i.e. the *object* on account of which 'objective reality' is forever inaccessible to the subject.

And the ultimate example of this convoluted exchange of places between the subjective and the objective is, of course, that of the *Gaze* itself. Nowhere is the gap between Theory and Post-Theory so obvious as apropos of the Gaze. Joan Copjec[60] asserts the proto-transcendental status of 'partial objects' (Gaze, voice, breast . . .), which are the 'condition of possibility' of their organ-counterparts: Gaze is the condition of possibility of the eye, i.e. of our seeing something in the world (we only see something insofar as an X eludes our eye and 'returns the Gaze'), voice is the condition of possibility of our hearing something, and so on. These partial *objets petit a* are neither subjective nor objective, but the short-circuit of the two dimensions: the subjective stain/stand-in that sustains the order of objectivity, and the objective 'bone in the throat' that sustains subjectivity.

Does this not provide the reason why, in so-called caper films, the act itself around which the story turns (usually a big robbery) is as a rule presented as a fantasmatic scene: all of a sudden, everyday 'reality' is suspended, we seem to enter another, ethereal dimension. The easiest way to achieve this effect is to deprive the depicted events of their vocal substance: the scene is shown from great distance, shot through glasses, so that persons seem to swim in thick air (recall the act of murder in Hitchcock's *Secret Agent* [1936]); instead of the realist background of sounds, the scene is accompanied by the off-voice commentary (in Robert Siodmak's *The Killers* [1946], we see the caper while a voice reads a later newspaper report on it; in his *Criss-Cross* [1948], it is the smoke enveloping the scene which creates an ethereal, quasi-magical atmosphere; in Kubrick's early masterpiece *The Killing* [1956], the circus masks worn by the robbers change them into mad, depersonalised dolls). The *act* itself, the traumatic, violent focus of the narrative, is supplied with a dream-like quality – a further demonstration of Lacan's thesis that, in a dream, the Real appears in the guise of a dream within a dream.

The result of experiencing and/or witnessing some excessively cruel (or otherwise libidinally invested) event, from intense sexual activity to physical torture, is that, when, afterwards, we return to our 'normal' reality, *we cannot conceive of both domains as belonging to the same reality*. The reimmersion in 'ordinary' reality renders the traumatic memory of the horror somewhat hallucinatory, derealising it. This is what Lacan is aiming at in his distinction between reality and the Real: we cannot ever acquire a complete, all-encompassing, sense of reality – some part of it must be affected by the 'loss of reality', deprived of the character of 'true reality', and this fictionalised element is precisely the traumatic Real.

This brings us back to Kieślowski: if there ever was a film-maker obsessed with this inner tension of our experience of reality, it is Kieślowski. In what is arguably his paradigmatic procedure (as exemplified by the short post-office sequence in *Decalogue* 6), he elevates a common phenomenon like the glass reflection of a human face into the momentous apparition of the Real for which there is no place in our experience of reality. And the same procedure is discernible at the narrative level itself: in an interview, Kieślowski remarks that, apropos of the Judge in *Red*, it is not certain whether he *exists at all* or if he is just the product of Valentine's imagination, her fantasy (the mythical figure who secretly 'pulls the strings of fate'). With the exception of two scenes, one never sees him with anyone other than Valentine:

> Does the Judge even exist? To be honest, the only proof . . . is the tribunal, the sole place where we see him with other people. Otherwise he could be merely a ghost, or better yet, a possibility – the old age that awaits Auguste, what might have happened if Auguste had not taken the ferry.[61]

There are echoes of this motif in other Kieślowski films: in *No End*, the deceased husband returns as a ghost to the wife: here, too, he doesn't exist, since he is a ghost (although *No End* seems to offer a rather clumsy earlier version of the more elegant later solutions). The fascinating denouement of M. Night Shyamalan's *The Sixth Sense* (1999) also points in the same direction: what we discover at the end of this story about a psychiatrist (Bruce Willis) who encounters a young kid with supernatural capacities (of materialising visions of the dead people who walk around seen only by him and unaware that they are dead) is that, without knowing it, the psychiatrist himself has been dead all the time, and is himself just a ghost evoked by the kid. So we have here the verbatim realisation of the scene from the Freudian dream in which the father who appears to the son *doesn't know that he is dead*, and has to be reminded of it. The shock of this denouement is that it turns around the standard discovery that I am alone, that all people around me are dead or puppets or aliens, that they do not exist in the proper human sense: what I discover is that *I myself* (i.e. the film's narrator through whom I see the film, my stand-in in the film) *do not exist*. The move here is properly anti-Cartesian: it's not the world around me which is a fiction, it is *I myself* who is a fiction.

One cannot but recall here the well-known exchange between Winston Smith and his interrogator from *1984*: ' "Does Big Brother exist? . . . Does he exist in the same way as I exist?" "You do not exist!" ' Along the same lines, although the Judge in *Red* is a 'real person', part of the film's diegetic reality, his symbolic-libidinal status is nonetheless that of a spectral apparition, of someone who exists as Valentine's fantasy creation. This unique procedure is the opposite of the standard revelation of the illusory status of (what we previously misperceived as) a part of reality: what is thereby asserted is rather, in a paradoxical, tautological move, *the illusory status of the illusion itself* – the illusion that there is some suprasensible, noumenal entity is rendered precisely as an 'illusion', as a fleeting apparition. And, again, what this means is that we cannot ever comprehend the 'whole' of reality that we encounter: if we are to be able to endure our encounter with reality, some part of it has to be 'derealised', experienced as a spectral apparition.

Part Two

THE PARTICULAR: SINTHOMS, SINTHOMS EVERYWHERE

Chapter Four
'Now I've got glycerine!'

The ultimate gap that gives rise to suture is ontological, a crack that cuts through reality itself: the 'whole' of reality cannot be perceived/accepted as reality, so the price we have to pay for 'normally' situating ourselves within reality is that something should be foreclosed from it: this void of primordial repression has to be filled in – 'sutured' – by the spectral fantasy. And this gap runs through the very core of Kieślowski's work.[1]

It was precisely a fidelity to the Real that compelled Kieślowski to abandon documentary realism – at some point, one encounters something more Real than reality itself. Kieślowski's starting point was the same as that of all cineasts in the socialist countries: the conspicuous gap between the drab social reality and the optimistic, bright image which pervaded the heavily censored official media. The first reaction to the fact that, in Poland, social reality was 'unrepresented', as Kieślowski put it, was, of course, the move towards a more adequate representation of real life in all its drabness and ambiguity – in short, an authentic documentary approach:

> There was a necessity, a need – which was very exciting for us – to describe the world. The Communist world had described how it should be and not how it really was. . . . If something hasn't been described, then it doesn't officially exist. So that if we start describing it, we bring it to life.[2]

Suffice it to mention *Hospital*, Kieślowski's documentary from 1977, in which the camera follows orthopaedic surgeons on a 32-hour shift. Instruments fall apart in their hands, there are frequent power-cuts and shortages of the most basic materials, but the doctors persevere hour after hour, and with humour . . . Then, however, the obverse experience sets in, best captured by the slogan used recently to publicise a Hollywood movie: 'It's so real, it must be a fiction!' – at the most radical level, one can render the

Real of subjective experience only in the guise of a fiction. Towards the end of the documentary *First Love* (1974), in which the camera follows a young unmarried couple during the girl's pregnancy, through their wedding and the delivery of the baby, the father is shown holding the newly born baby in his hands and crying. Kieślowski reacted to the obscenity of such unwarranted probing into the other's intimacy by referring to the 'fright of real tears'. His decision to pass from documentaries to fiction films was thus, at its most radical, an ethical one:

> Not everything can be described. That's the documentary's great problem. It catches itself as if in its own trap. . . . If I'm making a film about love, I can't go into a bedroom if real people are making love there. . . . I noticed, when making documentaries, that the closer I wanted to get to an individual, the more objects which interested me shut themselves off.
>
> That's probably why I changed to features. There's no problem there. I need a couple to make love in bed, that's fine. Of course, it might be difficult to find an actress who's willing to take off her bra, but then you just find one who is. . . . I can even buy some glycerine, put some drops in her eyes and the actress will cry. I managed to photograph some real tears several times. It's something completely different. But now I've got glycerine. I'm frightened of real tears. In fact, I don't even know whether I've got the right to photograph them. At such times I feel like somebody who's found himself in a realm which is, in fact, out of bounds. That's the main reason why I escaped from documentaries.[3]

The crucial intermediary in this passage from documentary to fiction is *Camera Buff* (1979), the portrait of a man who, because of his passion for the camera, loses his wife, child, and job – a *fiction* film about a *documentary* film-maker. So there is a domain of fantasmatic intimacy which is marked by a 'No trespass!' sign and should be approached only via fiction, if one is to avoid pornographic obscenity. This is the reason why the French Véronique in *The Double Life of Véronique* rejects the puppeteer: he wants to penetrate her too much, which is why, towards the film's end, after he tells her the story of her double life, she is deeply hurt and escapes to her father. And is not the figure of the Judge in *Red*, Kieślowski's last film, a kind of mega-puppeteer? The Judge's 'sin' (secretly listening to the private phone-conversations of his neighbours) involves precisely the unpardonable act of anonymously penetrating others' intimacy, of 'trespass'. So is it not as if the Judge is making documentaries which 'go all the way' and violate the barrier of intimacy? And, insofar as the Judge is, up to a point, Kieślowski's rather obvious self-portrait, does he not stand for a temptation of Kieślowski himself?

In Heiner Müller's short play *Der Mauser*, his reply to Brecht's 'learning play' *The Measures Taken*, the Chorus (which speaks from the exclusive position of revolutionary class struggle) asks the question: '*Was ist Mensch?*', 'What Is Man?', and its answer is: we do not know who or what man is, we know only *who the enemy is*, who has to be beaten and crushed so that a new man will emerge. Although Kieślowski is the ideological opposite of Müller, this is ultimately also his answer: all pathetic humanist celebrations of man are just so many obscene violations of the 'No trespass!' sign; the only proper thing to do is to maintain a distance towards the intimate, idiosyncratic, fantasy domain – one can only circumscribe, hint at, these fragile elements that bear witness to a human personality.

In this encroaching upon the Other's intimacy, we encounter the function of *shame* at its purest. Of course, one can feel ashamed for oneself (when one is caught in public doing something indecent). However, much more mysterious is the phenomenon of feeling ashamed for what *another* did – this is 'interpassivity' at its purest, where I am passive for (instead of) the other, assuming the feeling of shame for him or her.[4] It is clearly insufficient to account for this phenomenon in terms of empathy with the Other's embarrassment, or of transference (I am ashamed because I am secretly aware that the Other realised my unacknowledged desire; I am ashamed to see the Other, the subject supposed to know, humiliated, his impotence rendered public). *What makes me feel ashamed is not so much what the Other did, but, rather, the very fact that the Other is not ashamed of what he or she did.*[5] It is against this background that the threat of the human genome project becomes palpable: it opens up the prospect of the total 'transparency' of the human being: there will be nothing to hide, which means that the very notion of shame will be rendered irrelevant, as well as the notion of justice. As was pointed out by John Rawls, our most elementary notion of justice involves the reference to the 'veil of ignorance': justice *has* to be blind, it *has* to ignore the full specific context of those who demand justice and reduce them to 'abstract', equal subjects.

How, then, is Kieślowski's ban on real tears related to the Old Testament ban on images? A reference to Arnold Schoenberg's *Moses und Aaron*, the opera concerning the prohibition on making images (or its equivalent, *musica ficta*[6] – since Schoenberg's effort is precisely to tear music out of the imagistic-depicting frame), might be of some help here. In Schoenberg, the song approaches more and more the non-melodic *Sprechgesang*; as such, *Moses und Aaron* is to be set against the melodramatic excesses of someone like Puccini, in whose pathetic finales (from *La Bohème* onwards) the music overflows the stage. However, as Adorno remarked, *Moses und Aaron* gets caught here in a self-referential contradiction: 'The ban on images goes further than even Schoenberg himself was prepared to imagine ... To give great ideas immediate thematic expression in a work of art nowadays means depicting their after-image.'[7] In short, the prohibition on images affects the very musical medium, so the opera itself has to remain unfinished after its most 'efficient' scene (the Golden Calf), which *is* precisely, *musica ficta* – operatic spectacle. Significantly, *Moses und Aaron* ends with Moses' desperate cry, 'O Word, thou Word, that I lack!' What breaks down here is not Aaron's exuberant singing, but precisely its opposite, Moses' purity of Word. In a kind of Hegelian 'negation of negation', the negation of the image on behalf of the Word leads to the self-negation of the Word itself.[8]

Kieślowski seems to share the Old Testament injunction to withdraw the domain of what really matters from degrading visibility. However, in a spirit which runs counter to Old Testament iconoclasm, he supplements the prohibition to depict the intimate moments of 'real' life with, precisely, *fiction*, with 'false' images. While one should not show 'real' sex or intimate emotional moments, actors can *feign* them, even in a very 'realistic' way (as they definitely do in Kieślowski's films).[9] Is, then, Kieślowski's point simply that wearing a mask should serve as a kind of protective shield, as the sign of respect for what should remain concealed? Or is it rather that Kieślowski is fully aware of the dialectic of 'wearing a mask'? Our social identity, the person we assume to be in our intersubjective exchanges, is already a 'mask', it already involves the repression of our inadmissible impulses, and it is precisely in the conditions of 'just gaming', when the rules regulating our 'real-life' exchanges are temporarily suspended, that we can permit ourselves to display these repressed attitudes. Think of the stereotypical computer nerd who, while playing an interactive game, adopts the screen identity of a sadistic murderer and irresistible seducer. It is all too simple to say that this identity is just an imaginary supplement, a temporary escape from real-life impotence. The point is rather that, since he knows that the interactive game is 'just a game', he can 'show his true self', do things he would never have done in real-life interactions. In the guise of a fiction, the *truth* about himself is articulated.

As a proof of this dimension, one should evoke the uncanny feeling one gets when watching Kieślowski's documentaries: it is as if (real-life) persons *play themselves*, generating an uncanny overlapping of documentary and fiction; in Bentham's terms, they function as their own icons. When, in *From a Night Porter's Point of View* (1977), the factory porter – a fanatic of strict discipline, who extends his power even into his personal life as he tries to control everybody and everything – insists that 'rules are more important than people', he does not immediately display his innermost stance; it is rather that, in a reflective attitude, he 'plays himself' by way of imitating what he perceives as his own ideal image. It is to avoid *this* impasse that Kieślowski had to move to fiction: since, when we film 'real-life' scenes in a documentary way, we get people *playing* themselves (or, if not this, then obscenity, the pornographic trespass into intimacy), the only way to depict people *beneath* their protective mask of playing is, paradoxically, to make them *directly play a role*, i.e. to move into fiction. Fiction is more real than the social reality of playing roles.[10] If, in Kieślowski's documentaries, the protagonists seem to play themselves, then his late fiction films cannot but appear as documentaries about the brilliant and seductive performance of the beautiful actress (Binoche, Jacob).[11]

Today, however, this 'No trespass!' is increasingly undermined: our culture is one in which there is a pressure to 'tell everything', to probe into or publicly confess fantasies and intimate details of sexual lives, including the shape of the President's penis. The paradox, of course, is that this globalisation of discourse is the mode of appearance of its very opposite: the price we pay for the fact that 'everything is discourse' is that discourse becomes *impotent* in the face of the most common idiotic reality (recall the impotence of tolerant discourse in the face of meaningless raw violence).[12] The price we pay for the individual's unconstrained public confession/disclosure is that individuality itself is threatened. No wonder, then, that this utter 'subjectivisation' overlaps with utter 'objectivisation': unconstrained public confessions are supplemented by the obsession with genome, with the prospect of establishing what a human being 'objectively is'.

We confront these paradoxes in their purest form in what appears to be the anti-Kieślowski gesture *par excellence*, the recent endeavours to circumvent one of the fundamental prohibitions of narrative cinema by combining the 'hardcore' depiction of sex with the narrative, i.e. to include in it sex scenes which are played for real (we see the erect penis, actual penetration). Until recently, hardcore pornography itself respected the Kieślowskian ban: although it did show 'everything', real sex, the narrative which provided the frame for repeated sexual encounters was as a rule ridiculously non-realistic, stereotypical, stupidly comical, staging a kind of return to the eighteenth-century *commedia del'arte* in which actors do not play 'real' individuals, but one-dimensional types – the Miser, the Cuckolded Husband, the Promiscuous Wife. Is not this strange compulsion to make the narrative ridiculous a kind of negative gesture of respect: yes, we do show everything, but precisely for that reason we want to make it clear that it's all a big joke, that the actors are not really engaged?

Kieślowski's recourse to the theme of alternative realities is propelled by the same tension between documentary and fiction: since documentary shooting results in an overabundance of unco-ordinated material, in large part generated by unforeseeable contingencies, no single narrative line can organise it into a consistent whole, so the only way to bring about the necessary sense of unity is through organising the material along the lines of formal rhythmic patterns – documentary film-making and formalism are strictly correlative. The subterranean pattern of links and reverberations of visual and other motifs which underlies the narrative of Kieślowski's fiction films has nothing to do with any spiritualist mysticism: it is, on the contrary, the ultimate proof of his *materialism*. Even in his fiction films, Kieślowski *treats the footage as documentary material* which, consequently, should be decimated, so that all that remains are fragments which are never fully comprehensible, i.e. in whose final cut something – the element that would provide the crucial clarification – is always missing. Far from relying on anti-documentary ethereal spirituality, Kieślowski's openness to contingent encounters, coincidences and unexpected mysterious links, this much-celebrated 'mysterious' effect of his late feature films, is thus paradoxically grounded in the persistence of the documentary approach to the very end of his film-making.[13] The very notion of alternative realities is also grounded in the excess of documentary material which resists incorporation into a single narrative: it can only be organised as the texture of multiple narrative lines.

Therein, perhaps, resides the ultimate lesson of the dialectical tension between documentary reality and fiction: if our social reality itself is sustained by a symbolic fiction or fantasy, then the ultimate achievement of film art is not to recreate reality within the narrative fiction, to seduce us into (mis)taking a fiction for reality, but, on the contrary, to make us discern the fictional aspect of reality itself, to experience reality itself as a fiction. We are watching on screen a simple documentary shot in which, all of a sudden, the entire fantasmatic depth reverberates. We are shown what 'really happened', and suddenly, we perceive this reality in all its fragility, as one of the contingent outcomes, forever haunted by its shadowy doubles. This is what documentaries at their best can render.

And should we not interpret Kieślowski's final retreat into peaceful private life, his renunciation of film-making, as the *third* stage, which, in accordance with the inexorable inherent logic of his artistic development (the same logic responsible also for the silence of authors as different as Rimbaud and Dashiel Hammett), had to follow his 'documentary' and his 'fictional' stage?[14] If the passage from documentaries to fiction movies was caused by the 'fright of real tears', by the insight into the obscenity of directly rendering 'real-life' intimate experiences, was the abandonment of even the fiction movies not caused by an insight into how fictions are in a way even more vulnerable than reality? If documentaries intrude into and hurt the personal *reality* of the protagonists, fiction intrudes into and hurts *dreams themselves*, secret fantasies that form the unavowed kernel of our lives.

Chapter Five
Run, Witek, Run

Kieślowski's interest in the role of chance in determining the multiple possible outcomes of a dramatic situation (exemplarily in his *Blind Chance*, but also in *Véronique* and *Red*), offers yet another example of the well-known phenomenon of the old artistic forms pushing against their own boundaries by way of mobilising procedures which, at least from our retrospective view, seem to point towards a new technology that will be able to serve as a more 'natural' and appropriate 'objective correlative' to the life-experience the old forms endeavoured to render with their excessive experimentations.[15] It can thus be claimed that a whole series of narrative procedures in the nineteenth-century novel announces not only standard narrative cinema (recall the intricate use of 'flashback' in Emily Brontë or of 'cross-cutting' and 'close-ups' in Dickens), but sometimes even modernist cinema (recall the use of 'off-space' in *Madame Bovary*) – as if a new perception of life was already here, but was still struggling to find its proper means of articulation, until it finally found it in cinema.

It can be claimed that today we are approaching a homologous threshold: a new 'life experience' is in the air, a perception of life that explodes the form of the linear, centred narrative and renders life as a multiform flow; even in the domain of the 'hard' sciences (quantum physics and its multiple-reality interpretation; neo-Darwinism) we seem to be haunted by the chanciness of life and the alternative versions of reality – to quote Stephen Jay Gould's blunt formulation, which uses a cinema metaphor: 'Wind back the film of life and play it again. The history of evolution will be totally different.'[16] Either life is experienced as a series of multiple parallel destinies that interact and are crucially affected by meaningless contingent encounters, the points at which one series intersects with and intervenes in another (see Altman's *Short Cuts* [1993]),[17] or different versions/outcomes of the same plot are repeatedly enacted (the 'parallel universes' or 'alternative possible worlds' scenarios – even 'serious' historians themselves recently produced a volume of *Virtual Histories*, reading crucial historical moments, from Cromwell's victory over the Stuarts and the American War of Independence to the disintegration of Communism, as hinging on unpredictable and sometimes even improbable chance events). This perception of our reality as one of the possible, often even not the most probable, outcomes of an 'open' situation, this notion that other possible outcomes are not simply cancelled out but continue to haunt our 'true' reality as a spectre of what might have happened, conferring on our reality the status of extreme fragility and contingency, implicitly clashes with the predominant 'linear' narrative forms of our literature and cinema. It seems to call for a new artistic medium in which such multiplicity would not be an eccentric excess, but its 'proper' mode of functioning. One can argue that the cyberspace hypertext is such a new medium in which this life experience will find its 'natural', more appropriate objective correlative,[18] and that Kieślowski's seemingly 'obscurantist' dealing with the topic of the role of chance and of parallel alternative histories is to be perceived as yet another endeavour to articulate this new life experience in the old cinematic medium that promotes linear narrative. We find in Kieślowski three versions of alternative histories: direct presentation of three possible outcomes in *Blind Chance*, the presentation of two outcomes through the theme of the double in *Véronique* and the presentation of two outcomes through the 'flashback in the present' in *Red*. What interests Kieślowski in the motif of alternative histories is the notion of *ethical choice*, ultimately the choice between 'calm life' and 'mission'.

Is, however, this awareness of multiple universes really as liberating as it appears? The (false) ordinary perception that we live in one 'true' reality, far from containing us in a closed universe, relieves us from the unbearable awareness of the multitude of alternative universes which envelop us. That is to say, the fact that there is only one reality leaves the space open for other possibilities, i.e. for a choice: it might have been different ... If, however, these different possibilities are all in some way realised, we get a claustrophobic universe in which there is no freedom of choice precisely because *all* choices have already been realised. Perhaps it is the horrifying awareness of this absolute closure that is expressed by the desperate cry that opens Kieślowski's *Blind Chance*.

> *Blind Chance* (1981): Witek runs after a train. Three variations follow on how such a seemingly banal incident could influence the rest of his life. One: he catches the train, meets an honest Communist and himself becomes a Party activist. Two: while running for the train he bumps into a railway guard, is arrested, brought to trial and sent to unpaid labour in a park where he meets someone from the opposition. He, in turn, becomes a militant dissident. Three: he simply misses the train, returns to his interrupted studies, marries a fellow student and leads a peaceful life as a doctor unwilling to get mixed up in politics. He is sent abroad to a symposium; the plane he is on explodes in mid-air.

How do the three alternative narrative lines of *Blind Chance* relate to each other? The film opens with the 'primal scream' shot: a terrified male face looks into the camera and utters a cry of pure horror. Is this not Witek moments before his death, while the plane which was to take him to a medical symposium in the West is crashing minutes after its take-off from Warsaw airport (we learn this in the last shot of the film, at the end of the *third* narrative)? Is, then, the entire film not the flashback of a person who, aware that he is close to death, quickly runs not only through his life (as people are supposed to do when they know they will die shortly), but through his *three* possible lives? The scream that opens the film – the desperate 'Nooo!' of Witek falling to his certain death – is thus the zero-level exempted from the three virtual universes. One is tempted here to follow the hypothesis[19] according to which these three alternative versions are intertwined, so that the hero escapes from each one into the next one: the deadlock of the socialist apparatchik's career pushes him into dissidence, and non-satisfaction with dissidence into a private profession. Each version involves a reflexive stance towards the previous one, like the second Véronique, who seems to be aware of the experience of the first one.[20] It is only the third version which is 'real': just before dying, Witek runs through the two alternative life-stories in which he does not die ('What would have happened if I had caught the train; if, while running to catch it, I had bumpted into a railway guard?'), but they both end up in a deadlock which pushes him to the next story.

Tom Tykwer's *Run, Lola, Run* (1998) is a kind of post-modern frenetic remake of *Blind Chance*. Lola, a Berlin punk girl (Franka Potente), has twenty minutes to collect by any means 100,000 German Marks to save her boyfriend from certain death, and what follows are the three alternate outcomes: her boyfriend gets killed; she gets killed; she succeeds, *and* her boyfriend finds the lost money, so they end up happy together with the 100,000 DM profit. Here, also, a whole series of features signals that not only the heroine, but also even other people somehow mysteriously remember what happened in the preceding version(s). Although, in its tone (the frenetic, adrenalin-charged pace, the life-asserting energy, the happy end) *Lola* is the very opposite of *Blind Chance*, the formal matrix is the same: in both cases, one can interpret the film as if only the third story is the 'real' one, the other two staging the fantasmatic price the subject has to pay for the 'real' outcome.[21]

The interest of *Lola* resides in its tonality: not only in the fast rhythm, the rapid-fire montage, the use of stills (frozen images), the pulsating exuberance and vitality of the heroine, but, above all, in the way these visual features are embedded in the soundtrack – the constant, uninterrupted, techno-music soundscape whose rhythm renders Lola's heartbeat – and, by extension, ours, the spectators'. One should always bear in mind that, notwithstanding all the dazzling visual brilliance of the film, its images are subordinated to this musical soundscape, to its frenetic, compulsive rhythm which never stops – it only explodes in an outburst of exuberant vitality, in the guise of Lola's uninhibited scream which occurs in each of the three versions of the story. Which is why a film like *Lola* can only appear against the background of the MTV culture. One should accomplish here the same reversal Fredric Jameson proposed apropos of Hemingway's style: it is not that *Lola*'s formal properties adequately express the narrative; it is rather that the film's narrative itself was invented in order to be able to practise the style. The first words of the film ('the game lasts ninety minutes, everything else is just theory') provide the proper co-ordinates of a video game: as in the usual survival video game, Lola is given three lives. 'Real life' itself is thus rendered as a fictional video-game experience. One should resist here the temptation to oppose *Lola* and Kieślowski's *Blind Chance* along the lines of the opposition between low and high culture (Tykwer's video-game techno-rock MTV universe versus Kieślowski's thoughtful existential stance). Although this is in a way true – or, rather, a truism – the more important point is that *Lola* is much more adequate to the basic matrix of alternative spins of the narrative: it is *Blind Chance* which ultimately appears clumsy and artificial, as if the film is trying to tell its story in an inadequate form, while *Lola*'s form perfectly fits its narrative content.[22]

Kieślowski himself alludes to the virtualisation of reality in his claim that

> The theme of Red is in the conditional mood. . . . what would have happened if the Judge had been born forty years later. . . . It would be lovely if we could go back to the age of twenty. How many better, wiser things we could have done! But it's impossible. That's why I made this film – that maybe life can be lived better than we do.[23]

The theme of the 'double life' clearly resonates not only in *Red*, but also in *Blue* and *White*: in *Blue*, Julie desperately endeavours to (re-)create an alternative life for herself after the traumatic accident, while in *White*, Karol tries to invent a new career and life after his humiliating reduction to the status of social drop-out. There are traces of the alternative reality approach even in *Decalogue* 4, which was planned initially as three variations, on the model of *Blind Chance* (the father's story; the daughter's story; what really happened). Kieślowski wisely adopted a more complex procedure in which the three stories coexist in a kind of palimpsest: 'the variants are not successive (as in *Blind Chance* or *The Double Life of Véronique*), but present themselves simultaneously through the work's self-referential meditation on acting.'[24] The 'same' narrative shifts between different fantasmatic supports: sometimes, Anka acts as if there are no obstacles to her incestuous fantasy; at other times, father acts as if he and Anka are of the same age; at yet other times, the oppressive social reality makes itself felt.

Red presents us with a unique case of 'contemporary flashback': the Judge's alternative *past*, his missed opportunity, is staged as the *present* of another person (Auguste). Auguste's predicament is an exact repetition of the Judge's predicament thirty years previously. Auguste and the Judge are thus not two persons, but two versions of one and the same person – no wonder they never meet, since this meeting would function as the uncanny encounter of a double. The parallels in their respective lives are numerous: the Judge, like Auguste, was betrayed by a blonde woman two years older than him; his book also fell open at a particular page the night before his exam, where he was asked the very question answered on that page. No wonder, then, that the Judge says to Valentine: 'Maybe you're the woman I never met' – meeting her decades ago would have saved him in the way Valentine will *now* save Auguste.[25] One should approach *The Double Life of Véronique* in the same way: the image of two Véroniques should not deceive us – as the title says, we have the double life of (one) Véronique, i.e. the same person is allowed to redeem (or lose?) herself by being given another chance and repeating the fatal choice. All the mystique of being spiritually connected with another being is thoroughly misplaced.

The idea of the time–space continuum (time as the fourth dimension of space which can be traversed in two directions, forwards and backwards) in modern physics means, among other things, that a certain event (the encounter of multiple particles) can be much more elegantly and convincingly explained if we posit that only one particle travels forwards and backwards in time. Let us take Richard Feynman's classic space–time diagram of the collision between *two* photons at a certain point of time: this collision produces an electron–positron pair, each of the two going its separate way. The positron then meets another electron, they annihilate each other and create another *two* photons which depart in the opposite direction. What Feynman proposes is that, if we introduce the space–time continuum, we can explain the same process in a much simpler way: there is *only one* particle, an electron, which emits two photons; this causes it to reverse its direction in time. Travelling backwards in time as a positron, it absorbs two photons, thus becomes an electron again and reverses its direction in time, again moving forwards. This logic involves the static space–time picture described by Einstein: events do not unfold with the flow of time, but present themselves complete, and in this total picture, movements backwards and forwards in time are as normal as movements backwards and forwards in space. The illusion that there is a 'flow' of time results from our narrow awareness which allows us to perceive only a tiny strip of the total space–time continuum.[26] And is not something similar going on in the alternative narratives? Beneath ordinary reality, there is another shadowy, pre-ontological realm of virtualities in which the same person travels back and forth, 'testing' different scenarios: Véronique-electron crashes (dies), then travels back in time and does it again, this time surviving.

In *Véronique*, we are thus not dealing with the 'mystery' of the communication of two Véroniques, but with *one and the same* Véronique who travels back and forth in time. For that reason, the key scene of the film is the encounter of the two Véroniques in the large square in which a Solidarity demonstration is taking place. This encounter is rendered in a vertiginous circular shot reminiscent of the famous 360-degree shot from Hitchcock's *Vertigo*. Afterwards, when the French Véronique is introduced, it becomes clear that the perplexity of the Polish Weronika at this moment results from her obscure awareness that she was about to have an impossible encounter with her double (later, we see her photo taken at that moment by the French Véronique).[27] Consequently, is this camera's circular movement not to be read as signalling the danger of the 'end of the world', somehow like the standard scene in science-fiction films about alternative realities, in which the passage from one to another universe takes the shape of a terrifying primordial vortex threatening to swallow all consistent reality? The camera's circular movement thus signals that we are on the verge of the vortex in which different realities mix, that this vortex is already exerting its influence: if we were to take one step further – that is to say, if the two Véroniques were actually to confront and recognise each other, reality would disintegrate, because such an encounter of a person with her own double, with *herself* in another time–space dimension, is precluded by the very fundamental structure of the universe.

This encounter has a different meaning for each of the two Véroniques: for the Polish Weronika, it marks, in traditional Romantic mode, the encounter with death (and indeed she dies shortly afterwards), while to the French Véronique, the awareness that she has a double clearly confronts her with the possibility of choice – she may have chosen a different life (to pursue her singing career), which, again, would have led to her death. This is the reason why the double causes such anxiety: the double *is* the object that the subject refuses to be. In Wolfgang Petersen's thriller *Shattered* (1991), Tom Berenger barely survives a car accident. When, weeks later, he awakens in the hospital, with his face and body patched up by plastic surgery, he has total amnesia concerning his identity – he cannot remember who he is, although all the people around him, including a woman who claims to be his wife (Greta Scacchi), treat him as the head of a rich corporation. After a series of mysterious events, he goes to an abandoned warehouse where he is told that, in a barrel full of oil, the corpse of the person he has killed is hidden. When he pulls the body's head out of the liquid, he stiffens with horror – the head is his own.

The solution to the mystery is that he is not in fact the husband, but the lover of the woman who claims to be his wife. When he barely survives the accident while driving the husband's car, with his face disfigured beyond recognition, the wife kills her husband, identifies *him* as her husband and orders the surgeons to reconstruct his face on the model of her husband's. This horror of encountering oneself in the guise of one's double, outside oneself, is the ultimate truth of the subject's self-identity: in it, the subject encounters itself as an object.

Recall Humbert Humbert from Nabokov's *Lolita*: in a stroke of genius, Nabokov made his Christian name coincide with his surname – there is already the structure of the double in his very name! (And, in a gesture of supreme Nabokovian irony, Kieślowski named the hero of *White* Karol Karol.) Humbert Humbert thus *needs* Quilty, his obscene double who persecutes him and Lolita: Quilty is the paranoiac return in the Real of the paternal Name foreclosed from the symbolic (as signalled by Humbert Humbert's name, where the proper family name is missing). This is how *Lolita* signals the impossibility of sexual relationship: the liaison of Humbert Humbert and Lolita is simultaneously hindered and sustained by the intervention of a paranoiac Third. Although fanatically opposed to psychoanalysis, Nabokov was well aware of the link between the suspension of the paternal function and the murderous paranoiac relationship with one's double.[28] Consequently, it is wrong to read *Lolita* in a vulgar pseudo-Freudian way, as a case of 'repressed homosexuality': the point is not that Humbert Humbert chooses a nymphet in order to avoid a direct homosexual engagement with his double Quilty – on the contrary, Quilty is the necessary Third who supplements Humbert's impossible relationship with Lolita. The same goes for the two Véroniques. In the passage from the Polish Weronika to the French Véronique, after Weronika dies on the concert stage, we get the Dreyeresque shot from the grave (the impossible point-of-view shot of her corpse), which is then followed by a direct cut to Véronique making love and inexplicably feeling sad, as if she senses some unknown loss – the trace of her double interferes as the *Liebesstörer*, the intruder who disturbs the harmony of the sexual act. Again, the figure of the double is strictly correlative to the impossibility of sexual relationship.

So what is this impossibility? In Cuba, when one man boasts to another '*I had* that woman!', he implies not just 'straight' vaginal intercourse, but anal penetration – 'straight' intercourse is still considered a form of petting, of foreplay, and it is only the anal penetration that stands for the fully consummated sexual relation. Why is it so? Because the vagina is considered a pale, distorted copy of the anal opening: the anus is somehow like the pure Platonic Idea (a clear and simple round hole, with no hair or crevices), while the vagina is its distorted material realisation, full of protuberances and outgrowths, far from the ideal simplicity of the anus. Is this not yet another way to supplement the inexistence of the sexual relationship – 'natural' penetration is devalued as secondary in relation to its 'unnatural' ideal model? The male counterpoint to it is the difference phallus/penis, as mobilised in the standard porno shot of a woman being penetrated anally and at the same time displaying the hole of her spread vagina, as if to say, 'Although I am penetrated by *penis*, the hole is still open for *phallus*'. Some Hindu priests allegedly can do impossible things with their penises: not only fully controlling erection with their will; not only knowing how to ejaculate inside instead of outside, so that, instead of being released and spilled out, lost outside, the energy of orgasm gets back into the body and thus contributes to a heightened spiritual energy; they are even are able to suck small amounts of liquid like milk with their penises. The fascination of these cases resides in the fact that these priests seem to overcome the exceptional status of the penis, the way of its erection is independent of the subject's will – in short, in their unique case, penis and phallus *do* coincide.

Each of the three men in Neil LaBute's *Your Friends and Neighbors* (1998) is caught in his own solipsistic, fantasmatic space: the first one, the only decent 'good guy', can only find proper satisfaction in masturbation, and cannot satisfy his wife; the second one, the drama teacher, is a sleazy, fast-talking seducer who alienates his wife by talking all the time during the sexual act, communicating his (private, not shared) fantasies and thus spoiling the act by rendering public its fantasmatic support – in the middle of the act, the wife cruelly tells him to shut up and go on fucking; the third one, a cold, sadistic manipulator, engages in 'hot talk' one usually addresses to the feminine partner during the sexual act, while he effectively practises intensive body-building training. Their feminine partners are also frustrated (the teacher's wife, tired of his talking, engages in a lesbian relationship; the disappointed 'good guy's' wife searches for a lover among the other two men). The film is profoundly theological, pervaded by a bleak vision of a dark, 'godless' universe in which the solipsistic search for pleasure unavoidably ends in utter failure and despair (LaBute is a practising Mormon). All the characters are caught in a mechanic web of relations, like the puppets in some late-eighteenth-century French aristocratic chamber-comedy of manners. Exemplary here is the scene in the art gallery where five times different visitors ask the Nastassja Kinski character the same predictable set of questions and get the same answers ('Is this piece part of a series or does it stand alone?', ' Are you the artist?', etc.)[29]

However, one should not dismiss these frustrations as the result of a specific situation; a more radical deadlock lurks beneath them. In a TV movie about a global ecological catastrophe, the wife rejects her husband's love-making – her reproach to him is that he is doing it to her 'as if you want to make a statement'. This formulation renders succinctly what Lacan has in mind with his thesis that there is no sexual relationship: the sexual act is not possible in the mode of 'making a statement', as a symbolic assertion. Recall the first great Wagnerian love dialogue, that of the Dutchman and Senta from *The Flying Dutchman*: the two lovers seem to ignore each other's physical presence, they do not even look each other in the face, they simply engage each in his/her intimate fantasmatic vision of the other . . . 'There is no sexual relationship' means (among other things) that, during 'straight' intercourse, the man *qua* obsessional thinks of *another* woman, the true addressee of his passionate whispers, reducing the woman he holds in his hands to the material support of the fantasmatic *objet petit a*; in an inverse way, the woman *qua* hysteric doesn't want to be the object-cause of her man's (other's) desire, so she imagines some other woman, not her, in bed with her partner, while she is 'somewhere else'.[30] What, however, if these two fantasies *overlap*, so that, during intercourse, the other woman – the woman whom the 'actual' woman engaged in the sexual act fantasises as the one who is in bed with her partner – is the very woman the male partner imagines in bed with him? What if they are only able to do it because he secretly identifies with a lesbian woman and she *is* a lesbian, so that, at the fantasmatic level, the act is effectively that of a lesbian couple doing it with a dildo? The fantasmatic support of a 'straight' sexual relationship is never the scenario of 'straight sex', but always a mixture of 'perverse' elements. Maybe, therein resides the only possible 'harmony' in sex – Lacan himself says somewhere that sexual relations can work if the man's and the woman's fantasies overlap.

The feminine fantasy of being someone else in the relation with her husband also accounts for what is, perhaps, the ultimate melodramatic scenario, detectable from Rudolph Maté's *No Sad Songs for Me* (1950) to *Stepmom* (1998): the idea of a woman who, dying of cancer or some other mortal disease, in her last weeks organises things so that, after her death, a new, younger woman will replace her as the new partner of her husband and the new mother to her children. (The title of one of the TV movies in this series is indicative: *When I Am No Longer There* – does this not provide the most succinct formula of the fantasy Gaze, i.e. of the subject erasing herself out of the picture, remaining only as the pure disembodied spectral gaze observing the idyll that emerges in her absence?) This is the paradigmatically feminine fantasy of obliterating the inexistence of sexual relationship: if she erases herself out of the picture, the new relationship of her husband will be a full one . . . As Joan Copjec convincingly demonstrated, this same basic fantasmatic matrix is at work in King Vidor's *Stella Dallas* (1937): Barbara Stanwyck does not sacrifice herself for her daughter; she rather 'erases herself out of the picture' in order to be able to assume the position of a pure Gaze witnessing through the window-frame (of fantasy) the newly established perfect family of her daughter and her ideal parental couple, her father and his new, appropriate wife.[31] This fantasy of the feminine self-withdrawal, self-erasure from the picture, finds its ultimate expression in Richard Strauss's *Der Rosenkavalier*, in the words of the Marschallin which open the final trio: 'I chose to love him in the right way, so that I would love even his love for another!'

Something similar happens in Goethe's *Elective Affinities* where, during sexual intercourse between wife and husband, each of them fantasises about embracing another partner he/she is really in love with (the husband Ottilie, the wife Hauptmann). What we thus obtain is the paradox of *marital fidelity in the guise of double unfaithfulness*. This ideal-impossible, purely fantasmatic couple of Hauptmann and Ottilie is nonetheless not without material incidence: the child born from this act of marital copulation *qua* double treachery gives body to this impossible couple, i.e. he has the hair and face of Ottilie and the eyes of Hauptmann, and thus renders visible the illicit desire of both husband and wife. No wonder that he dies soon after his birth.

And, perhaps, this possibility of overlapping fantasies is what sustains the subtle literary figure of the 'vanishing mediator' who brings together a couple by intentionally mistranslating their messages to each other. In a story by Guy de Maupassant, some schoolchildren intend to play a cruel joke on their shy teacher by arranging for a date between him and the poor cleaning woman of the school. They tell each of the two the invented story of how the other confided in them that he/she has a concealed love interest in him/her. Hidden under the roof, they then observe the encounter, expecting a good laugh at the couple's embarassment when they discover that they are the victims of a cruel practical joke. However, when they finally meet, the couple forms a relationship (falsely) assured of the other's feelings, and end up happily married . . .[32] In all these cases, a double lie results in a final harmony.

This hysterical refusal to be the body that one has is today clearly discernible in the two opposed stances with regard to woman's body: in the late liberal promiscuous tolerance, women freely expose themselves as part of universalised capitalist prostitution, while religious fundamentalism forces women to wear veils, so that nothing is visible of them but their two eyes. This dichotomy itself is significant: crucial is the structural ambiguity as to its meaning – on the one hand, one can say that the covered woman designates the victim of extreme patriarchal domination, as opposed to the woman in liberal Western society, who is free to enjoy her body; on the other hand, one can say that the Western woman is turned into a sexual object exposed to the male Gaze, in contrast to the veiled woman, who retains at least some dignity. The paradox, of course, is that the very fact of compelling women to be covered in order to retain their dignity asserts what it wants to deny: it automatically assumes that the view of a woman's body reduces it to an object for male sexploitation, so that the way to counteract this is not to change the nature of the male Gaze, but to cover its object (which, of course, in this way becomes even more fascinating). On the other hand, and in a complementary way, one can claim that, in the concrete conditions of our late-capitalist society, the freedom of a woman to dispose of her body is ultimately the freedom to prostitute herself, to sell herself as an object of exchange to men. We are definitely dealing here with a kind of Hegelian 'identity of the opposites'.

Another aspect of this same tension is discernible in cases where a gynaecologist is accused of finding sexual pleasure in touching the intimate parts of his patients; the reproach here is that he does not *objectivise* his feminine patient enough, that he does not treat her as simply an object of the medical Gaze. Around the turn of the century, sexually frustrated hysterical ladies from upper-class families regularly visited doctors who applied a hand-massage to their genitals in order to relieve them of their pathological tension and unrest – to masturbate a female patient was considered a painful and delicate medical duty, not a perversion. This is the reason why doctors welcomed the invention of (electrical and mechanical) machines to 'massage' the feminine genitalia (what today we call vibrators): these machines were not considered sex toys, but medical instruments. Does this strange example not tell us a lot about shifts in the discursive formation of sexuality, i.e. about how a certain form of sexual (dis)satisfaction was depersonalised-objectivised, reduced to a pathological tension to be appeased through the doctor's intervention? The enigma here is: did they all, doctors and patients alike, just feign and play an obscene game, being well aware that it was all about sexual (dis)satisfaction, or did they effectively treat the dissatisfaction as an objectivised illness ('hysterical tension') to be properly treated (by the masturbatory massage)? Perhaps it *was* possible to 'desubjectivise' sexual dissatisfaction into an objective affliction.

So, for Lacan, 'there is no sexual relationship' because there are always *at least three* in it, never just the two (if they are two) engaged partners – and *this* is what complicates the issue of homosexuality: it is never just the relationship between the two persons, so the true enigma is: *who is the fantasised Third*? In a lesbian relationship, this Third could well be a paternal phallic figure (which is why 'lesbian phallus' is a pertinent category). The need for this fantasmatic Third arises from the excess which escapes the (sexual) partner's grasp: on the women's side, it is the feminine Mystery beneath the provocative masquerade, forever eluding the male grasp; on the male side, it is the drive which makes him stick unconditionally to his (political, artistic, religious, professional) vocation. The eternal male paranoia is that the woman is jealous of this part of him which resists her seductive charm, and that she wants to snatch it from him, to induce him to sacrifice that kernel of his creativity for her (afterwards, of course, she will drop him, because her interest for him was sustained precisely by that mysterious ingredient which resisted her grasp). This aspect accounts for the popularity of Colleen McCullough's *The Thornbirds*, in which Father Ralph is torn between his love for Maggie and his unconditional religious vocation – paradoxically, a chaste priest is one of the emblematic figures of the non-castrated Other, of the Other not bound by the symbolic Law.

Lacan provided the ultimate formulation of this impossibility in his 'formulae of sexuation': the masculine side combines universality with its constitutive exception, while the feminine side asserts the non-all as the paradoxical obverse of the lack of exception.[33] One should read the two levels that define each position as 'appearance versus truth': the upper level provides the 'appearance', while the lower level discloses its 'truth'.[34] The 'appearance' of the masculine position is that of Universality, while its 'truth' is the constitutive Exception/transgression (say, the Hero-Master who violates the Law in order to constitute it); the 'appearance' of the feminine position is the mysterious Exception, the Feminine which resists the universal symbolic order, while its 'truth' is that *there is nothing outside* the symbolic order, no exception. If, then, the masculine stance is that of the Law-suspending, exceptional violence of the Master concealed behind Universality, i.e. the Exception that grounds the Universality, the feminine stance designates the hysterical split – a woman focuses on something 'in her more than herself', her narcissistic secret treasure that escapes the male Master's universal grasp, and the truth of it is that *there is no secret*, that femininity is a masquerade concealing nothing (as was clear to Otto Weininger, who equated femininity with the ontological Nothingness). The standard opposition of the masculine subject fully integrated into the symbolic law and the feminine subject partially resisting it is thus thoroughly misleading: it is the masculine position which involves the Exception, while in the feminine position, there is nothing that is *not* inscribed into the 'phallic' symbolic function.

Chapter Six
Children of a Lesser God

Kieślowski's universe of alternative realities is thoroughly ambiguous. On the one hand, its lesson seems to be that we live in the world of alternative realities in which, as in a cyberspace game, when one choice leads to the catastrophic ending, we can return to the starting point and make another, better, choice – a suicidal mistake can be rectified the second time round, so that the opportunity is not missed. In *The Double Life of Véronique*, Véronique learns from Weronika, avoids the suicidal choice of singing and survives; in *Red*, Auguste avoids the mistake of the Judge; even *White* ends with the prospect of Karol and his French bride getting a second chance and remarrying. The very title of Annette Insdorf's recent book on Kieślowski, *Double Lives, Second Chances*, points in this direction: the other life is here to give us a second chance, i.e. 'repetition becomes accumulation, with a prior mistake as a base for successful action'.[35] However, while it sustains the prospect of repeating past choices and thus retrieving the missed opportunities, this universe can also be interpreted in an opposite, much darker, way. There is a material feature of Kieślowski's films which long ago attracted the attention of some perspicacious critics. Suffice it to recall the use of filters in *A Short Film About Killing*:

> The city and its surroundings are shown in a specific way. The lighting cameraman on this film, Sławek Idziak, used filters which he'd made specially. Green filters so that the colour in the film is specifically greenish. Green is supposed to be the colour of spring, the colour of hope, but if you put a green filter on the camera, the world becomes much crueller, duller and emptier.[36]

Furthermore, in *A Short Film About Killing*, the filters are used 'as a kind of mask, darkening parts of the image which Kieślowski and Idziak did not

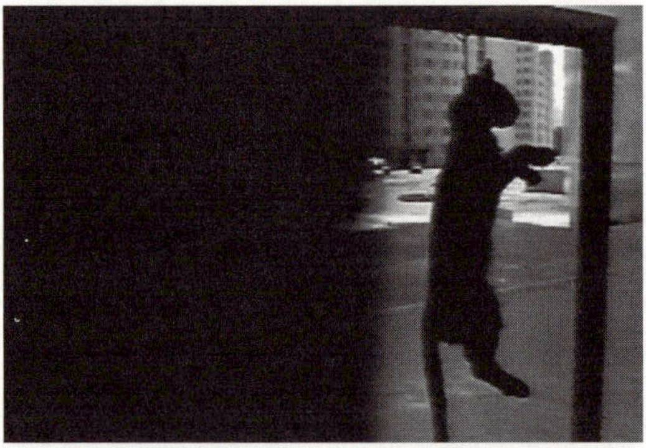

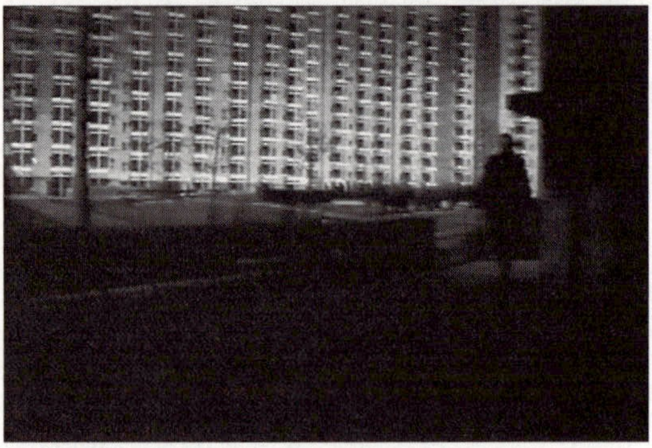

wish to show'.[37] This procedure of having 'large chunks smogged out'[38] – not as part of the formulaic depiction of a dream or a vision, but in shots rendering grey, everyday reality – directly evokes the Gnostic notion of the universe, which was created imperfect and is as such not yet fully constituted. The closest one can get to it in reality is, perhaps, the countryside in extreme places like Iceland or Tierra del Fuego at the southernmost tip of South America: patches of grass and wild hedges intersected by the barren raw earth or gravel with cracks out of which gush sulphuric steam and fire, as if the pre-ontological primordial Chaos is still able to penetrate the cracks of the imperfectly constituted/formed reality.

Kieślowski's universe is one created by a perverse, confused and idiotic God who screwed up the work of Creation, producing an imperfect world, and then tried to save whatever could be saved by repeated new attempts – we are all 'Children of a Lesser God'.[39] In mainstream Hollywood itself, this uncanny, in-between dimension is clearly discernible in what is arguably the most effective scene in *Alien Resurrection* (1997): the cloned

Ripley (Sigourney Weaver) enters the laboratory room in which the previous seven aborted attempts to clone her are on display. Here she encounters the ontologically failed, defective versions of herself, including the almost successful version with her own face, but with some of her limbs distorted so that they resemble the limbs of the Alien Thing. This creature asks Ripley to kill her, and, in an outburst of violent rage, Ripley destroys the entire horror-exhibition.[40]

This idea of multiple imperfect universes can be discerned at two levels in Kieślowski's opus: 1) the botched character of reality as depicted in his films, and the ensuing repeated attempts to (re-)create a new, better, reality; 2) with regard to Kieślowski himself as author, we also have the repeated attempts to tell the same story in a slightly different way (not only the difference between the TV and movie versions of *Decalogue* 5 and 6, but also his idea to make twenty different versions of *Véronique* and play them in different theatres in Paris – a different version for each theatre). In this eternally repeated rewriting, the 'quilting point' is forever missing: there never is a final version, the work is never done and actually put in circulation, delivered from the author to the big Other of the public. (Is the recent fashion of the later release of the allegedly more authentic 'director's cut' also not part of the same economy?) What does this absence of the 'final version' *mean* – this everlasting deferral of the moment when, like God after his six days' work, the author can say, 'It's done!' and take a rest?

The 'virtualisation' of our life-experience, the explosion/dehiscence of the single 'true' reality into the multitude of parallel lives, is strictly correlative to the assertion of the proto-cosmic abyss of a chaotic, ontologically not yet fully constituted reality – this primordial, pre-symbolic, inchoate 'stuff' is the very neutral medium in which the multitude of parallel universes can coexist. In contrast to the standard notion of one fully determined and ontologically constituted reality, of which all other realities are its secondary shadows, copies, reflections, 'reality' itself is thus multiplied into the spectral plurality of virtual realities, beneath which lurks the pre-ontological proto-reality, the Real of the unformed ghastly matter. The first person to articulate this pre-ontological dimension clearly was F. W. J. Schelling with his notion of the unfathomable Ground of God, something in God that is not-yet-God, not yet the fully constituted reality.[41]

Recall, in Lynch's *Wild at Heart* (1990), the repeated extreme close-ups of a burning match – as if this intensity of fire stands for the excessively intense life-experience of the hero, an intensity that cannot be contained within the narrative line and continuously threatens to explode it (the closest the narrative comes to this intensity is, towards the beginning of the film, the violent outburst of Sailor's rage against the African-American thug sent by his lover's stepfather to beat him up – in one of the most nauseating scenes in all of Lynch, Sailor goes on beating the head of the African-American even when the brains are already spilling out). The title

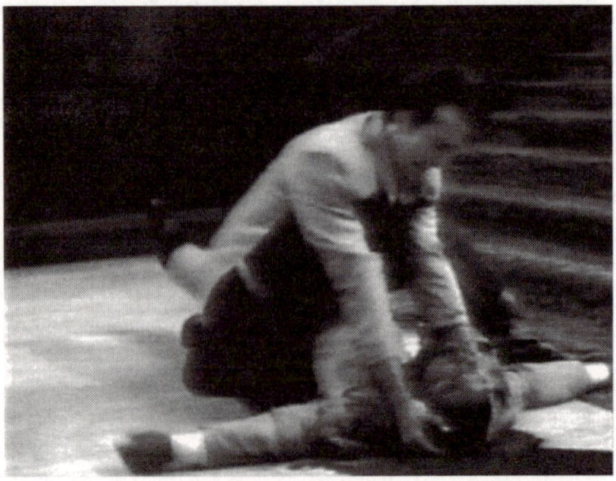

of the *Twin Peaks* cinema prequel *Fire Walk With Me* (1992) thus points towards a key constituent of Lynch's universe: the Real of an excessive life-intensity threatening to explode the framework of reality.[42] In *Lost Highway*, such intensities are the two moments of excessive light and darkness: towards the end of the first part of the film, it seems as if Fred is swallowed by the excessive darkness of his bedroom; in contrast to this, after the love-making scene in the desert, it is as if the couple is swallowed by the excessive light.

This, then, is what one is tempted to call the minimum or the basic level of cinematic *materialism*: this inertia of a pre-symbolic motif that insists and returns as the Real in different symbolic contexts. A materialist analysis should thus discern an intermediate domain of transversal links, associations, echoes, which are not yet properly signifying in the precise sense of a differential symbolic network that generates meaning. In a memorable scene from *Le Mépris* (1963), Godard shoots the dialogue between Paul

(Michel Piccoli) and Camille (Brigitte Bardot) in a continuous lateral movement of the camera: instead of the standard shot/reverse-shot procedure, the camera drifts from one character to the other and back again. However, this movement does not simply follow the rhythm of their exchanges in the conversation, focusing each time on the character who is speaking; rather, it follows its own disparate rhythm, so that it is as if the 'official' line of the exchange of phrases is redoubled by the movement of the camera, which follows its own syntax in counterpoint to the spoken word.

In the alternative-reality comedy of manners *Sliding Doors* (1998), after being sacked from her job, a young PR woman (Gwyneth Paltrow) decides to go home earlier than usual. In one version, she just catches the tube train, returning home in time to catch her boyfriend in bed with another woman; in the alternative version, she misses the train, takes a cab, gets involved in an accident and comes home hours later, after her boyfriend has had the time to clean the appartment of the traces of his clandestine love encounter. The interest of this movie resides in how it resists the trap of making the pseudo-Hegelian point that accidents are just accidents which cannot change the underlying basic pattern of events: whether she catches her partner with his pants down or not, there must be something wrong in their relationship, so that, if not for this reason, they would have split for another (or, as the standard evolutionary Marxist doxa on the role of individuals in history goes: they can slow down or speed up a historical process, but they cannot change its fundamental direction – even if Napoleon had been killed in his youth, there would have been another figure like him, because the outcome of the French Revolution was necessarily 'Napoleonic', demanding a strong dictatorial figure). Of course, *Sliding Doors* is full of coincidences and echoes between the two alternative series of events; however, these coincidences do *not* occur at the level of the basic underlying matrix of events, so that we do *not* get the same elementary course with a different set of accidents (the final outcome is even radically different: in one, Gwyneth Paltrow dies, in the other, she survives). These echoes occur precisely at the level of small, 'meaningless' gestures and accidents which reverberate between the two series. In both series, Paltrow gets dizzy at the same moment, utters the same words to a different man, drinks the same beer in a different context, and so on.

In parallel to Donald Davidson's semantic 'principle of charity', one could also claim that there is a Freudian charity principle which forms the very basis of the psychoanalytic treatment: everything that the patient will say, even the most confused free associations, *has a meaning*, is to be interpreted. However, Lacan's problem is that, at a certain point, this charity principle breaks down: when we pursue the work of interpretation far enough, we encounter *sinthoms* (as opposed to symptoms, bearers of a coded message), formations with no meaning guaranteed by the big Other, 'tics' and repetitive features that merely cipher a certain mode of *jouissance* and insist from one to another totality of meaning. And is this how one should read the uncanny cross-resonances in Kieślowski's work which repeat themselves from film to film? Kieślowski displays a breathtaking mastery in rendering drab, contingent, everyday reality: his films are full of the ominous intrusions of the extra-narrative, raw Real that can be (or not) read as a sign. When, in *Decalogue* 1, Paweł hurries to school, he sees a dead dog who has been run over by a car and is lying on the roadway, stiff, frozen, with its eyes wide open, yellow and glazed-over. Paweł stretches out his hand to touch the animal, feels its rough, erect fur, withdraws and goes on – a premonition of *his own* frozen state after his drowning? As Paweł's father puts it in a response to his son's query, people die either of cancer or of a heart-attack – this depressing option is the ultimate version of the Kieślowskian choice. Underlying the 'official' narrative development, these *sinthoms* form a dense texture (of visual motifs, gestures, sounds, colours) that provides substantial 'tensile strength' to the narrative line.[43] Therein resides the link between *sinthoms* and alternative narrative universes: *sinthoms* are real in the precise sense of that which *remains (returns as) the same in all possible (symbolic) universes*.

At the very beginning of *Decalogue* 9, after learning that he is permanently impotent, Roman succumbs to suicidal temptation and almost crashes his car on the long drive home from the south of Poland – the barely avoided catastrophe actually occurs at the beginning of *Blue*. Roman's impotence, as well as his secret observation of his wife's meeting with her lover, point towards *White*, while his secret listening to his wife's phone conversations anticipates the figure of the Judge in *Red*. Furthermore, while Roman is on his duty at the hospital, a young girl approaches him with the problem which is exactly that of *Véronique* (should she abandon her singing career because of her heart condition?). Even more important than these narrative echoes are the multiple material and visual reverberations: the excessive close-ups of old-fashioned black phones, evoking the threatening dimension of communication; the shots which contain their counter-shot by way of including some medium (mirror, glass partition) which renders what is absent, invisible within the frame; when he sits alone at home, desperately brooding, Roman drinks milk from the same glass bottle which appears in every instalment of *Decalogue*; etc.

In *Decalogue* 1, the frozen bottle of milk signals that the ice is thick enough for Paweł to go skating. (Ironically, the motif of milk first occurs when a TV crew visits Paweł's school in order to make a report on milk-distribution to the pupils.) When, later, the ice cracks, since the water was too warm, is this not like the bottle of milk defreezing itself? Furthermore, when, at the time of Paweł's drowning, the ink bottle spills on the father's table, making an uncanny green pool, is this not a signal of the melted milk? The effect of this spill is properly uncanny, the magic appearance of the stain of the Real in reality which, a couple of seconds later, after the first surprise, is accounted for rationally. In addition, at the beginning of *Decalogue* 2, the old doctor goes out to buy a bottle of milk; the same goes for the father towards the end of *Decalogue* 4. And, of course, the bottle of milk is prominent in *Decalogue* 6: Tomek distributes milk in order to have contact with Magda; in despair, Magda spills the bottle of milk on her table. And is this spilling of milk not echoed in the red stain of blood that gradually fills the washbasin after Tomek's suicide attempt, when he cuts his wrists and then immerses his hands in the water? Is this not the same intrusion of the Real as the blood that emerges from the toilet sink when the detective flushes it in Coppola's *The Conversation* (1974)? The same magic effect occurs in what is arguably the best scene in Minghella's *The Talented Mr Ripley* (1999): Ripley is at the opera, watching Tchaikovsky's *Eugene Onegin*; at the end of Act II, a man is shot in a duel and, while he collapses, his vividly red coat spills out and extends, as if a gigantic blood pool were amplifying itself in an uncannily exaggerated way. This is sublimation at its purest: the moment at which, by means of some simple trick of theatrical staging, the 'other scene' of the hero's traumatic act of murder finds unexpected resonance, generating the deceptive appearance of the trace of the murder. Therein resides the origin, the condition of possibility, of fiction: not in the escape from reality, but in the return, in the guise of a fiction, of the Real which had to be foreclosed so that the subject could gain access to consistent reality.

Kieślowski's films display here a profound ambiguity, oscillating between what one is tempted to designate as the Freudian and the Jungian approaches. Freud is thoroughly modern: the Freudian notion of a symptomatic act (say, a slip of tongue) emphasises its radical contingency, i.e. the Freudian interpretation does not discern in it a 'deeper meaning' ('it was predetermined that this will happen to me'), but simply renders visible how, in a thoroughly contingent way, an unconscious 'wish' has attached itself to an everyday superficial element or event in no way inherently connected to it. (Even more radically, the very basic constituents of the subject's identity – the signifiers around which his/her symbolic universe has crystallised itself, the fundamental fantasy which provides the co-ordinates of his/her desire – result from a series of contingent traumatic encounters.) Jean-Claude Milner[44] emphasised that modern science is strictly correlative to the assertion of universal contingency (which, of course, is not opposed to causal necessity, but functions as its inherent obverse: causal necessity works in the guise of rules which regulate the endless 'contingent' – meaningless – interaction of elements). What Freudian interpretation involves is thus a 'modern', materialist theory of *meaning itself*: as to its ontological status, meaning is strictly *secondary*, a way to 'internalise' the traumatic shock of some preceding contingent encounter. There is no 'deeper meaning' beneath the contingency of events; it is, on the contrary, meaning itself which designates the way a finite subject is able to cope with the unbearable contingency of the 'way of all flesh'. So, when I truly, passionately fall in love, it seems that 'all my previous life was but a preparation for the magic moment of encountering you'; the point of Freudian interpretation is precisely to 'deconstruct' this retroactive illusion by unearthing the symbolic features on account of which I fell in love.[45]

In clear contrast to Freud, Jung's reinscription of psychoanalysis into the confines of pre-modern wisdom involves the *massive resubstantialisation of sexuality*: the Masculine and the Feminine are posited as the two complementary aspects of the human psyche, whose balance is to be maintained (each man has to rediscover the feminine aspect of his psyche and vice versa) – the very opposite of constructionism *à la* Judith Butler, which conceives of sexual identity as discursively produced by performative sedimentation. James Redfield's *Celestine Prophecy* is a prime example of this anti-modernist twist of New Age wisdom: it posits as the first 'new message' which will open the path to humanity's 'spiritual awakening' the awareness that there are no contingent encounters: since our psychic energy participates in the energy of the universe itself, which secretly determines the course of things, contingent external encounters always bear a message addressed to us, to our concrete situation; they occur as an answer to our needs and questions (for example, if I am bothered by a certain problem and then something unexpected happens – a long-forgotten friend visits me, something goes wrong in my work place, etc. – this accident certainly contains a message concerning my problem).[46]

With regard to this point, Hegel's thought is also thoroughly ambiguous. On the one hand, one can claim that Hegel is *the* philosopher of the 'sublation' (cancellation) of the idiotic (meaningless, contingent, inert) presence of the Real, of its *derealisation*: one can be sure that, in the end, even the most traumatic and contingent experience will be reintegrated in some totality of meaning. Even if some event obviously happened for contingent reasons, its very contingency harbours some deeper meaning: Alexander had to die young (to mark the impossibility and necessary failure of his project to resuscitate Greek culture), Napoleon had to be deposed twice (first in 1813, then, again, in 1815). On the other hand, does this very strategy of generating meaning to account for contingencies not already presuppose – and thus rely on – the paradigmatically modern experience of the ultimate contingency of Being? And do we not also find a homologous tension, a homologous oscillation (and coincidence) between the reign of chance and the underlying secret interconnection between events in Kieślowski: is there a deeper meaning beneath contingency, or is the meaning itself the outcome of a contingent turn of events? The first reading seems to impose itself, which is why many of today's theorists abhor Kieślowski as a New Age obscurantist – is there any way to read the finale of *Red*, other than that it miraculously brings together all the threads of the trilogy? However, the ambiguity is radical, as with Tarkovsky, Kieślowski's Russian counterpart.

What ultimately redeems Tarkovsky from his ideological obscurantism is his *cinematic materialism*, the direct physical impact of the texture of his films: this texture renders a stance of *Gelassenheit*, of pacified disengagement that suspends the very urgency of any kind of quest.[47] What pervades Tarkovsky's films is the heavy gravity of the earth, which seems to exert its pressure on time itself, generating an effect of temporal anamorphosis, extending the dragging of time well beyond what we perceive as justified by the requirements of narrative movement (one should confer here on the term 'earth' all the resonance it acquired in late Heidegger). Perhaps Tarkovsky is the clearest example of what Deleuze called the time-image replacing the movement-image. This time of the Real is neither the symbolic time of the diegetic space nor the time of the reality of our viewing of the film, but an intermediate domain whose visual equivalent are perhaps the protracted stains which 'are' the yellow sky in late van Gogh or the water or grass in Munch: this uncanny 'massiveness' pertains neither to the direct materiality of the colour stains nor to the materiality of the depicted objects – it dwells in a kind of intermediate spectral domain of what Schelling called *geistige Körperlichkeit*, spiritual corporeality. From the Lacanian perspective, it is easy to identify this 'spiritual corporeality' as materialised *jouissance*, '*jouissance* which turned into flesh'. This inert insistence of time as Real, rendered paradigmatically in Tarkovsky's famous slow five-minute tracking or crane shots, is what makes Tarkovsky so interesting for a materialist reading: without this inert texture, he would be just another Russian religious obscurantist. That is to say, in our standard ideological tradition, the approach to spirit is perceived as elevation, as getting rid of the burden of weight, of the gravitational force which binds us to earth, as cutting links with material inertia and starting to 'float freely'; in contrast to this, in Tarkovsky's universe, we enter the spiritual dimension only via intense direct physical contact with the damp heaviness of earth (or stagnant water) – the ultimate Tarkovskian spiritual experience takes place when a subject is lying stretched on the earth's surface, half submerged in stagnant water; Tarkovsky's heroes do not pray on their knees, with the head turned upwards, towards Heaven, but while intensely listening to the silent palpitation of the damp earth. One can see, now, why Lem's *Solaris* exerted such an attraction on Tarkovsky: the planet Solaris seems to provide the ultimate embodiment of the Tarkovskian notion of a heavy, damp matter (earth) which, far from functioning as the opposite of spirituality, serves as its very medium; this gigantic 'material Thing which thinks' literally gives body to the direct coincidence of matter and spirit.

In a homologous way, Tarkovsky displaces the common notion of dreaming, of entering a dream: in Tarkovsky's universe, the subject enters the domain of dreams not when he loses contact with sensual material reality around him, but, on the contrary, when he abandons the hold of his intellect and engages in an intense relationship with material reality. The typical stance of the Tarkovskian hero on the threshold of a dream is to be on the lookout for something, with his senses fully focused and alert; then, all of a sudden, as if through a magic transubstantiation, this most intense contact with material reality changes it into a dreamscape.[48] One is thus tempted to claim that Tarkovsky stands for the attempt, perhaps unique in the history of cinema, to develop an attitude of *materialist theology*, of a deep spiritual stance which draws its strength from its very abandonment of intellect and its immersion into material reality.

In order to locate this feature properly, one should read it against the background of capitalist dynamics as deployed by Marx. On the one hand, capitalism entails the radical secularisation of social life – it mercilessly tears apart any aura of authentic nobility, sacredness, honour. However, the fundamental lesson of the 'critique of political economy' elaborated by the mature Marx in the years after *The Communist Manifesto* is that *this reduction of all heavenly chimeras to brutal economic reality generates a spectrality of its own*. When Marx describes the mad, self-enhancing circulation of capital, whose solipsistic path of self-fecundation reaches its apogee in today's meta-reflexive speculation on futures, it is far too simplistic to claim that the spectre of this self-engendering monster that pursues its path disregarding any human or environmental concern is an ideological abstraction, and that one should never forget that, behind this abstraction, there are real people and natural objects on whose productive capacities and resources capital's circulation is based and on which it feeds like a gigantic parasite. The problem is that this 'abstraction' is not only in our (financial speculator's) misperception of social reality, but that it is 'real' in the precise sense of determining the structure of the very material social processes: the fate of whole strata of the population and sometimes of whole countries can be decided by the 'solipsistic' speculative dance of capital, which pursues its goal of profitability in blessed indifference to how its movement will affect social reality. This material spectrality of capital also allows us to locate properly the logic of Tarkovsky's spiritualism, i.e. of how his return to spiritual values in a properly dialectical way simultaneously involves the return to the heavy material inertia of the earth.

If, then, *Stalker* (1979) is Tarkovsky's masterpiece, it is above all because of the direct physical impact of its texture: the physical background (what T. S. Eliot would have called the objective correlative) to its metaphysical quest, the landscape of the Zone, is a post-industrial wasteland with wild vegetation growing over abandoned factories, concrete tunnels and railways full of stagnant water in which stray cats and dogs wander. Nature and industrial civilisation are here again overlapping, but through a common decay – civilisation in decay is in the process of again being reclaimed (not by idealised harmonious Nature, but) by nature in decomposition. The ultimate Tarkovskian landscape is that of a damp nature, a river or pool close to some forest, full of the debris of human artifice (old concrete blocks or pieces of rotten metal). The actor's faces themselves, especially Stalker's, are unique in their blend of ordinary ruggedness with scars, dark or white spots and other signs of decay, as if they have all been exposed to some poisonous chemical or radioactive substance, but still emanate a fundamental naive goodness and trust.

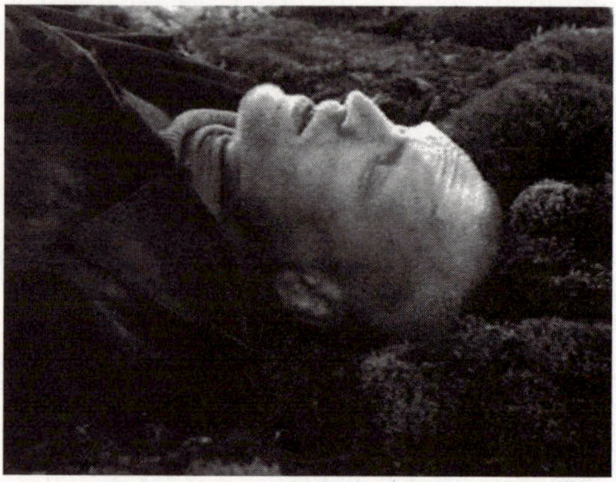

Here we can see the different effects of censorship: although censorship in the USSR was no less stringent than the infamous Hayes Production Code in Hollywood, it nonetheless allowed a movie so bleak in its visual material that it would never pass the Production Code test. Recall, as an example of Hollywood material censorship, the representation of dying from an illness in *Dark Victory* (1939) with Bette Davis: upper-middle class surroundings, painless death . . . the process is deprived of its material inertia and transubstantiated in an ethereal reality free of the bad smells and tastes. It was the same with slums – recall Goldwyn's famous quip, when a reviewer complained that slums in one of his films look too nice, without real dirt: They'd better look nice, since they cost so much! The Hayes Office censorship was extremely sensitive on this point: when slums were depicted, they explicitly demanded that the set of the slum be constructed so that it did not evoke real dirt and bad smell – at the most elementary level of the sensuous materiality, censorship was thus in Hollywood much stronger than in the Soviet Union.

Tarkovsky is to be opposed here to the ultimate American paranoiac fantasy, that of an individual living in a small, idyllic Californian city, a consumerist paradise, who suddenly starts to suspect that the world he lives in is a fake, a spectacle staged to convince him that he lives in a real world, while all the people around him are actors and extras in a gigantic show. The most recent example of this is Peter Weir's *The Truman Show* (1998), with Jim Carrey playing the small-town clerk who gradually discovers the truth that he is the hero of a 24-hour-a-day TV show: his home town is constructed on a gigantic studio set, with cameras following him permanently. Among its predecessors, it is worth mentioning Philip K. Dick's 1959 novel *Time Out of Joint*, in which a hero living a modest daily life in a small, idyllic Californian city of the late 50s gradually discovers that the whole town is a fake staged to keep him satisfied. The underlying experience of *Time Out of Joint* and of *The Truman Show* is that the late-capitalist, consumerist Californian paradise is, in its very hyperreality, in a way *irreal*, substanceless, deprived of material inertia. So it is not only that Hollywood stages a semblance of real life deprived of the weight and inertia of materiality – in late-capitalist, consumerist society, *'real social life' itself somehow acquires the features of a staged fake*, with our neighbours behaving in 'real' life as stage actors and extras. Again, the ultimate truth of the capitalist, utilitarian, despiritualised universe is the dematerialisation of 'real life' itself, its reversal into a spectral show. Among others, Christopher Isherwood gave expression to this unreality of American daily life, exemplified by the motel room: 'American motels are unreal! ... they are deliberately designed to be unreal. ... The Europeans hate us because we've retired to live inside our advertisements, like hermits going into caves to contemplate.'[49]

It is only now that we confront the crucial dilemma of any interpretation of Tarkovsky's films: is there a distance between his ideological project (of sustaining meaning, of generating new spirituality, through an act of meaningless sacrifice) and his cinematic materialism? Does his cinematic materialism provide the adequate 'objective correlative' for his narrative of spiritual quest and sacrifice, or does it secretly *subvert* this narrative? There are, of course, good arguments for the first option: in the long obscurantist-spiritualist tradition leading up to the figure of Yoda in Lucas's *The Empire Strikes Back* (1980), a wise dwarf who lives in a dark swamp, rotting nature in decay is posited as the 'objective correlative' of spiritual wisdom – the wise man accepts nature the way it is, he renounces any attempt at aggressive domination and exploitation, any imposition of artificial order on it. On the other hand, what happens if we read Tarkovsky's cinematic materialism in the opposite way: what if we interpret the Tarkovskian sacrificial gesture as a very elementary ideological operation, as a desperate strategy of beating the meaninglessness of existence by its own means, i.e. of engendering meaning – of overcoming the unbearable Otherness of meaningless cosmic contingency – through a gesture that is itself utterly meaningless?

This dilemma is discernible in the ambiguous way Tarkovsky uses natural ambient sounds[50] – their status is ontologically *undecidable*, as if they were still part of the 'spontaneous' texture of non-intentional natural sounds, and simultaneously already somehow 'musical', displaying a deeper spiritual structuring principle. It seems as if nature itself miraculously starts to speak, the confused and chaotic symphony of its murmurs imperceptibly passing over into music proper. These magic moments, in which nature itself seems to coincide with art, lend themselves, of course, to the obscurantist reading (the mystical art of spirit discernible in nature itself), but also to the opposite, materialist reading (the genesis of meaning out of natural contingency). Therein resides also the ambiguity of the role of chance in Kieślowski's universe: does it point towards a deeper fate secretly regulating our lives, or is the notion of fate itself a desperate stratagem to cope with the utter contingency of life?

Part Three

THE INDIVIDUAL: *LACRIMAE RERUM*

Chapter Seven
Displaced Commandments

How, exactly, does Kieślowski's *Decalogue* relate to the Ten Commandments? The majority of interpreters take refuge in the alleged ambiguity of this relationship: one should not correlate each instalment with a single Commandment, the correspondences are more fuzzy, sometimes a story refers to a multitude of Commandments. Against this easy way out, one should emphasise the *strict* correlation between the episodes and the Commandments: each instalment refers to only one Commandment, but with a 'shift of gear': *Decalogue* 1 refers to the second Commandment, etc., until, finally, *Decalogue* 10 brings us back to the first Commandment.[1] This *décalage* is indicative of the displacement to which the Commandments are submitted by Kieślowski. What Kieślowski does is very close to what Hegel is doing in his *Phenomenology of Spirit*: he takes a Commandment and then 'stages' it, actualises it in an exemplary life situation, thereby rendering visible its 'truth', the unexpected consequences which undermine its premises. One is almost tempted to claim that, in a strict Hegelian way, this displacement of each Commandment generates the next Commandment:

One: 'Thou shalt have none other Gods but me.' *Decalogue* 10 renders this Commandment in the guise of its opposite, of the unconditional 'passionate attachment' to the trivial activity of collecting stamps. We have here the logic of sublimation at its most elementary: a common activity (collecting stamps) is elevated to the dignity of the Thing for which one sacrifices all – the job, family happiness, even one's kidney. The underlying premise of *Decalogue* 10 is thus the Hegelian infinite judgment in which the highest and the lowest coincide: revering God = collecting stamps.[2] No wonder, then, that the introductory song (performed by the younger of the two sons) is the only place in the entire *Decalogue* series where the list of Commandments is mentioned – significantly, in the inverted form of injunctions to *violate* the Commandments: 'Kill, rape, steal, beat up your mother and father . . .' This subversive reversal of prohibition into obscene injunction to transgress the Law is entailed by the very formal procedure of Kieślowski's 'dramatisation of a law':[3] since the prohibitive Law is in itself a suprasensible Idea, its dramatic staging automatically cancels (purely intellectual) negation, shifting the focus on to the imposing image of the act of, say, killing, irrespective of its ethical preamble (+ or −, recommended or prohibited). Like the Freudian unconscious, the dramatic staging knows of no negation. In his famous reflections on negativity and the Decalogue, Kenneth Burke reads the Commandments through the opposition between the notional level and the level of imagery: 'though the injunction "Thou shalt not kill" is in essence an *Idea*, in its role as *imagery* it can but strike the resonant gong: "Kill!"'[4] This is the Lacanian opposition between the symbolic Law and the obscene call of the superego at its purest: all negations are powerless and turn into mere denegations, so that what remains is the obscene intrusive reverberation of 'Kill! Kill!'

This reversal of prohibitions into imperatives is a strictly *tautological* gesture: St Paul himself already asserts that the Law itself generates the desire to violate it.[5] The God who appears here is thus the 'cruel' God of Division, the God from Matthew 10:37, 10:34–5, or 23:9, the God who came to 'set the son against his father', the God who suspends all positive order, the God of absolute negativity. So when Christ says 'call no one your father on earth, for you have one Father – the one in Heaven', the metaphoric chain of paternal authority (Father in Heaven, beneath him the rulers, fathers of our social community, and, finally, the father of the family) is suspended: the function of the Divine Father is ultimately purely negative, i.e. to revoke the authority of all earthly paternal figures.[6] The 'truth' of the first Commandment is the next Commandment, prohibiting images, since only the Jewish God is without an image – all other gods are present in the guise of images, of idols.

Two: 'Thou shalt not make to thyself any graven image . . . For I the Lord thy God am a jealous God, and visit the sins of the fathers upon the children.' In *Decalogue* 1, the 'graven image' is materialised in the computer as the fake god-machine which generates icons and thus stands for the highest violation of the prohibition to make images. Consequently, God punishes the father by way of 'visiting the sin of the father upon the son', who drowns while skating on thin ice.[7] The 'truth' of this Commandment is the dialectical undermining of the very opposition between word and image: the ban on *images* ends up in the prohibition on pronouncing the very *name* of God. So we get the third Commandment.

Three: 'Thou shalt not take the name of the Lord thy God in vain.' In *Decalogue* 2, the embittered old doctor, asked if the husband will survive, consciously lies and swears to God in order to prevent an abortion, a mortal sin. (The key lines are left out of the film – one finds them only in the scenario: 'He doesn't stand a chance.' 'Swear to it in God's name.' [*The doctor is silent.*] 'Swear to it in God's name.' 'As God is my witness!'[8]) The struggle for the unborn child's life or death constitutes a common thread between *Decalogue* 1 and 2: in 1, the child unexpectedly dies, while in 2, he unexpectedly stays alive (i.e. is born); both times, the cause is a miraculous rupture in the order of causality: the ice unexpectedly melts down, the husband unexpectedly survives cancer. (The further link is that, due to the malfunctioning of the heating system in the apartment block in *Decalogue* 2, its inhabitants have problems with hot water: in a conversation, the doctor asks Dorota what she is doing to obtain hot water; the excess of hot water in *Decalogue* 1 is symmetrically matched with the lack of it in *Decalogue* 2.) The 'truth' of this Commandment is that, since one cannot even fully pronounce the divine name, the only thing that remains is to *abstain* from doing anything on the Sabbath day and thus mark God by the very absence of any act.

Four: 'Remember that thou keep holy the Sabbath day.' In *Decalogue* 3, the hero breaks the prohibition (leaves the family alone on Christmas Eve, when one is supposed to suspend the rhythm and worries of ordinary life) in order to save the life of his ex-mistress. In its tonality and mood, *Decalogue* 3 announces *Blue*: not only is blue its predominant colour, but its universe is cold and distanced. However, in contrast to *Blue*, coldness and distance are here 'objectivised': they are not the coldness and distance of the heroes themselves, but pertain to the very cinematic mode of presenting them. We cannot ever fully identify with them (as we do with Julie in *Blue*, so that we experience the cold, distanced mode as expressing her own detachment). *Decalogue* 3 furnishes clues, but also precludes 'identification with the people for whom they are significant, and knowledge of quite what they might signify for them'.[9] Even when, at the end, we learn the sad predicament of Ewa, we somehow cannot feel full compassion for her. *Decalogue* 3 is thus unique in its intended blockage of the spectator's full emotional or ethical engagement: we are reduced to the position of the observing detective who, on the basis of sparse clues, has to guess what is really going on with Ewa. The 'truth' of this Commandment is that, since God is only present as absent, the only way one can properly celebrate Him is not by directly addressing Him, but by treating one's neighbours properly, especially one's parents.

Five: 'Honour thy father and thy mother.' *Decalogue* 4 gives an ironic twist to this Commandment: the daughter 'honours her father' in the guise of a burning incestuous desire for him. The question is again: is it better *not to know* certain things (the burning of the letter that answers the question whether he is really her father)? The 'truth' of this Commandment is that, since family stands for the ultimate guarantee of the social order, not honouring one's father and mother leads to the disintegration of all constraints: when paternal authority is suspended, everything is permitted, including the ultimate crime, murder. (As David Lynch's counterpoint to *Decalogue* 4, *Fire Walk With Me*, demonstrates, incest – not honouring one's father – ends up in murderous violence.)

Six: 'Thou shalt not kill.' *Decalogue* 5 again gives an ironic twist to this Commandment: is the *repetition* of the murder by the state apparatus also a murder and thus a violation of this Commandment? Kieślowski does not simply oppose the shock of a unique, traumatic encounter to the somniferous daily rhythm of repetitions: the ultimate force of his films resides in how he submits the unique trauma itself, in all its emotional violence, to a repetition. The result is *not* the trauma's 'renormalisation': although, through its repetition, the traumatic event is viewed with a cold, impersonal distance, as part of a meaningless global machinery that automatically runs its course, this shift makes the impact even more unbearable – what is really unbearable in *Decalogue* 5 is the *second* murder (punishment).[10] The 'truth' of this Commandment is contained in the very opposition of killing and loving: is love really an antidote to killing, or is there a murderous dimension lurking in (at least a certain kind of) possessive/impotent love?

> Love of a woman is possible only when it does not consider her real qualities, and so is able to replace the actual psychical reality by a different and quite imaginary reality. The attempt to realise one's ideal in a woman, instead of the woman herself, is a necessary destruction of the empirical personality of the woman. And so the attempt is cruel to the woman; it is the egotism of love that disregards the woman, and cares nothing for her real inner life. . . . Love is murder.[11]

Or, as Lacan put it in the last chapter of his *Four Fundamental Concepts of Psycho-Analysis*: 'I love you, but, because inexplicably I love in you something more than you – the *objet petit a* – I mutilate you.'[12] The passage from *Decalogue* 5 to 6 can also be formulated in the opposite way: deprived and insensitive as Jacek is, his redeeming feature is his search for love. He kills the taxi-driver due to a lack of love, as a (perverted) means to gain love. It is thus logical that the next instalment directly tackles love, exposing its murderous potential.

Seven: 'Thou shalt not commit adultery.' One should be attentive to the uncanny resemblance between the two young men, Jacek from *Decalogue* 5 (and its long version, *A Short Film About Killing*) and Tomek from *Decalogue* 6 (and its long version, *A Short Film About Love*), which could also have been entitled *A Short Film About Self-Killing*: Tomek's love for Magda is fundamentally false, a narcissistic attitude of idealisation whose necessary obverse is a barely conceived lethal dimension. *Decalogue* 6 should thus be read against the background of 'slasher' films, in which a Peeping Tom male character stalks and harasses a woman who traumatises him, finally attacking her with a knife: *Decalogue* 6 is a kind of introverted 'slasher' in which the man, instead of striking at the woman, turns his murderous rage against himself. The concise formula of the final lesson of *Decalogue* 6 is thus: there is no (full, reciprocal) love, there is only an immense *need* for love; every actual love encounter fails and throws us back into our solitude.[13] Perhaps, it is only when one is in love that one can fully confront one's fundamental solitude. The 'truth' of this Commandment is contained already in the psychoanalytic cliché according to which, when one doesn't get love, one steals (in order to get another thing that one can get). One should bear in mind that the very first scene of *A Short Film About Love* depicts Tomek breaking into a storage room and stealing a telescope in order to observe Magda.

Eight: 'Thou shalt not steal.' The specific twist that *Decalogue* 7 gives to this Commandment is provided in a short conversation between Majka and her ex-partner: 'You've never stolen anything, never killed anyone.' 'But can you steal something that belongs to you?' A biological mother (named Majka, which, in Slavic languages, *means* mother!) steals little Anna from the woman who functions socially as Anna's mother (and this symbolic mother is none other than Majka's own biological mother). The symmetry with the Lacanian notion of love cannot but strike the eye: in love, you give what you don't have, while in *Decalogue* 7, you steal what is already yours. Is this also love? The 'truth' of this Commandment is that, since stealing can only occur within the order of property, i.e. of *symbolic* obligations, the thief, in his/her social interactions, *has* to 'bear false witness against his neighbours'. The problem with stealing is not primarily the appropriation of another's material property, but rather the implicit violation of his/her *symbolic veracity*.

Nine: 'Thou shalt not bear false witness against thy neighbour.' In *Decalogue* 8, the entire life of the old professor of ethics has been marked by the fact that, in her youth, during World War II, she 'bore false witness against her neighbour', the fellow Resistance fighter whom she unjustly suspected of collaborating with the Nazis. There is an intriguing self-referential twist in what is otherwise the weakest episode of the *Decalogue*: in the course of a university seminar, one of her students presents the case of a moral dilemma which exactly fits the dilemma of *Decalogue* 2; the professor's comment is: 'The main thing here is that the child is alive.' The irony of this is, of course, that, in the tense situation during World War II, *she herself* acted differently, as if there *were* things which *are* more important than the child's survival. One can speculate that she became a professor of ethics, dedicating her life to philosophy, in order to clarify her mistake, i.e. to account for why and how, at a crucial moment, she made the wrong choice. (And is it not more than plausible to claim that the same goes for Paul de Man: his intense theoretical activity after World War II was an attempt to account for, and thus undo, the mistake of his wartime pro-Nazi engagement?) The 'truth' of this Commandment concerns the properly dialectical tension between telling the truth and lying: one can lie in the guise of truth (this is what obsessionals are doing, when, in statements which are factually entirely accurate, they conceal or disavow their desire), one can tell the truth in the guise of a lie (the hysterical procedure, or a simple slip of tongue which betrays the subject's true desire). 'Bearing false witness against one's neighbour' is thus not primarily a matter of factual accuracy, but of the desire which sustains my position of enunciation when I tell the truth (or lie): so if I denounce my neighbour's wife to her husband, accusing her of adultery and thus (perhaps) ruining their lives, this accusation, even if factually 'true', is false if and insofar as it is sustained by my desire for her, by my 'coveting my neighbour's wife'. I do it out of jealousy, because she did not choose *me* as her lover.

Ten: 'Thou shalt not covet thy neighbour's wife.' In *Decalogue* 9, this most Hitchcockian of all of Kieślowski's films, the twist to which the Commandment is submitted is homologous to that of *Decalogue* 7: the impotent husband covets *his own* wife (in a parallel to Majka, who steals what is hers). One would expect the Commandment to refer to the young physics student, the wife's lover who 'covets his neighbour's wife'; however, in a true stroke of genius, Kieślowski transposes it to the cuckolded husband himself. Is the film's solution – the reconciliation through double pain – the only one feasible? Would it not be possible to arrive at the same result through the empty gesture, the gesture made to be rejected? What if the impotent husband were to offer his wife the freedom to sleep around with other men without telling him, *expecting her to reject this offer*? Or – the opposite empty gesture – what if she were to offer him to renounce sex, *expecting him to allow her to sleep around*? The 'truth' of this Commandment is that, as long as one remains within the confines of the interpersonal relationship, there is no way out of the deadlock – *even coveting one's own wife is a sin*. The only way out is in what Brecht, in *The Mother*, called '*Lob der dritten Sache*' ('praise of the third thing'). One breaks out of the deadlock by focusing on a third agency, which is ultimately God Himself; the circle is thus closed, we are back at the first Commandment.[14]

The Decalogue (1988):

One: Krzysztof's small son, Paweł, is well versed in the mysteries of the personal computer. It is winter and Paweł, anxious to try out his new pair of skates, asks his father if he can go out to the nearby pond which has just frozen over. They consult the computer: the ice will hold the boy's weight, he can go. However, Paweł doesn't return home: the computer was wrong, there was a freak local thaw and Paweł drowned. Krzysztof runs to a church in despair and, in an outburst of rage, demolishes the altar. Candle wax splashes over the painted face of the Black Madonna, appearing as her tears.

Two: Dorota is pregnant, but not by Andrzej, her husband, who seems to be dying of cancer in the hospital. She asks the doctor in charge of her husband, an embittered old man who lives in the same block, whether there is any chance that Andrzej will survive. If he lives, she will have to have an abortion; if he dies, she can have the child. Although the doctor is not certain of the outcome, in order to save the unborn child, he tells Dorota that Andrzej doesn't have a chance. However, Andrzej miraculously recovers; Dorota tells him that they are going to have a baby which he thinks is his.

Three: On a Christmas Eve, a night when families are together and nobody wants to be alone, Ewa tricks Janusz, a taxi-driver and her ex-lover, away from his family and, under various pretexts, keeps him with her for the night, roaming around the deserted streets. In the morning, just before he returns home, Janusz learns that he has inadvertently saved Ewa's life: Ewa's husband abandoned her long ago, she now lives alone, and, the previous evening, she made a desperate vow that, if she had to spend the night of Christmas Eve alone, she would kill herself.

Four: Anka's mother is dead and she lives with Michał, her father. They get on well together, more colleagues than father and daughter. While Michał is on a trip abroad, Anka finds an envelope in his room with the inscription: 'Not to be opened before my death.' Inside that envelope is another, in her mother's handwriting, addressed to her. Instead of opening it, Anka forges a new letter in which her mother reveals that Michał is not her real father. Upon Michał's return, Anka shows him this forged letter and offers herself to him, since she is not his daughter. Michał gently, but firmly, rejects her sexual advances and leaves on another trip. Anka runs after him and confesses her forgery – her mother's true letter is still unopened. The two return home and burn the letter, preferring not to know the truth.

Five: Piotr, who has just passed his law exams and been admitted to the bar, is to defend Jacek, a youth who has randomly and brutally murdered a taxi-driver and then planned to escape the city with the next-door girl. There is no evidence for the defence and no apparent motive: Jacek is found guilty and executed by hanging. Before his execution, Jacek asks Piotr to take care of his dead sister's grave. Piotr, after his first case, is left with bitter doubts about the legal system.

Six: From his bedroom in a large dreary concrete apartment block, Tomek, a young post clerk, spies each evening and night on Maria Magdalena (sic), a mature, sexually attractive and promiscuous woman who lives in the same block, opposite his backyard. His activity is not limited to passively observing her sexual prowess; step by step, he intervenes in her life, sending her false notices of money-orders so that she will come to his window in the post office, calling plumbers to her apartment in the middle of her love-making, etc. When, finally, he gathers courage, contacts her and discloses that he is the source of her recent nuisances, her curiosity is aroused. She entices him into a humiliating sexual game which ends in his premature ejaculation. Shattered, he runs home and cuts his wrists. He survives and, after his return from the hospital, their respective roles are reversed: stirred by her guilt, she frantically endeavours to contact him, whereas he now ignores her.

Seven: Six-year-old Ania is being brought up by Ewa in the belief that Majka, Ewa's daughter, is her elder sister, whereas Majka is really her mother. Tired of living this lie and desperate to have Ania love her as a mother, Majka kidnaps Ania and runs away from her parents. She seeks refuge with Wojtek, Ania's father, who got her pregnant when he was her teacher (in order to avoid the scandal, Ewa adopted the child as her own). Ewa, jealous of Ania's love, looks for her everywhere and phones Wojtek. Majka seizes Ania and continues to run; she will only return home if her mother will allow her to bring up her own daughter. At a nearby train station, Ewa tracks down Majka and Ania. Ania wakes up, sees Ewa, calls 'Mummy!' and runs towards her. A train arrives and Majka jumps on it, leaving her family for good.

Eight: Elżbieta, researching the fate of Jewish war survivors, is visiting from New York and attends lectures in ethics at the University of Warsaw. She approaches Zofia, the professor, and tells her that she is the little Jewish girl whom Zofia refused to shelter from the Nazis during the Occupation. As Zofia explains the reason for this apparent cowardice – the man who brought the little Elżbieta to her apartment was suspected of being a Nazi informer – her long-standing sense of guilt is cleared. She takes Elżbieta to this unjustly accused man, who now works as a tailor. Still embittered, he ignores Elżbieta's questions concerning their wartime experience, and treats her politely as just another customer.

Nine: Roman learns he's impotent. Recognising his wife's, Hanka's, sexual needs, he encourages her to take a lover. She is reluctant, since she loves Roman, but does have an affair with Mariusz, a student. Roman becomes excessively jealous and obsessed with the thought that Hanka might have taken a lover. He spies on her and learns of her affair, unaware of the fact that Hanka has just broken it off. Desperate, he tries to commit suicide by crashing his car, but he survives. In a phone conversation, he is reconciled with Hanka.

Ten: A lonely old man dies, leaving an extremely valuable stamp collection to his two sons, Jerzy, a pop singer, and Artur, a clerk. Although they know very little about stamps, they are unwilling to sell them. They learn that one very rare stamp is needed to complete a valuable set. To acquire the stamp, Artur donates his kidney – the man in possession of the stamp is in need of a kidney for his daughter. Returning from hospital, Jerzy and Artur find that their father's apartment has been burgled, and the entire stamp collection has been stolen. Shamefully, they confess that they each suspected the other, and are reconciled by taking up their father's vocation of stamp-collecting.

Network

Decalogue 1 and 10 both stand out in the series: the first is the zero-level story of a traumatic intrusion of the meaningless and contingent Real, and lacks the intersubjective tension of the other instalments, while the last is a satyr play which introduces a comic mode into the otherwise sombre series. Since a detailed reading of all ten instalments is beyond the scope of this book,[15] we should limit ourselves to some of the motifs which provide a common thread between the episodes, beginning with the motif of the thread itself, of the invisible network connecting people. In the opening sequence of *Red*, Kieślowski's last film, after a hand dials a phone number, the camera traces the call's journey to its distant destination via the lead to the plug socket, the cables that lead underground and beneath the sea, to the flashing red light in the local exchange which tells us the line is busy. The topic of the film is thus clearly designated: the exploration of the hidden forces that affect communication between individuals. However, virtuoso as it is, this opening sequence's attempt to render visible the irrepresentable flow of signals comes dangerously close to the ridiculous: is it not just one step from the naive anthropomorphisation of digital circuitry in Disney's *Tron* (1982), in which electronic signals are rendered as small humanoids who run along the microchip's pathways?

The basic problem here is the relationship between this 'external' electronic network that supports communication and the 'deeper' New Age notion of the invisible hand of some immaterial network which connects people in a mysterious, incomprehensible way, pulling the strings of their destinies (say, in *Red* itself, the Fate which mysteriously selects the heroes of the *Colours* trilogy as the only survivors of a ferry catastrophe, or the extrasensory way the two Véroniques are able to communicate).[16] No wonder that Kieślowski is often perceived (and dismissed) as a preacher of New Age obscurantism: because of the very irrepresentability of what goes on behind the interface screen, cyberspace itself was from its very beginnings colonised by the Gnostic imagination, perceived as a space haunted by secret spiritual powers. The prospect of the digital global network not only gave rise to a renewed Gnostic New Age spirituality (precisely the spirituality associated with Kieślowski's late films), but that this spirituality even actively sustained the digital technological development – the notion of 'TechGnosis' is fully justified as the designation of what Louis Althusser would have called the 'spontaneous ideology' of the cyber-scientists. As we have already seen, Kieślowski's very theme of alternative realities points towards digital technology.

It is thus crucial *not* to read *Decalogue* 1 as simply asserting the unreliable and cheating nature of the 'false God' of reason and science: its lesson is *not* that, when our reliance on the false idol of science (embodied in the father's personal computer) fails, we are confronted with a 'deeper' religious dimension; on the contrary, when science fails us, our religious foundation is also shattered – *this* is what happens to the desperate father at the end of *Decalogue* 1. Is the same structure not displayed in the shift in Kieślowski's work with regard to representation? As we have already seen, Kieślowski's first move was to fight false representation (the lack of an adequate image of social reality) in Polish cinema through documentaries; then he noticed that, *when you let go of false representation and directly approach reality, you lose reality itself*, so he abandoned documentaries and moved into fiction. Furthermore, does his very timely/untimely death not involve the same structure? When he renounced film-making, he lost also the alternative to it, the calm of 'real life' itself – didn't he in this way confirm that, outside film-making, there was no 'simple life' for him?

In order to disentangle the meaning of Kieślowski's films, it often helps to compare the film itself with the scenario.[17] In the scenario of *Decalogue*

1, the reason why the computer's calculation of the thickness of the ice went wrong is specified (the nearby power station released some hot water into the lake during the night), while in the film there is no explanation, and thus the field is open for a more metaphysical speculation. For example, what about the mysterious 'angel' (a Christ-like bearded homeless young man who appears in most of the *Decalogue* stories as a silent observer at key moments), who is seen keeping himself warm by a fire at the lake's shore – did the heat of his fire contribute to the melting of the ice? In the film, the warm water which caused the catastrophe is thus more

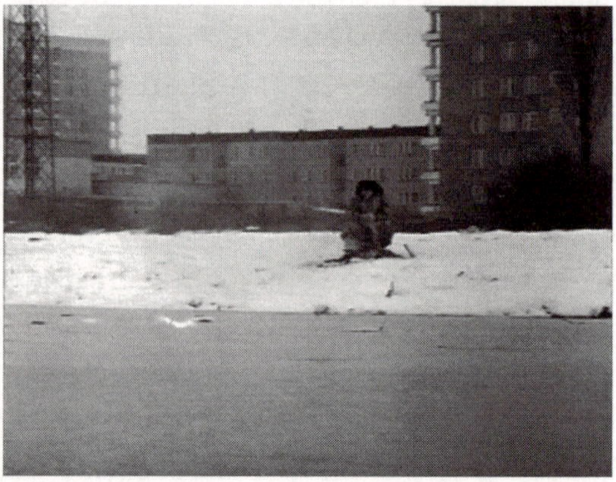

a kind of Jansenist miracle, readable as such only to those who believe. Among other appearances of this figure, suffice it to mention *Decalogue* 3, where he is the strangely illuminated tram-driver with a calming smile, who prevents Janusz and Ewa from committing suicide by driving their car straight into the tram; *Decalogue* 4, where he walks past Anka at the two crucial moments of decision – when she intends to burn the mother's letter and when, at the end, she decides to tell the truth to her father; and *Decalogue* 5, where he is seen just before Janek brutally murders the taxi-driver, as a last warning, a last chance of salvation. Is this angelic figure not, much more than a Christ-like figure, the good God of Gnosticism? (Since our material universe was created and is ruled by the evil Demon, this God is reduced to the role of an impotent observer: unable to intervene in our predicament and prevent catastrophe, all he can do is sympathise with our misery.) Does the fact that this figure appears in the very first shot of *Decalogue* 1 not make him into the ideal impotent/compassionate spectator of the whole series who, like us, sitting comfortably in our chairs, cannot effectively intervene in order to prevent the tragic outcome, but can only imitate the 'primitive' spectator who, on seeing that a hero is unaware of approaching danger, shouts at the screen: 'Turn around and look! You will be hit in a second!'

Decalogue 1 thus sets the basic matrix of the entire series: the intrusion of the meaningless Real which shatters any complacent immersion in socio-symbolic reality and thereby gives rise to the desperate question: '*Che vuoi?*' – what do you really want from me? Why did it happen? The crucial difference between the scenario and the film of *Decalogue* 1 concerns the end. In the scenario, before going to the church and acting out his despair in a destructive fury directed at the altar, the distraught father searches for answers in a dialogue with the computer which, mysteriously, seems to have switched on by itself (the computer is here mystified into an almost Stephen-Kingesque status of the Green Evil Object, at the same time a malevolent subject and an indifferent blind machine, the other – evil – side of God). While the screen glows with an ominous green light, the father bombards it with questions: 'Are you there? Why? Why take a small boy? Listen to me. Why take a small boy? I want to understand. If you are there, give me a sign.' In the film, these words are addressed *directly* at God Himself in the empty church where the enraged father goes after he gets no answer from the computer. There, in an impotent outburst of destructive rage, he knocks over the altar, causing the burning candles to fall; the wax of the overturned candles drips down a painting of the Virgin Mary, creating an image of tears – an ambiguous sign that God nonetheless *did* answer. The paradox here is that this 'answer of the Real', the sign of a divine compassion with the hero's misery, only takes place when he reaches the depth of the utmost despair, rejecting divinity itself – following the steps of Christ, one is united with God only in the experience of utter abandonment by Him. Significantly, this melting wax is the last link in the chain of metonymic displacements of the motif of melting down: firstly, the frozen milk melts; then, the ice that covers the nearby lake melts, causing the catastrophe; finally, the wax melts. Is *this* the final answer of the Real, the proof that we are not alone, that 'someone is out there', or just another stupid coincidence?

To Live a Lie

Another important difference between scenario and film occurs in *Decalogue* 4. At the very end of the scenario, Michał tells Anka the story (left out in the film itself) about a man who was able to race through traffic on his bicycle because he didn't see well; once he put on glasses, he could no longer move – a nice way to emphasise how excessive knowledge can block active participation in life, and, as such, a justification for burning the letter, i.e. for rejecting the knowledge that might render the peaceful coexistence of father and daughter untenable. As such, *Decalogue* 4 has to be read as the middle term in the triad of *Decalogue* 2, 4 and 9, which all turn around the same problem: is it acceptable to lie (or even to *live a lie*) in order to maintain peace or save a person from sin? Can one build one's life on a basic formative *lie*? Instead of imposing a clear and final choice, Kieślowski just proposes three versions.

In *Decalogue* 2, the doctor lies to the pregnant wife to prevent an abortion, and, furthermore, the 'happy' couple of wife and husband with a child live a lie, since the husband believes he is the child's father; a lie is here celebrated as a saving device, preventing a mortal sin and reuniting the couple.

In *Decalogue* 4, the father and the daughter jointly burn the mother's letter, thereby endorsing ignorance as the basis of their relationship – not a lie, but a consensual withdrawal from truth, an attitude of 'it's better not to know'. Here, in order to maintain the fragile and delicate libidinal balance of daily life, the letter should *not* arrive at its destination.

In *Decalogue* 9, the couple discovers that you cannot bypass problems by 'not talking about certain things', by just silently doing them: this solution miserably fails, engendering the husband's pathological jealousy and driving him to attempted suicide.

The stakes of this debate are much higher than may appear. Until recently, a standard opposition between the conservative, moralistic Right and the enlightened Left was that the Right insisted on the necessity of maintaining (proper) appearances: even if we know that we all have our dirty secrets, it is crucial to sustain the sacred dignity of power by not probing too much into these secrets ... This attitude was elaborated already by Pascal, not to mention Romantic conservatives à la

Chateaubriand, who acknowledged that, at the origin of the existing legal order, there always lurks the horror of some unspeakable crime – for that reason, one should not dig to deeply into it, since this scrutiny may undermine the charisma of power and thus ultimately entail the disintegration of the entire social edifice. Against this conservative stance of 'appearances matter', standard leftist radicalism advocated the thorough scrutiny of 'secrets best left in shadow': is not the basic thesis of Freud that the uncompromising analysis of the libidinal foundations of morality will, far from undermining the stability of the social edifice, exert a liberating effect? The public radio discussion between Theodor Adorno and Helmut Schelsky in the late 50s is here exemplary: Adorno sustained the emancipatory potential of radical demystification, while Schelsky claimed that the vast majority of ordinary people cannot endure the radical demystification of their existence, and need a comforting lie, a semblance of stability and authority. (Today, however, the usual roles are reversed – in the Clinton–Lewinsky scandal, the fundamentalist moralistic Right endorsed the uncompromising probing into intimacy which undermined the charisma of authority, while the liberal Left desperately evoked the dignity of power and the limits of privacy. By the very form of their procedure, the conservative defenders of the dignity of power undermine their proclaimed goal.)

All nostalgic fans of Westerns remember John Ford's provocative quote along the lines of 'When the truth becomes legend, print the legend.' The two outstanding cases of such an attitude in Ford's opus are *Fort Apache* (1948), in which Henry Fonda plays a cruel commander whose military blunder is posthumously elevated into a heroic sacrifice and *The Man Who Shot Liberty Valance* (1962), in which the non-aggressive politician, played by James Stewart, builds a political career on the legend that he shot Valance, the psychopathic killer, while Valance was actually shot by his anonymous friend, who ends his life in poverty. What makes these two films subversive is that Ford, while endorsing the myth, simultaneously *renders visible the mechanism of its fabrication*. A line can be traced to Kevin Costner's *The Postman* (1997), a film focused on the structural necessity of the ideological lie (of narrative fiction) as the condition for reconstituting the social link – the only way to restore the USA after a global catastrophe is by pretending that the Federal Government *still exists*, so that people start to believe in it and behave accordingly, and the lie becomes truth (the hero sets in motion the reconstitution of the USA by starting to deliver mail as if he is acting on behalf of the US postal system). The film (and David Brin's novel on which it is based) affirms this recognition in the call of the fictitious idelogical agency against the two alternate positions: the survivalist, neo-feudal order and the neo-hippy notion of everyday life relieved of the burden of ideological belief.[18]

We encounter here the inherent limitation of the otherwise sublime effort of the Truth and Reconciliation strategy in post-apartheid South Africa: anyone who accepted to tell publicly the truth about his acts, often in front of his or her former victims themselves, was promised clemency, no matter how heinous his or her acts. However, what about – among others – the case of the secret police officers who brutally murdered the black activist Steven Biko? They came forward and, with a cynical smile, without the minimum of remorse, told the story of his torture and death in all its grisly details ... We all sensed that there was something wrong here, that the strategy had somehow misfired. The procedure relied on the premise that the public confession of the crime would have a cathartic, redeeming effect on the perpetrator, reconciling him with the victims and reintegrating him into the space of human dignity – the premise which is rendered inoperative the moment we are dealing with a cynical subject unaffected by the act of confession.

Along similar lines, Berel Lang's *Heidegger's Silence*, the study of Heidegger and the Holocaust,[19] argues that Heidegger's stance is in a way more evil than those of the Nazi perpetrators themselves, inclusive of their revisionist defenders. The perpetrators who tried to erase the traces of their crimes, as well as today's revisionists who deny that the Holocaust took place, implicitly admitted that the Holocaust was and/or would have been a horrible crime – hence the attempt to conceal it or to prove its non-existence. Heidegger, on the contrary, denies nothing: he simply asserts his fundamental *indifference* towards it, a kind of philosophically grounded 'So what?' His rare references to the Holocaust either conceive of it as just another example of the reduction of dying to an industrial process grounded in the essence of technology, or relativise it to other similar acts, purporting that these other acts may even be worse – see his remark, in a letter to Herbert Marcuse from 20 January 1948:

> To the serious legitimate charges that you express 'about a regime that murdered millions of Jews . . .' I can merely add that if instead of 'Jews' you had written 'East Germans', then the same holds true for one of the allies, with the difference that everything that has occurred since 1945 has become public knowledge, while the bloody terror of the Nazis in point of fact had been kept a secret from the German people.[20]

The way Heidegger dismisses traumatic events like the Holocaust or the defeat of Fascism as epochally-ontologically irrelevant is more ambiguous than it may appear: not *all* such 'ontic' events are dismissed in this way – the fate of Germany, of the German people, was definitely *not* ontologically irrelevant for Heidegger. Heidegger was through his whole life in search of an 'ontic' event with 'ontological' relevance – therein resides the philosophical grounds of his engagement with Nazism (when he withdrew from politics in the mid-30s, he often emphasised that he still supported Hitler; his point was that he now considered the Nazi regime the best pragmatic political option in the present circumstances, no longer endowing it with the epochal mission of enacting the answer to the threat of nihilism inherent in modern technology). Heidegger liked to emphasise that the most distressing thing today is the very absence of distress, i.e. the distressing fact that we are not sufficiently distressed at the crisis of our entire being. Is it not possible to apply this lesson to him too, to his own response to Nazism?

The Silent Father

Is there another, more authentic, mode of silence? Although the tailor appears only in the very last scene of *Decalogue* 8, he is the key person, the one against whom Zofia, the ethics professor, has borne false witness during World War II. This tailor who refuses to talk about his wartime trauma stands for the ultimate Kieślowskian figure of the reserved silent father – the resigned and reconciled figure to whom the heroine can return at the end, as Véronique does at the end of *The Double Life of Véronique*.[21] This paternal figure is to be opposed to the successful work of mourning accomplished by the two women in *Decalogue* 8: they come to terms with the past and pardon each other, verbalising their traumatic past encounter, while the tailor *remains silent*, is not ready to speak, cannot verbalise his predicament – as such, he and only he is the one who 'knows it all'. *Decalogue* 4

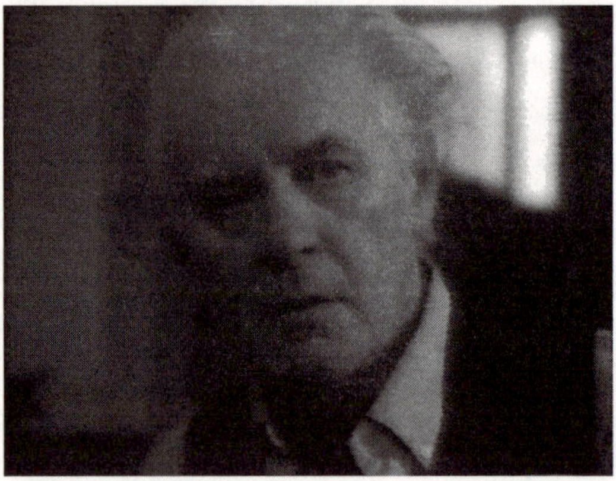

demonstrates Kieślowski's awareness of the explosive, incestuous danger which always lurks beneath the surface of such a reliable desexualised relationship: at any moment, such an attachment can explode into the open demand for an incestuous link. The true counterpoint to *Decalogue* 4 is David Lynch's *Fire Walk With Me*, which ends with what is arguably the ultimate Lynchean death-and-redemptive-transubstantiation scene: incest in its lethal, most brutal dimension, in contrast to Kieślowski, where the couple of father and daughter are able to stop before the precipice.

This father is not the bearer of paternal authority, of the symbolic Law, but something incomparably more ambiguous and mysterious – a non-paternal father, if there ever was one. In *Lassie Comes Home* (1943), the old bearded blacksmith observes Lassie who, each day exactly on time, passes the main village street on its way to wait for the boy in front of the school. When, after months of absence, the wounded, bleeding and tired dog again passes the street on time, the blacksmith just silently nods, understanding the unconditional *drive* that sustains the faithful dog. A similar Gaze occurs in Randa Haines's *Children of a Lesser God* (1986): the charismatic teacher (William Hurt) is trying to entice his deaf-mute pupils into an exciting and amusing social game; everybody falls for it, with the notable exception of a fat boy who just sits silently, ignoring the teacher's advances. Later, however, when the teacher is deeply depressed because his love (Marlee Matlin) has left him, and is unable wholeheartedly to perform his amusing tricks, he exchanges a passing glance with the silent boy – a magic exchange in which the boy lets the teacher know that *now* he fully empathises with his despair. This silence is the silence of the drive, which means that the final return to the silent paternal figure in a number of Kieślowski's films is the recourse of the hysterical woman, caught in the vertiginous dialectics of desire, to the stability of the drive's eternal return.

One should thus correlate the two couples in Kieślowski's universe: the daughter attached to the enigmatic figure of the silent father, and the innocent/violent boy confronted with an 'overripe', sexualised, mature woman. The couple of Tomek and Magda from *A Short Film About Love* has a long prehistory which reaches back to the *fin-de-siècle* emergence of the (self-) destructive *femme fatale*. Of special interest here is 'Language in the Poem', Heidegger's seminal essay on Georg Trakl's poetry, the *only* place where he approaches the topic of sexual difference:

> A human cast, cast in one mold and cast away into this cast, is called a kind [*Geschlecht*]. The word refers to mankind as a whole as well as to kinship in the sense of race, tribe, family – all of these in turn cast in the duality of the sexes. The cast of man's 'decomposed form' is what the poet calls the 'decomposing' kind. It is the generation that has been removed from its kind of essential being, and this is why it is the 'displaced' kind.
>
> What curse has struck this humankind? The curse of the decomposing kind is that the old human kinship has been struck apart by discord of *Geschlechter*. Each of the *Geschlechter* strives to escape from that discord into the unleashed turmoil of the always isolated and sheer wildness of the wild game. Not duality as such, the discord is the curse. Out of the turmoil of blind wildness it carries each kind into an irreconcilable plot, and so casts it into unbridled isolation. The 'fallen *Geschlecht*', so cleft in two, can on its own no longer find its proper cast. Its proper cast is only with that kind whose duality leaves discord behind and leads the way, as 'something strange', into the gentleness of simple twofoldness following in the stranger's footsteps.[22]

This, then, is Heidegger's version of 'there is no sexual relationship' – the reference and indebtedness to Plato's myth from *Symposion* is obvious here, and this unproblematic reference to metaphysics should give us to think: the undead, pale-faced, ethereal boy Elis ('Elis in wonderland', one is tempted to add) stands for the gentle sex, for the harmonious duality of the sexes, not their discord. What this means is that, in the ambiguous series of discords, sexual difference ('the duality of the sexes') occupies a privileged role – it is in a way the generating site of the 'decomposition': all other levels are 'decomposed' insofar as they are infected by the fundamental discord of sexual difference, by what Heidegger, later in this essay, refers to as the 'degenerate kind' ('*entartete Geschlecht*').[23]

The first thing to do (and which is not done by Heidegger) is to situate this figure of a pre-sexual boy into its context, whose first reference is Edvard Munch's paintings: is this 'unborn' fragile boy not the very terrified asexual figure of *The Scream*, or the figure squeezed *between the two frames* in his *Madonna*, the same foetus-like, asexual figure floating among the droplets of sperm. One of the minimal definitions of a modernist painting concerns the function of its frame. The frame of the painting in front of us is not its true frame; there is another, invisible, frame, the frame implied by the structure of the painting, which frames our perception of the painting, and these two frames by definition never overlap – there is an invisible gap separating them. The pivotal content of the painting is not rendered in its visible part, but is located in this dislocation of the two frames, in the gap that separates them. This dimension in-between-the-two-frames is obvious in Malevich (what is his *Black Square on White Surface* if not the minimal marking of the distance between the two frames?), in Edward Hopper (recall his lone figures in office buildings or diners at night, where it seems as if the picture's frame has to be redoubled with a window-frame, or, in the portraits of his wife close to an open window, exposed to sunlight, the opposite excess of the painted content itself with regard to what we actually see, as if we see only the fragment of the whole picture, the shot with a missing counter-shot), and, again, in Munch's *Madonna* – the droplets of sperm and the small foetus-like figure from *The Scream* squeezed in between the two frames. The horror of this figure is *not* the Heideggerian anxiety (*Angst*), but a suffocating horror pure and simple.

And one is tempted to insert in the same series the famous shot in the scene at the florist's early in Hitchcock's *Vertigo*, in which Scottie observes

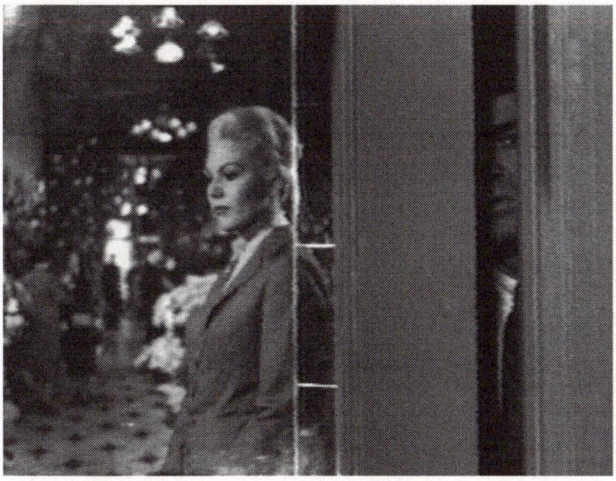

Madeleine through a crack in a half-open door close to the big mirror. Most of the screen is occupied by the mirror-image of Madeleine; on the right side of the screen, between the two vertical lines (which function as the double lines of the frame), there is Scottie looking at her, resembling the dwarf on the border of the mirror who answers the evil queen's questions in the Grimm brothers' *Snow White*. Although we see only the image of Madeleine, while Scottie is there in reality, the effect of the shot is nonetheless that it is Madeleine who is really there, part of our common reality, while Scottie is observing her from a crack in our reality, from the pre-ontological shadowy realm of the hellish underworld. Furthermore, one is tempted to recall here the most disturbing scene in Lynch's *Wild at Heart*, in which Willem Dafoe harasses Laura Dern: although a man harasses a younger woman, a series of clues (Laura Dern's boyish fair face, Dafoe's obscenely distorted 'cuntface') signals that the underlying fantasy scenario is that of a vulgar, overripe woman harassing an innocent boy. And what about, in Lynch's *The Lost Highway*, the boyish Pete confronted with the woman's face, contorted by sexual ecstasy, displayed on a gigantic video screen? Perhaps the outstanding example of this confrontation of the asexual boy with the woman are the famous shots, from the beginning of Ingmar Bergman's *Persona* (1966), of a pre-adolescent boy with large glasses, examining with a perplexed gaze the giant, unfocused screen-image of a feminine face; this image gradually shifts to a close-up of what seems to be another woman who closely resembles the first one – yet another exemplary case of the subject confronted with the fantasmatic

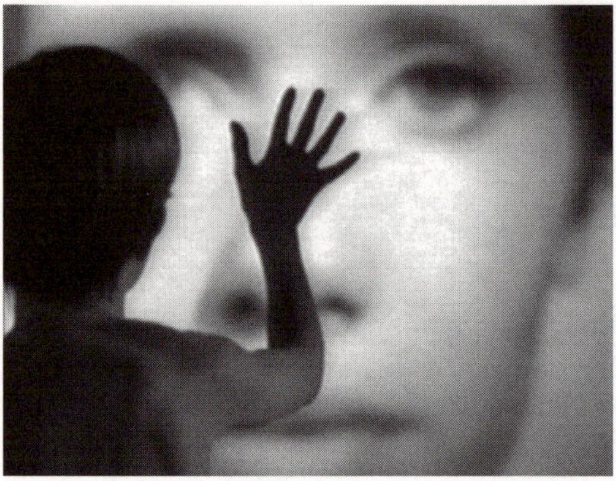

interface-screen. And should one not risk here a further step and put in the same lineage the paradigmatic image of the war or Holocaust victim, the starved, asexual boy with a terrified look?

There is, however, a superb example of the *feminine* version of this asexual, angelic/monstrous entity: Ruth Rendell's (Barbara Vine's) masterpiece *A Dark-Adapted Eye*, which focuses on the dual/imaginary relationship between two sisters, the elder, maternal Vera and the younger, beautiful and promiscuous Eden. While serving at military headquarters during World War II, Eden gets pregnant and leaves the child in Vera's care; after the war, when Eden forces Vera to return the child to her through the courts, the strain between the two sisters mounts and Vera slaughters Eden. We are dealing here with the tension between 'woman' and 'mother' as symbolic identities and as biological entities: Vera, the biological non-mother, is the symbolic mother, while Eden, a 'whore', is the biological mother. When Lacan claims that 'woman doesn't exist', one should not forget that woman *does* exist *qua Mother*, *quod matrem.*[24] From Medea onwards, the relationship mother/woman is the site in which violence threatens to explode; the violence which explodes in *A Dark-Adapted Eye* is the opposite of Medea's violence: it is not the violence of the woman who, betrayed as a woman, takes revenge as a mother, but the violence of the betrayed mother. However, in *A Dark-Adapted Eye*, the little boy is merely the *enjeu* of the relationship of *l'hainamoration*, love-hate, between the two sisters. Violence explodes out of their absolute proximity: Vera and Eden are excessively intimate, they form a self-enclosed couple silently talking to each other for hours, excluding all the world around them; after repeatedly knifing her, Vera gently holds Eden's head in her hand and whispers into her ear. Eden is for Vera the *absolutely idealised object* to whom 'everything is permitted' – it is significant that her name means 'paradise' and is rather gender-neutral. One should recall here the enigmatic figure of the corrupted angel, a golden-haired, ethereal, hermaphroditic figure which embodies the utter degeneration of absolute *jouissance*. Vera is the 'practical', serving counterpoint to this idealised figure of 'no use': she finds fulfilment in taking care of others – she breaks down and passes to (the murderous) act when she is deprived of this fulfilment. The two sisters thus form a perfect couple of the Ideal and Real, of remote coldness and warm, caring emotion, in Lacan's mathems, of *á* and *a*, of *ideal-ego* and *ego* – a recipe for the explosion of murderous violence.

One should recall here again the key scene from Syberberg's *Parsifal*, the transformation of the boy-Parsifal into the girl-Parsifal after Parsifal rejects Kundry's advances, all this played out against the background of the gigantic interface-Thing, the spectral contours of Wagner's head. When the boy repudiates (his fascination with) the woman, he at the same time loses his boyishness and turns into a blue-faced, monstrously cold young woman. The message of this is not some obscurantist hermaphroditism, but, on the contrary, the violent reinscription of sexual difference into the spectral-undead, boyish figure.

In short, what Heidegger's reading does not take into account is how the very opposition between the asexual boy and the discordant *Geschlecht* is sexualised as the opposition between a *boy* and a *woman*. The discordant *Geschlecht* is not neutral, but feminine, and the very apparent gender-neutrality of Elis makes him a boy. So when Heidegger claims that

> The boyishness in the figure of the boy Elis does not consist in the opposite of girlishness. His boyishness is the appearance of his stiller childhood. That childhood shelters and stores within it the gentle two-fold of sex, the youth and the 'golden figure of the maiden',[25]

he misses the key fact that sexual difference does not designate the two sexes of the human stock/species, but, in this case, the very difference between the asexual and the sexual: to put it in the terms of Laclau's logic of hegemony, sexual difference is the Real of an antagonism, since, in it, the external difference (between the sexual and the asexual) is mapped on to the internal difference between the two sexes. Furthermore, what Heidegger (and Trakl) already hint at, and what Kieślowski makes clear, is that, precisely as pre-sexual, this innocent, 'undead' child confronted with the overripe and overblown female body is properly *monstrous*, one of the figures of evil itself:

> Spirit or ghost understood in this way has its being in the possibility of *both* gentleness *and* destructiveness. Gentleness in no way dampens the ecstasy of the inflammatory, but holds it gathered in the peace of friendship. Destructiveness comes from unbridled licence, which consumes itself in its own revolt and thus is active evil. Evil is always the evil of a ghostly spirit.[26]

Perhaps, one should insert the figure of Elis into the series of similar figures from horror stories *à la* Stephen King: the 'undead', white, pale, ethereal, monstrous, asexual child returning to haunt the adults. Is, at a different level, Highsmith's Tom Ripley not also such a subject, uniting ruthless destructiveness with angelic innocence, since his subjective position is in a way not yet marked by sexual difference? To go to the end of this series, is, in Kieślowski's *Decalogue*, the mysterious, Christ-like, homeless young man who appears to the hero in decisive moments, not also such an asexual, ghost-like presence? And is it not the ultimate irony that this Trakl-Heidegger vision of the asexual, angelic entity found its latest expression in Michel Houellebecq's *Les Particules elementaires*? At the end of this bestseller from 1998,[27] which triggered a large debate all around Europe, humanity collectively decides to replace itself with genetically modified asexual humanoids in order to avoid the deadlock of sexuality.

In music, this complicity of gentle innocence and the brutal outburst of evil is the topic of Giya Kancheli's *Lament* (music of mourning in memory of Luigi Nono for violin, soprano and orchestra) of 1994.[28] Kancheli's pure expressionism, in which the subject articulates his pain, homelessness and vulnerability, is imbued by an almost unbearable antagonistic tension. There are the repeated attempts to express subjectivity in a modest, proto-ontological melody – more of a rehearsal, outline or fragment – using the violin, piano or voice, which are the three main modes of expressing subjectivity. However, these phantom-like fragments disappear even before they fully appear; they not only fail to develop into a full sonata form, or whichever musical shape, but immediately pass into a *fortissimo* explosion, a violent, cataclysmic *tutti*, the eruption of the Real in all its brutality. It is as if there is no proper measure of symbolic articulation: we have either the ethereal, imaginary, fleeting, not yet fully constituted forethought of subjectivity, or the overwhelming violence that crushes and destroys it. The moment the subject – with hesitation, fear and shame – takes the risk to put himself forward, the Other strikes back with all ferocity, like the brutal parent who, in a grotesque disparity between action and reaction, beats the child black and blue for every modest, imperceptible gesture of putative defiance or self-assertion. And therein resides the ambiguity of *Lament*: are these two poles effectively opposed? Is it really that fragile, intimate subjectivity, its innerness, is crushed by the violent reaction of the external Real? Or is it rather that there is the ultimate *identity* of the two poles, i.e. that, today, the moment one tries to express innocent, fragile subjectivity, its true nature explodes in all its violence? Kancheli seems to misrecognise this coincidence of opposites: if he were to assert it, he would be compelled to leave behind the domain of 'musical expression' and pass into the puppet-like post-psychological universe of *Sprechgesang*.

Chapter Eight
Retrieved Choices

There is a well-known case of a German officer who helped Jews at the risk of his own life (finally, he was caught and shot by the Gestapo): as a person, he was a conservative, upper-class anti-Semite; he despised Jews and avoided any contact with them, and fully supported the initial legal-economic measures of the Nazis aimed at curbing the 'excessive' Jewish influence. All of a sudden, however, when he fully realised what was going on (the total annihilation of the Jews), he started to help Jews by all means possible, out of the simple, unshakeable conviction that something like this cannot be tolerated. It would be totally wrong and misleading to interpret this sudden shift along the lines of the 'ambiguity' of the Gentile's attitude towards Jews, oscillating between hatred and attraction: in the officer's sobering decision to help the Jews, a totally different order intervenes, an order which has nothing whatsoever to do with emotions and their fluctuations – the ethical dimension proper in the strict Kantian sense.

This dimension is to be opposed to morality. From my high-school days, I remember the strange gesture of a good friend of mine which shocked me considerably at the time. The teacher gave us an essay to write on 'What satisfaction does it provide to accomplish the good deed of helping one's neighbour?' – the idea being that each of us should describe the profound satisfaction that comes from the awareness that we did something good. This friend of mine put the pen and paper down on the table and, in contrast to the others, who quickly scribbled their notes, just sat motionless. When the teacher asked him what was wrong, he answered that he was unable to write anything, because he had simply never felt either the need for or the satisfaction at such acts – he had never done anything good. The teacher was so shocked that she gave him a special dispensation: he could write his paper at home after school – surely he would remember some good deed. The next day, my friend came to school with the same blank paper, stating that he had thought a lot about it the previous afternoon – there was simply no good deed of his that he could recall. The desperate teacher then blurted out: 'But could you not simply invent some story along these lines?', to which my friend answered that he had no imagination that would run in this direction – it was beyond his scope to imagine things like this. When the teacher made it clear to him that his stubborn attitude could cost him dearly – he would get the lowest grade, which would seriously damage his standing – my friend insisted that he could not help it, he was completely powerless, since it was beyond his scope to think along these lines, his mind was simply blank. This refusal to compromise one's attitude is ethics at its purest, ethics as opposed to morality, to moral compassion. That is to say, needless to add that this friend of mine was in his deeds an extremely helpful and 'good' person; what was absolutely unpalatable for him was to find narcissistic satisfaction in observing himself doing good deeds – in his mind, such a reflexive turn equalled the profoundest ethical betrayal.

And, in this precise sense, Kieślowski's topic is ethics, *not* morality: what actually takes place in each of the instalments of his *Decalogue* is *the shift from morality to ethics*. The starting point is always a moral commandment, and it is through its very violation that the hero(ine) discovers the proper ethical dimension. *Decalogue* 10 is exemplary of this choice between ethics and morality which runs through Kieślowski's entire opus: the two brothers opt for their dead father's vocation (stamp-collecting) at the expense of their moral obligations (the elder brother not only abandons his family, but even sells his kidney, paying for his symbolic vocation with the proverbial pound of flesh). This choice, staged at its purest in *The Double Life of Véronique* – the choice between vocation (leading to death) and a quiet satisfied life (when/if one compromises one's vocation) – has a long tradition (recall E. T. A. Hoffmann's tale of Antonia, who also chooses singing and pays for her choice with death). The staging of this choice in the narrative of Kieślowski's films is clearly *allegorical*: it contains a reference to Kieślowski himself. Was not his choice that of the Polish Weronika – aware of his heart condition, he chose art/vocation (not singing, but film-making), and then died of a sudden heart attack? Kieślowski's fate is prefigured already in his *Camera Buff* (1979), the portrait of a man who forsakes happy family life for the attitude of observing and recording reality through a distant camera lens. In the final scene of the film, when his wife is leaving him for good, the hero turns the camera on himself and his wife, recording her departure on film: even in this traumatic, intimate moment, he does not get fully involved, but persists in his observing attitude – the ultimate proof that he has truly elevated filming into his ethical cause. *Camera Buff* finds its counterpoint in *Calm* (1976), which describes the destiny of Antek, who has just been released from prison. All he wants are the simple things in life: work, somewhere clean to sleep, something to eat, a wife, television and peace. Caught in criminal manipulations at his new workplace, he ends up being beaten by his colleagues, and, at the film's end, just mutters, 'Calm ... calm.' The hero of *Calm* is not alone: even Valentine, the heroine of *Red*, claims that all she wants is to live in peace, without any excessive professional ambitions.

This choice between ethics and morality again renders palpable the ultimate ambiguity of Kieślowski's matrix of salvation through repetition: from a certain perspective, the message of his films is the optimistic one: we *are* given a second chance, we *can* learn from the past. However, the opposite reading of this topic of repeated choices also imposes itself, according to which 'wise' repetition entails ethical betrayal, the choice of life versus the cause (the French Véronique compromises her desire).[29] This, then, accounts for the difference between the two Véroniques: 'the adventure of a brutal, direct approach to the essential, crowned by a musical mort in a perfect but inexplicit note' versus 'a conscious voyage, mediated by the literary allegory' reflected through the experience of the Other (the projected novel of the puppeteer).[30] Véronique is thus melancholic and reflective, in contrast to Weronika's direct enthusiasm for the cause; to put it in Schiller's terms, she is *sentimental*, in contrast to Weronika's *naivety*. It is not simply that Véronique profits from her awareness of the suicidal character of Weronika's choice, but also that she accomplishes the act of ethical betrayal. The presence of this tragic choice is what prevents us from reducing *Véronique* to a New Age tale of spiritual self-discovery – there already *is* a New Age obscurantist remake of Kieślowski's *Véronique*: *Veronika Decides to Die*, Paul Coelho's bestseller of 1999,[31] the story of a 24-year-old librarian from – of all places – Ljubljana, Slovenia, a healthy, attractive and intelligent woman, who all of a sudden decides to die, because the prime of her youth is already behind her, so that all that awaits her from now on is slow but inexorable decay, a foretaste of which she gets in the daily portion of depressing news from the media. Fortunately, she is discovered before the suicidal pills take their full effect and hospitalised in a psychiatric ward, where the poison is pumped out of her stomach. There she learns that the coma has nonetheless fatally weakened her heart: experiencing strong heart palpitations at regular intervals, she is informed that she has only a couple of days to live. Only now is she able to appreciate and fully to savour each remaining moment. What she does not know is that she is involved in a therapeutic experiment by the wise and benevolent doctor who treats her: he has induced her strong heart palpitations with harmless drugs, since his wager is that only the experience of the proximity of death will resuscitate her will to live. An old piano that she finds in the hospital awakens her old passion for music; soon afterwards, she leaves the hospital, fully recovered and intent on pursuing her musical vocation. The difference from Kieślowski cannot but strike the eye: any notion of the inherent and irreconcilable *tension* between leading a satisfied life and the pursuit of a (musical or other) vocation is absent, since Coelho's is a universe in which the pre-established harmony of the two dimensions reigns.

This ethical choice between mission and life around which Kieślowski's films turn is repeated in different guises in a series of recent films, although they never quite achieve Kieślowski's poignancy. Is Anand Tucker's *Hilary and Jackie* (1998), the story of Hilary and Jacqueline du Pré, both musical prodigies in 1950s England, not yet another variation on this motif? While Hilary chooses to start a family, Jackie quickly rises to international fame, dazzling audiences with her unbridled passion for music, and soon marries the renowned pianist and conductor Daniel Barenboim. However, the constant touring becomes a strain on Jackie: she longs for the seemingly simpler family life that Hilary has built; on an unannounced visit, a lonely and depressed Jackie reveals that she also longs for her sister's husband – and, in the supreme act of mercy, her sister obliges her. (This most 'scandalous' moment of the relationship between Jackie and Hilary, the fact that, with her sister's approval, Jacqueline had an affair with Hilary's husband, is so unbearable because it involves a reversal of the standard Lévi-Straussian logic of women as objects of exchange between men: in this case, it is the *man* who serves as the object of exchange between women.) As if punished for her ruthless dedication, Jackie dies after a long, debilitating illness that cuts short her musical career, constraining her to a wheelchair. *Hilary and Jackie* is thus a variation on the Véronique motif: instead of the two Véroniques, we get, more 'realistically', the two sisters, each of them standing for a different ethical choice.[32] There is a double hysteria in the relationship between Hilary and Jackie: each of the two perceives the other as the woman who knows how to desire (the 'subject supposed to desire'), and, at some point, at least, paints herself out of the picture, with the wager that her absence will constitute the ideal image of a couple or a family. For Jackie, Hilary and her family is the ideal unit she longingly observes, while for Hilary, Jackie playing with her own husband and children is such an ideal, in which there is ultimately no place for her.

The film is divided into two parts: the story is first told from Hilary's and then from Jackie's perspective. This division is fully justified by the fact that the couple Hilary–Jackie is the latest version of the couple Ismene–Antigone, i.e. the 'normal' emotional woman versus the woman utterly dedicated to her cause: firstly, we see the extraordinary, monstrous even, Object-Thing (Jackie) through the eyes of her 'normal' compassionate sister; finally, we are transposed into the point of view of the impossible Thing itself, i.e. the Thing itself gets subjectivised, starts to speak. Since we are dealing with the impossible Thing, her subjectivisation can only consist in the story of her decline and fall. Jackie's mental breakdown during a concert performance is rendered through a supreme reversal of the standard procedure of 'sublime' transubstantation, in which we pass from the deficient, miserable song performed in reality to the perfect magic of singing or playing in the fantasy space: her actual concert goes fine, while she *imagines* striking the wrong notes and producing ugly, dissonant sounds.

Is Jackie's relationship with her cello not best captured by the motif of 'death and the maiden'? Is her cello not the *objet petit a*, the partial object that threatens to swallow the subject by dragging her into its lethal, non-phallic *jouissance*? Is it not the exception with regard to the series of intersubjective partners/lovers (not a phallic exception, but the non-phallic excess), so that we have 1+1+1+1... +*a*? To put it in somewhat naive psychological terms, the mystery of Jackie's life is: why did she – while still a happy, promiscuous girl in her early twenties – choose as her privileged piece Elgar's melancholic cello concerto, the masterpiece of his old age, and give such a deeply felt interpretation of it? Is it not like Oscar Wilde who, while still enjoying full public success, already had a premonition of his ultimate failure (clearly discernible in his *The Picture of Dorian Gray*)? This pseudo-teleological premonition is *not* to be reduced to an expression of ideological censorship which demands that women pay the price for engaging themselves fully in their art and treating men as serial lovers. There is more in it, the intimate link that seems to join femininity and the death drive.[33]

Neil LaBute's *In the Company of Men* (1997) gives a much more sinister twist to this choice: the film should be accredited for restaging the sadist project in a way that fits today's ideology of victimisation. As the director himself pointed out in an interview, the idea of the film germinated from a phrase he once overheard: 'Let's really hurt somebody!' Significantly, this notion of 'really hurting somebody' is no longer situated at the level of physical torture or even economic ruin, but at the level of what one usually refers to as 'psychological torture'. The two managers, obliged to stay in a small mid-western town for six weeks, complain to each other about being ruthlessly dropped by their female partners; so they decide to take revenge on womankind: they will pick out a lone, vulnerable woman who has already abandoned all hopes of a fulfilling love life; they will both court her passionately and endeavour to seduce her. Pleasantly surprised by this double attention and by the unexpected problem of deciding whom to choose, she will find new hope in her life; and then, just as she is in the full bloom of her new happiness, the two men will jointly inform her that it was all a practical joke on her intended to hurt her, that they do not give a damn about her. She will never be able to regain her composure after this shock; she will be condemned to long, sleepless nights, her life ruined forever, deprived of any hope. So, if either of the two men is again trampled on by a woman or humiliated by his boss, he will find comfort in the fact that his trouble is as nothing compared to the sad lot of that woman – at least once, he did something much more hurtful to another human being. The story then follows a predictable line: they pick out a deaf office girl, one of the guys falls for her for real, and since he is the uglier of the two and the poor girl prefers the other guy, he – in order to win her over – breaks the rules of their game and tells her directly of the experiment of which she is the victim, etc. He is a knavish weakling, his evil is in a way 'still human', while the other guy's evilness is closer to a perverted ethical stance – for him, evil is a mission, while for the weakling, it is part of coping with life.

Significantly, at the film's end, we learn that the truly evil guy had not been abandoned by his girlfriend at all – they all the time maintained their link: his story was just a fabrication. His intention to hurt someone was not an act of revenge, but in a perverted sense purely ethical. What, however, if the true target of his act was not the poor girl, but the apparently more 'honest' and 'human' partner in crime? What if the evil guy's intention was to hurt *him*, his partner in crime, by way of humiliating him and destroying the last vestiges of his sense of self-respect? At the film's end, one cannot say who of the two perpetrators is worse: the question is properly undecidable. The guy who breaks the rules of the game by 'opening himself up' and spilling it out to the girl is in a way even more brutal (as, when he tells the girl that, because of her deafness, she is in no position to choose partners); although he is unable to sustain really hurting someone, he effectively hurts the girl even more.

Two recent films which, although made by different directors, have to be read as a couple, provide further versions of the same choice: David Lynch's *The Straight Story* (1999) and Anthony Minghella's *The Talented Mr Ripley*. The very beginning of David Lynch's *The Straight Story*, the words that introduce the credits, 'Walt Disney Presents – A David Lynch Film', provide what is perhaps the best resumé of the ethical paradox that marked the end of the twentieth century: the overlapping of transgression and the norm. Walt Disney, the brand of conservative family values, takes under its umbrella David Lynch, the author who epitomises transgression, who brings to light the obscene underworld of perverted sex and violence that lurks beneath the respectable surface of our lives.

Today, more and more, the cultural-economic apparatus itself, in order to reproduce itself under competitive market conditions, has not only to tolerate, but directly to incite stronger and more shocking effects and products. Suffice it to recall recent trends in the visual arts: gone are the days when we had simple statues or framed paintings – what we get now are exhibitions of frames themselves without paintings, dead cows and their excrement, videos of the inside of the human body (gastroscopy and colonoscopy), inclusion of smell into the work, etc. Here, again, as in the domain of sexuality, perversion is no longer subversive: the shocking excesses are part of the system itself, the system feeds on them in order to reproduce itself. So, if Lynch's earlier films were also caught in this trap, what then about *The Straight Story*, based on the true story of Alvin Straight, an old farmer who motored across the American plains on a John Deere lawnmover to visit his ailing brother? Does this slow-paced story of persistence imply the renunciation of transgression, a turn towards the naive immediacy of a direct ethical stance of fidelity? The very title of the film undoubtedly refers to Lynch's previous opus: this is the straight story with regard to the 'deviations' into the uncanny underworld from *Eraserhead* (1976) to *The Lost Highway*. However, what if the 'straight' hero of Lynch's last film is actually much more subversive than the weird characters who people his previous films? What if, in our post-modern world, in which radical ethical commitment is perceived as ridiculously anachronistic, he is the true outcast? One should recall here G. K. Chesterton's perspicacious remark, in his 'A Defence of Detective Stories', about how the detective story

> keeps in some sense before the mind the fact that civilization itself is the most sensational of departures and the most romantic of rebellions. When the detective in a police romance stands alone, and somewhat fatuously fearless, amid the knives and fists of a thieves' kitchen, it does certainly serve to make us remember that it is the agent of social justice who is the original and poetic figure, while the burglars and footpads are merely placid old cosmic conservatives, happy in the immemorial respectability of apes and wolves. [The police romance] is based on the fact that morality is the most dark and daring of conspiracies.[34]

What, then, if this is the ultimate message of Lynch's film – that ethics is 'the most dark and daring of all conspiracies', that the ethical subject is the one who in fact threatens the existing order, in contrast to a long series of weird Lynchean perverts (Baron Harkonnen in *Dune* [1984], Frank in *Blue Velvet*, Bobby Peru in *Wild at Heart* . . .) who ultimately sustain it? In this precise sense, the counterpoint to *The Straight Story* is Anthony Minghella's *The Talented Mr Ripley,* based on Patricia Highsmith's novel of the same name. The film tells the story of Tom Ripley, an ambitious but broke young New Yorker, who is approached by the rich magnate Herbert Greenleaf, in his mistaken belief that Tom was at Princeton with his son Dickie. Dickie is off idling in Italy, and Greenleaf pays Tom to go to Italy and bring his son back and to his senses, to take his rightful place in the family business. However, once in Europe, Tom gets more and more fascinated not only by Dickie himself, but also by the polished, easy-going, upper-class life that Dickie inhabits. All the talk about Tom's homosexuality is here misplaced: Dickie is for Tom not the object of his desire, but the ideal desiring subject, the transferential subject 'supposed to know [how to desire]'. In short, Dickie becomes for Tom his *ideal ego*, the figure of his imaginary identification: when he repeatedly casts a covetous side-glance at Dickie, he does not thereby betray his erotic desire to engage in sexual commerce with him, to *have* Dickie, but his desire to *be* like Dickie. So, to resolve this predicament, Tom concocts an elaborate plan: on a boat trip, he kills Dickie and then, for some time, assumes his identity. Acting as Dickie, he organises things so that, after Dickie's 'official' death, he inherits his wealth; when this is accomplished, the false 'Dickie' disappears, leaving behind a suicide note praising Tom, while Tom again reappears, successfully evading the suspicious investigators, even earning the gratitude of Dickie's parents, and then leaves Italy for Greece.

Although the novel was written in the mid-50s, one can claim that Highsmith foreshadows today's therapeutic rewriting of ethical commandments into 'Recommendations' which one should not follow too blindly. Ripley simply stands for the last step in this rewriting: thou shalt not kill – *except when there is really no other way to pursue your happiness*. Or, as Highsmith herself put it in an interview: 'He could be called psychotic, but I would not call him insane because his actions are rational. . . . I consider him a rather civilized person who kills when he absolutely has to.' Ripley is thus not any kind of 'American psycho': his criminal acts are not frenetic *passages à l'acte*, outbursts of violence in which he releases the energy hindered by the frustrations of everyday yuppie life. His crimes are calculated with simple pragmatic reasoning: he does what is necessary to attain his goal, the wealthy quiet life in the exclusive suburbs of Paris. What is so disturbing about him, of course, is that he somehow seems to lack an elementary ethical sense: in daily life, he is mostly friendly and considerate (although with a touch of coldness), and when he commits a murder, he does it with regret, quickly, as painlessly as possible, in the same way one performs an unpleasant but necessary task. He is the ultimate psychotic, the best exemplification of what Lacan had in mind when he claimed that normality is the special form of psychosis – of not being traumatically caught in the symbolic web, of retaining 'freedom' from the symbolic order.

However, the mystery of Highsmith's Ripley transcends the standard American ideological motif of the capacity of the individual to radically 'reinvent' him/herself, to erase the traces of the past and assume a thoroughly new identity; it transcends the post-modern 'Protean Self'. Therein resides the ultimate failure of the movie with regard to the novel: the film 'Gatsbyises' Ripley into a new version of the American hero who recreates his identity in a murky way. What gets lost here is best exemplified by the crucial difference between the novel and the film: in the film, Ripley has the stirrings of a conscience, while in the novel, the qualms of conscience are simply beyond his grasp. This is why making Ripley's gay desires explicit in the film also misses the point. Minghella implies that, back in the 50s, Highsmith had to be more circumspect to make the hero palatable to the large public, while today we can say things in a more overt way. However, Ripley's coldness is not the surface effect of his gay stance, but rather the other way round. In one of the later Ripley novels, we learn that he makes love once a week to his wife Heloise, as a regular ritual. There is nothing passionate about it – Tom is like Adam in paradise, prior to the Fall, when, according to St Augustine, he and Eve *did* have sex, but it was performed as a simple instrumental task, like sowing the seeds on a field. One way to read Ripley is thus to claim that he is angelic, living in a universe which precedes the Law and its transgression (sin), i.e. the vicious superego cycle of guilt generated by our very obedience to the Law, described by St Paul. This is the reason why Ripley feels no guilt or even remorse after his murders: he is not yet fully integrated into the symbolic Law.

The paradox of this non-integration is that the price Ripley pays for it is his inability to experience intense sexual passion – a clear proof of how there is no sexual passion outside the confines of the symbolic Law. In one of the later Ripley novels, the hero sees two flies on his kitchen table and, upon looking at them closely and observing that they are copulating, squashes them with disgust. This small detail is crucial – Minghella's Ripley would *never* have done something like this: Highsmith's Ripley is in a way disconnected from the reality of flesh, disgusted at the Real of life, of its cycle of generation and corruption. Marge, Dickie's girlfriend, provides an adequate characterisation of Ripley: 'All right, he may not be queer. He's just a nothing, which is worse. He isn't normal enough to have *any* kind of sex life.' Insofar as such coldness characterises a certain radical lesbian stance, one is tempted to claim that, rather than being a closet gay, the paradox of Ripley is that he is a *male lesbian*. (Here, one is tempted to evoke the biographical fact that Highsmith herself was lesbian: no wonder that she felt such proximity to the figure of Ripley.) The true enigma of Ripley is why he persists in this shuddering coldness, retaining a psychotic disengagement from any passionate human attachment, even after he reaches his goal and recreates himself as a respectable art-dealer living in a rich Paris suburb. This disengaged coldness that persists beneath all possible shifting identities, perhaps the ultimate truth of the 'post-modern subject', somehow gets lost in the film.

Furthermore, the cinema version of *The Talented Mr Ripley* enables us to discern clearly what is wrong with the basic post-modern move of 'filling in the gaps' (through sequels, prequels, retelling the story from a different perspective, or the simple filling in of the blanks of the original text), the procedure that cuts across the divide of high and low, since it can be found in popular culture products as well as in high art (the two new versions of *Hamlet*, Tom Stoppard's *Rosencrantz and Guildenstern Are Dead*, retelling the story from the point of view of two minor characters, and John Updike's prequel *Gertrude and Claudius*). So what is in principle wrong with such a procedure? According to Richard Maltby's perspicacious analysis,[35] *Casablanca* (1942) mobilises two different registers of reading, the 'naive' reading which fully complies with the rules of the infamous Production Code, and a more sophisticated register in which the spectator discerns in the film's texture multiple indications of transgressive behaviour. So we have the 'official' storyline, in which the Gaze of the big Other *qua* 'innocent observer' cannot find anything morally/ideologically problematic, and the whole series of possible alternative storylines imagined by the spectator, lines which clearly violate the predominant sexual, political, etc. prohibitions. These two readings are not simply opposed: it is *because* the cinematic text takes good care to remain innocent in the eyes of the big Other (all events and actions can be accounted for in the terms of the 'official' storyline) that it can afford to allow the spectator to indulge in prohibited pleasures.[36]

Today's 'post-modern' films seem to reverse this procedure: we no longer get the 'official' storyline which we can then supplement by multiple fantasised alternatives – the public text that we see *directly proposes itself as one of the variations*. This shift is clearly perceptible in the passage from a novel to its film version: in traditional Hollywood, the cinema version represses (censors) its literary source, which starts to function as the film's alternative obscene, publicly disavowed text (say, a prostitute in the novel is changed into a bar singer); today's post-Code cinema versions, on the contrary, directly *bring out* what was allegedly 'repressed' in the original (see, precisely, the case of *The Talented Mr Ripley*, which renders the hero explicitly gay). Van Sant's remake of *Psycho* followed the same path of 'showing it all': Norman is shown masturbating while he peeps on Marion before slaughtering her – and, again, the point to be made is that such a 'radicalisation' is the form of appearance of its opposite, of the *retreat* from the actual monstrosity of the figure of Norman.[37]

The example of *Ripley* makes it clear what is wrong with this procedure which appears to be 'more radical than the original', bringing out its implicit, repressed content: what mattered in the original was not only the 'repression' of the allegedly prohibited (sexual, etc.) content, but *the void of this 'repression' as such*. What is lost in the gesture of filling in the gaps of Ripley is his non-psychological cold monstrosity, which is uncannily close to a weird 'normality'. In other words, what if, by way of 'filling in the gaps' and 'telling it all', what we retreat from is the void as such, which, of course, is ultimately none other than the void of subjectivity (the Lacanian 'barred subject')? What Minghella accomplishes is the move from the void of *subjectivity* to the inner wealth of *personality*: instead of a polite person who is at the same time a monstrous automaton with no inner turmoil, we get a person full of psychic traumas – in short, we get someone whom we can, in the fullest meaning of the term, *understand*. The move to 'fill in the gaps' thus obeys the compulsion to understand, to 'normalise', and, in this way, to avoid the void that is subjectivity.

Perhaps, the opposition of Lynch's 'straight' hero and Highsmith's 'normal' Ripley determines the extreme co-ordinates of today's late-capitalist ethical experience – with the strange twist that it is Ripley who is uncannily 'normal', and Lynch's 'straight' man who is uncannily weird, even perverted. We have thus the unexpected opposition between the *weirdness of the thoroughly ethical stance* and the *monstrous 'normality' of the thoroughly unethical stance*. How, then, are we to break out of this deadlock? Both heroes have in common a ruthless dedication to the pursuit of their goal, so the way out may seem to be to abandon this common feature and plea for a more 'warm', compassionate humanity ready to accept compromises. Is, however, such a 'soft' (in short: unprincipled) 'humanity' not the predominant mode of subjectivity today, so that the two films merely provide its two extremes? In the late 20s, Stalin defined the figure of a Bolshevik as the unity of Russian passionate obstinacy and American resourcefulness. Perhaps, along the same lines, one should claim that the way out is rather to be sought in the impossible *synthesis* of the two heroes, in the figure the Lynchean 'straight' man who pursues his goal with the cunning resourcefulness of Tom Ripley.

We have thus the same basic choice repeated at three different levels: firstly, in Kieślowski, as a direct choice between mission-cause and life; then, in LaBute, as two modes of evil, ethical-radical and pathological; finally, in Lynch and Minghella, as the two modes of detachment from ordinary life. And is the topic of our first chapter, the choice between Theory and Post-Theory, not yet another case of the ethical choice between event and Being, between ethics and morality, between mission and life? In

Freudian terms, this choice is, of course, the choice between the pleasure principle and the (death) drive beyond the pleasure principle: between a 'good life' oriented towards happiness, the 'care of the self', the wisdom of moderation, etc., and a life caught in a compulsion which we are compelled to follow irrespective of our own good. Sometimes, these two options coexist in one and the same mode of activity. Although Minghella's *The Talented Mr Ripley* totally deforms the original Ripley figure from the Highsmith novel, it is nonetheless an interesting film in its own terms – it neatly renders the paradox of Ripley's situation at the end: on the one hand, he succeeds, he is 'in', by assuming Dickie's identity, he is rich, free to do whatever he wants, to pursue his happiness, to lead what he considers a good life; on the other hand, after the first murder, he is caught in a compulsive logic, forced to commit further murders, since the only way open to him is to persist to the end in the way he has chosen. Perhaps it is this tension and not his 'guilt' that justifies his nightmares.

Kieślowski advocates neither the moralistic dismissal of life on behalf of the mission nor the cheap wisdom of advocating simple life against mission; he is fully aware of the mission's limitation. Exemplary here is *The Scar* (1976), the story of an honest Communist cadre who, as a director, comes to a small provincial town to construct a new chemical factory. He wants to make local people happier, bring progress; however, the factory not only causes environmental problems and undermines traditional ways of life, it also conflicts with the short-term interests of the townspeople. Disillusioned, he gives up his post . . . The problem here is that of the good – who knows what is good for others, who can impose *his* good on others? This inconsistency of different forms of good is the topic of the film: although the director succeeds socially (the factory is built), he is aware that he has failed ethically. We see here why Freud was sceptical towards the ethical motto 'Do to others only what you would like them to do to you.' The problem with it is not that it is too idealistic, overestimating the ethical capacity of man; Freud's point is rather that, if one takes into account the basic *perversion* of human desire, then the very application of this motto leads to strange results – one certainly wouldn't like a *masochist* to follow this precept.

The same complexity marked Kieślowski's personal choice: after finishing *Red*, he retired to the countryside in order to spend his remaining days fishing and reading – in short, to realise the fantasy of a quiet retired life, redeemed of the burden of vocation. However, in a tragic way, he lost on both accounts: the choice 'vocation or quiet life' proved false, it was already too late, so that, after choosing peace and retirement, he died – or does his sudden death signal that the retirement into a quiet country life was a false issue, a fantasy screen effectively functioning as a metaphor for death, i.e. that, for Kieślowski, the only way to survive was to continue filming, even if this were to mean constantly courting death? Did Kieślowski not, at least from our retroactive view, *die at a proper moment*: although premature, his death – like Alexander the Great's or Mozart's – seemed to occur precisely when his opus was rounded up? Is this not the ultimate case of miraculous coincidences around which his films turn? It is as if his fatal heart-attack was a free act, a staged death, striking at the right time – just after he announced that he would no longer be doing films.

Should we, then, read Weronika's second (unethical) choice as a new version of the traditional sublime reversal found, among others, in Charles Dickens' *Great Expectations*? When, at his birth, Pip is designated as a 'man of great expectations', everybody perceives this as the forecast of his worldly success; however, at the novel's end, when he abandons London's false glamour and returns to his modest childhood community, we become aware that he did live up to the forecast that marked his life – it is only by way of finding strength to leave behind the vain thrill of London's high society that he authenticates the notion of being a 'man of great expectations'. We are dealing here with a kind of Hegelian reflexivity: what changes in the course of the hero's ordeal is not only his character, but also the very ethical standard by which we measure his character. And did not something of the same order happen at the opening ceremony of the 1996 Olympic games in Atlanta, when Muhammad Ali lit the Olympic flame, the hand holding the torch shaking heavily on account of his severe illness? When the journalists claimed that, in doing this, he truly was 'The Greatest' (a reference to Ali's boasting self-designation decades ago, the title of the film about himself in which he starred and of his autobiography), they, of course, wanted to emphasise that Muhammad Ali had achieved true greatness now, through his dignified endurance of his debilitating illness, not when he was enjoying the full swing of popularity and smashing his opponents in the ring.[38] And what if it's the same with the Kieślowskian second choice – there are things more important than singing, like the simple human goodness radiated by Véronique?

The Double Life of Véronique (1991): Poland. Weronika, who sings beautifully, suffers from a heart condition. She has to choose – to continue singing, with all the strain and stress which this involves, and risk her life or to give up her singing career and lead a normal life. She wins a singing contest and chooses her career. During a concert she suffers a heart attack and dies.

France. Véronique is Weronika's double. She, too, has a beautiful voice and a heart condition. When Weronika suffers, Véronique senses that she must avoid the situation which leads to the pain: she rejects her singing career and teaches music at a primary school. One day, Alexandre, a puppeteer and story writer, visits her school and performs for the pupils. Days later she receives mysterious messages, among them a cassette recording of sounds made in a station café. She locates the café, goes there and sees Alexandre waiting for her. In the hotel where they make love, Alexandre finds the photographs which Véronique took when she visited Poland; on one of them, she sees Weronika, her double. Alexandre makes two puppets, one of Véronique, the other, an identical one, of Weronika, explaining to Véronique that she has a double; he wants to use Véronique's life for the purposes of his new story. Shattered and feeling exploited, Véronique leaves and returns home to her father.

When and why, exactly, does Véronique return to her father in order to find there a safe haven of calm? After her puppeteer lover stages for her the (unconscious) choice that structured her life, in the guise of the two marionettes. So what is Véronique retreating from when she abandons her lover? She perceives this staging as a domineering intrusion, while it is actually the very opposite: the staging of her ultimate unbearable *freedom*. In other words, what is so traumatic for her in the puppeteer's performance is not that she sees herself reduced to a puppet whose strings are pulled by the hidden hand of destiny, but that she is confronted with what F. W. J. Schelling called the primordial decision-differentiation (*Ent-Scheidung*), the unconscious atemporal deed by means of which the subject 'chooses' his/her eternal character which, afterwards, within his/her conscious-temporal life, s/he experiences as the inexorable necessity, as 'the way s/he always was'.[39] This paradox of the atemporal choice accounts for

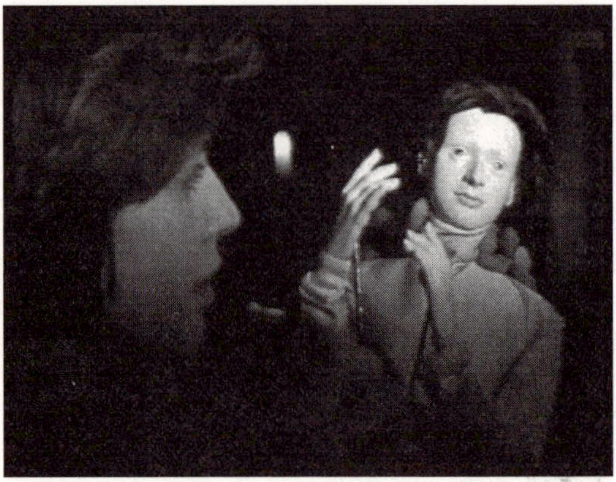

the ambiguous tension between chance and necessity in the Kieślowskian universe of alternative realities: while the choice is radically contingent, determinism is complete *within* each of the three realities of *Blind Chance* – Witek *necessarily* misses the train, hits the railway guard, catches the train.

What does a puppet (more precisely: a marionette) stand for as a subjective stance? One should turn here to Heinrich von Kleist's essay *Über das Marionettentheater* from 1810,[40] which is crucial with regard to his relationship to Kant's philosophy (we know that reading Kant threw Kleist into a shattering spiritual crisis – this reading was *the* traumatic encounter of his life). Where, in Kant, do we find the term 'marionette'? In a mysterious subchapter of his *Critique of Practical Reason* entitled 'Of the Wise Adaptation of Man's Cognitive Faculties to His Practical Vocation', in which he endeavours to answer the question of what would happen to us if we were to gain access to the noumenal domain, to the *Ding an sich*:

> instead of the conflict which now the moral disposition has to wage with inclinations and in which, after some defeats, moral strength of mind may be gradually won, God and eternity in their awful majesty would stand unceasingly before our eyes. . . . Thus most actions conforming to the law would be done from fear, few would be done from hope, none from duty. The moral worth of actions, on which alone the worth of the person and even of the world depends in the eyes of supreme wisdom, would not exist at all. The conduct of man, so long as his nature remained as it is now, would be changed into mere mechanism, where, as in a puppet show, everything would gesticulate well but no life would be found in the figures.[41]

So, for Kant, direct access to the noumenal domain would deprive us of the very 'spontaneity' which forms the kernel of transcendental freedom: it would turn us into lifeless automata, or, to put it in modern-day terms, into 'thinking machines'. What Kleist does is to present the *obverse* of this horror: the bliss and grace of marionettes, the creatures who have direct access to the noumenal divine dimension, who are *directly* guided by it. For Kleist, marionettes display the perfection of spontaneous, unconscious movement: they have only one centre of gravity, their movements are controlled from only one point. The puppeteer has control only of this point, and as he moves it in a simple straight line, the limbs of the marionettes follow inevitably and naturally because the figure of the marionette is completely co-ordinated. Marionettes thus symbolise beings of an innocent, pristine nature: they respond naturally and gracefully to divine guidance, in contrast to ordinary humans, who have to struggle constantly with their ineradicable propensity to evil, which is the price they have to pay for their freedom. This grace of the marionettes is underscored by their apparent weightlessness: they hardly touch the floor – they are not bound to the earth, for they are drawn up from above. They represent a state of grace, a paradise lost to man, whose wilful 'free' self-assertions make him self-conscious. The dancer exemplifies this fallen state of man: he is not upheld from above, but, rather, feels himself bound to the earth, and yet must appear weightless in order to perform his feats with apparent ease. He must try consciously to attain grace, which is why the effect of his dance is affectation rather than grace. Therein resides the paradox of man: he is neither an animal wholly immersed in his earthly surroundings, nor the angelic marionette gracefully floating in the air, but a free being who, due to his very freedom, feels the unbearable pressure that attracts and ties him to the earth where he ultimately does *not* belong.

It is in terms of this tragic split that one should read figures like Kätchen von Heilbronn from Kleist's play of the same name, this fairy-tale figure of a woman who wanders through life with angelic equanimity: like a marionette, she is guided from above and fulfils her glorious destiny by merely following the spontaneous assertions of her heart. What Kleist is not able to confront is not only the fact that such an angelic position is impossible due to human finitude, but also the more disturbing fact that, if this position were to be realised, it would amount to its opposite, to a horrible, lifeless machine. The very metaphor Kleist uses (marionette) is tell-tale: in order for it to function, Kleist has to exclude the machinic aspect of it.

Chapter Nine
'Happiness also has its tears'

How does the Decalogue (the traumatically imposed divine Commandments) relate to its modern obverse, 'human rights'? Kieślowski's *Colours* trilogy implicitly refers to human rights: the three colours stand for the three catchwords of the French Revolution. Blue: Liberty, white: Equality, red: Fraternity. In our post-political, liberal-permissive society, human rights are ultimately reduced to *the rights to violate the Ten Commandments*. 'The right to privacy' – the right to commit *adultery*, done in secret, when no one sees me or has the right to probe into my life. 'The right to pursue happiness and to possess private property' – the right to *steal* (to exploit others). 'Freedom of the press and of the expression of opinion' – the right to *lie*. 'The right of free citizens to possess weapons' – the right to *kill*. And, ultimately, 'freedom of religious belief' – the right to celebrate false gods.

This degradation of human rights is inscribed into their very notion: human rights generate their own excess in the guise of *libertinage*.[42] How, then, are we to bridle this excess? The lesson of libertinage seems to be that rights without Commandments unavoidably change into mutual enslavement and exploitation: in his violation of the Commandments, a libertine enslaves and exploits other people as the means for his unbridled pleasures. However, the *Colours* trilogy proposes another way out, beyond the notion that the exercise of rights should be kept in check by Commandments. Insofar as *Decalogue* relates to the Old Testament Commandments, one is tempted to read the *Colours* trilogy as implicitly referring to the three New Testament virtues: Faith, Hope, Charity (Love); the triad of Liberty-Equality-Fraternity can only function in an authentic way if supported by the *other* triad, Faith-Hope-Charity. Liberty is true freedom only if sustained by Charity, the loving acceptance of others (in *Blue,* Julie takes the path from a cold abstract freedom to the concrete freedom of lovingly embracing others);

Equality relies on a reciprocity which is never fully realised, but remains a utopian Hope (*White*, the film about Equality, ends with the hero observing his imprisoned beloved – there is hope they will be reunited); Fraternity relies on Faith – without Faith, it remains a cold abstract codependence (in *Red*, it is only through a fundamental faith, trust, in others that the Judge can re-enter the 'fraternity' of human beings). It is interesting to recall here that, in the initial conception of *Decalogue*, the housing block in which its protagonists live was to blow up in a gas explosion, killing them all – a pun on the Last Judgment, and a confirmation that the God of *Decalogue* is the cruel, jealous and punitive God of the Old Testament, in whose eyes we all have to pay the price for our sins (in clear contrast to the *Colours* trilogy, in whose finale there also is a large disaster, the sinking of the ferry; however, the chosen ones, i.e. the protagonists of the three films – the three couples of Julie and Olivier, Karol and his wife, and Valentine and Auguste – miraculously survive the catastrophe).[43]

One is thus tempted not only to oppose *Decalogue* and the *Colours* trilogy along the lines of the Old versus the New Testament (the cruel merciless God versus the conciliatory power of Love), but also along the axis of sexual difference.[44] *Decalogue* is male-centred: almost all its stories are told from the perspective of the male hero, and the women are reduced to the standard role of agents of hysterical outbursts who disturb the male hero's calm. Women are excessive, a danger to themselves and to others: as wives, they are unfaithful, striking at their husbands when they are most vulnerable (when they have cancer, as in *Decalogue* 2, when they are impotent, as in *Decalogue* 9); as *femmes fatales*, they humiliate the innocent boy who has a crush on them (in *Decalogue* 6); as daughters, they explode in incestuous rage (in *Decalogue* 4). In both *Decalogue* 3 and 4, the heroine stages a hysterical spectacle which addresses the man with an excessive unconditional demand: the ex-lover has to abandon his family on Christmas Eve in order to help her find her husband; the father has to confront the daughter's incestuous provocation. In *Decalogue* 6, once aware of being observed, Magda – instead of simply pulling the curtains down – enters into a perverse game with Tomek; in *Decalogue* 7, Majka disrupts the fragile family balance by escaping with her (biological) daughter. Is this not yet again the basic figure of the hysterical woman threatening the man's stab-

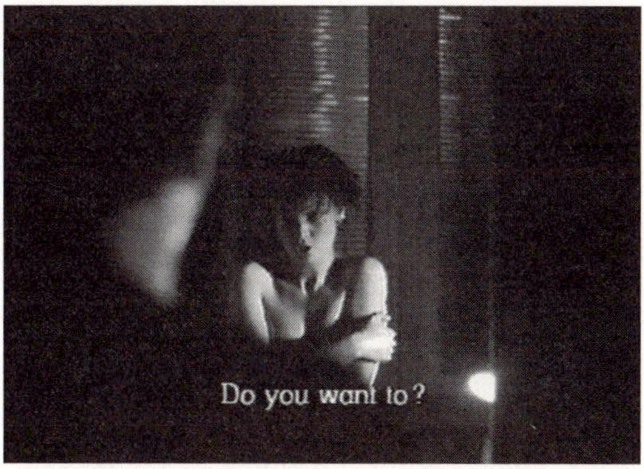

ility, even his very identity, the figure articulated at the end of the nineteenth century from Richard Wagner and Otto Weininger to August Strindberg and Edvard Munch?

In *Véronique* and the *Colours* trilogy, the change is discernible already at the level of physical appearance and clothing: in *Decalogue*, Kieślowski either selected sexually unattractive actresses, or (in 2, 4, and 6) he portrayed the beautiful ones in such a way that their beauty is clearly devalued – they are badly dressed, unkempt, and shot under a harsh lighting that ruthlessly accentuates all their flaws. Compare this with Irène Jacob, Julie Delpy and Juliette Binoche, who are not only intrinsically beautiful, but *also treated as such* by the camera which lovingly traverses their bodies.[45] In these films, the story is told from the female perspective (with the significant exception of *White*, which finishes in a courtly love model of the cruel lady admired in her inaccessibility): the woman (Irène Jacob, Juliette Binoche) not only provides the focus and perspective of the story, but also embodies a deeper intuitive insight into the situation:

> She 'knows' because she is endowed with a female talent which men completely lack, an extra-rational insight below the surface of things, a gift of illumination that permits an instantaneous penetration of the heart of a matter which men would require a long and complex investigation to reach.[46]

This passage is quoted not because of our agreement with it, but because it renders adequately the ideology that sustains these films: in its very elevation of the 'female', it reduces women to a pre-rational intuition:

> The phrase that falls most frequently from the lips of Véronique, Julie and Valentine is 'I don't know', a kind of declaration of helplessness with regard to a certain way of knowing or gaining knowledge. Were they consciously to grasp the nature of their contact with the world, perhaps they would use such phrases as 'I see' or 'I foresee'.[47]

'Were they consciously to grasp . . .' – but the whole point is that they are unable to do it. Is it not clear that this apparent reassertion of the 'feminine', far from amounting to an actual threat to the patriarchal universe, is merely the exact obverse and supplement of the above-mentioned figure of the hysterical women prone to excessive theatrical outbursts? A woman is good insofar as she retains her pre-rational, intuitive, passive attitude, renouncing any aggressive drive to assert herself – the moment she succumbs to this temptation, she turns into a pathetic hysterical monster that is a threat to everybody, including herself.

One should emphasise here the thematic proximity between the existential mystery of the women in Kieślowski's films and in the narratives of Christa Wolf, the literary beacon of the former GDR. Wolf's masterpiece, *The Quest for Christa T.*, renders – through the prism of the narratrix who collects memoirs, letters and other of Christa T.'s writings, combining them with her own recollections and reflections – the life-story of a young woman, born in 1927, who grows up in a small village, as the only child of the village schoolteacher. After studying at the gymnasium, she is forced to flee her village due to the invasion of the Red Army. In the first post-war years, she teaches at an elementary school and falls in love once or twice. In about 1951 she decides to return to the University of Leipzig to study German literature. As she seeks more meaning in her life, she has doubts about her profession and even contemplates suicide. However, she does manage to complete her degree in 1954 and becomes a teacher at a high school, where she has several run-ins with rigid functionaries and finds it difficult to impart humanistic lessons to her students. After she meets Justus, a young veterinarian, and becomes pregnant, they marry, and she decides to seek refuge with him from her meaningless job in a small town in the north. Here she hopes to write and dedicate herself to her family. However, she cannot escape into a country idyll. While she and her husband begin building a new house, she is overcome by the senselessness of her 'new life', has a brief affair with a forester, and then learns just before she and her husband are to move into the new house that she has leukemia; she dies in 1963.

Simple as such a story may appear, one should avoid a whole series of traps here, from the anti-Communist thesis that Christa T. effectively dies not of leukemia, but because of the oppressive GDR system, where the drabness of day-to-day life offered no space for authentic personal fulfilment, up to the proto-Heideggerian reading of the heroine's ultimate failure as the necessary outcome of her metaphysical nihilism, of the excessive assertion of her subjectivity – a reading which conceives of Christa T. as the last in the great line of modern European novel heroes and heroines, from Don Quixote through Julien Sorel and Madame Bovary to Josef K., all victims not of constraining social circumstances, but, rather, of their own subjectivist *hubris*, of their unreadiness to accept life the way it is, independent of the grand metaphysical projects they want to impose on it.

There is something odd about Christa T., something strikingly different, which makes her seem out of step with her times (this same prodigious life-asserting energy of the feminine subject is also the topic of what are arguably the two archetypal GDR movies: Heiner Carow's *Die Legende von Paul und Paula* from 1973[48] and Konrad Wolf's *Solo Sunny* from 1980). To put it in Althusserian terms, her story is the story of a failed ideological interpellation, of the failure – or, at least, the vacillation – in fully recognising oneself in one's socio-ideological identity:

> When her name was called: 'Christa T.!' – she stood up and went and did what was expected of her; was there anyone to whom she could say that hearing her name called gave her much to think about: Is it really me who's meant? Or is it only my name that's being used? Counted in with other names, industriously added up in front of the equals sign? And might I just as well have been absent, would anyone have noticed?[49]

Is this gesture of 'Am I that name?', this probing into one's symbolic identification, rendered by Johannes R. Becher's quote which Wolf put at the very start of the novel, 'This coming-to-oneself – what is it?', not hysterical provocation at its purest? In an apparently opposite move, one should simultaneously conceive of *Christa T.* as a failed version of the *Ankunftsroman*, the novel of 'arrival in a [new socialist] reality', the new GDR version of the old tradition of the *Bildungsroman*, in which a group of young East Germans learns to abandon their excessive romanticised expectations and to accept the reality of the GDR as the space of their personal fulfilment. (Perhaps it is more than a mere coincidence that the key figure of this tradition, Brigitte Reimann, the author of the 1961 novel *Ankunft im Alltag*, also died of cancer at approximately the same age as Christa T.) *The Divided Heaven*, Wolf's earlier, breakthrough novel, still fits the co-ordinates of the *Ankunftsroman*, with Rita, the heroine, at the end getting over her suicidal crisis and accepting the reality of the GDR, and, specifically, her work collective as the place which offers the solidarity necessary to overcome her personal crises. In *Christa T.*, the 'arrival in reality' fails to occur, so the novel ends with a meaningless death.[50]

How, then, are we to conceive of this exuberant life-potential of Christa T.? It undermines the opposition between identifying with the 'official' ideology and the resigned, cynical retreat into private life: it stands for a naive fidelity to the utopian potential of the 'official' socialist ideology itself – ultimately, for (feminine) desire itself. Freud's dream of Irma's injection is *the* dream, the inaugural dream, because of its reflexivity: its message is that it undermines Freud's (the dreamer's) own desire to master the hysterical subject (Irma). That is to say, which *is*, ultimately, the desire realised in it, in the very failure of Freud's desire to master Irma? *Desire as such*, Irma's hysterical desire. What this dream stages is the inaugural scene of the emergence of (female) desire in its subversive dimension, as that which remains impenetrable, which cannot be controlled by the male master. Desire is thus literally *realised* – not 'fulfilled', but actualised, rendered visible, as desire. And is not something of the same order taking place in Kieślowski's films? Do they not ultimately tell the story of the birth of feminine desire out of the spirit of mourning and melancholy?

There is, however, yet another, more radical, level at which the *Colours* trilogy marks a break and signals the emergence of a new dimension in Kieślowski's work. From Kieślowski's early documentaries to *Véronique* runs the straight line of reflection upon the fundamental ethical choice between mission and life: the spontaneous flow of life tending towards calm is interrupted by the violent intrusion of interpellation. If, in (ideological) interpellation as well as in paranoia, the subject 'hears a voice' that calls him, in what, then, resides the difference? The naive and direct answer that imposes itself is: in interpellation, the call is 'real', while in paranoia, it is imagined, i.e. the subject hears a non-existent voice – but is this not all too simple? Is it not that the very idea of a big Other 'really' addressing us from the outside is *the very definition of paranoia*, so that this distinction cannot but remind us of the way (evoked by Lévi-Strauss)[51] the fully qualified magicians in Indian tribes dismiss their less qualified imitators: although they are well aware that they also cheat, they, at least, do it in a proper way. The terms should thus be reversed: the 'normally' interpellated subject knows that the voice addressing him or her 'does not really exist', that it comes from within him or her, that it is a fiction, while the paranoiac believes the voice really comes from the outside. In other words, if, as Althusser makes clear, interpellation (recognition in the call) is performative in the sense of positing the (very) big Other in whose call the subject 'recognises' himself, is then interpellation as such paranoiac? No: it is precisely in paranoia that the voice heard by the subject is fully *real* (a hallucination). The difference thus concerns the *status* of the voice: is it part of the (barred) big Other, the *symbolic* order, or does it emanate from (is it located in) the *Real*?

The *Colours* trilogy introduces a new element in this choice between life and interpellation, a third term, the 'zero-level' of utter contraction/self-withdrawal, of symbolic death, which is neither mission nor life, but their obscure ground, their 'vanishing mediator'. Each part of the trilogy focuses on the voyage from a certain mode of radical self-withdrawal to the acceptance of others, the reintegration into the social universe: *Blue*'s Julie travels from 'night of the world' to *agape*, *White*'s Karol from being reduced to a social outcast (to an economic and sexual failure) to regaining his wealth and his wife, *Red*'s the Judge from cold, cynical observation to reaching out his hand. Here we have the three modes of entering (passing through) the domain between the two deaths: Julie withdraws from the world into solitude, she dies for the symbolic community; Karol is reduced to nothing, robbed of his wife and all his possessions – and, as the first step

Three Colours: Blue, White, Red (1993/4)

Blue (Liberty): Julie loses her husband Patrice, a renowned composer, and their young daughter Anna in a car accident which she barely survives. After the accident, she learns that Patrice had a mistress, Sandrine, who is now expecting his child. Under the shock of this double loss, she tries to cut herself off from all her previous ties and begin a new life: she moves to an area in Paris where she believes no one will find her. Olivier, her husband's collaborator who is secretly in love with her, locates her and solicits her to complete the husband's unfinished score, a song dedicated to a united Europe. She refuses, desperately trying to erase all traces of the past which threaten her new freedom; however, fragments of her husband's – or is it her own? – music haunt her, until she finally decides to finish the composition, and then makes love to Olivier, reconciled with the world and all the persons in it who meant a lot to her and to her husband, including Sandrine.

White (Equality): Karol, a Polish hairdresser in Paris, is humiliated. He has become impotent and his wife throws him out on to the streets. He meets a fellow countryman who helps to smuggle him back into Poland. On home ground, Karol tries to be 'more equal' than others and plots revenge on his wife. No longer happy with the small-time hairdressing establishment which he ran with his brother, he tries his hand at making quick money. Through connivance and cunning, he makes himself a fortune, and feigns his own death. When his wife appears at his 'funeral', Karol first discloses himself to her, successfully making love to her, and then plants false clues on account of which she is condemned for his murder. He smuggles himself into the prison, where he can observe her behind the bars. Smiling, she signals to him that her love for him is resurrected and that, now that they are equal, she is ready to marry him again after her release. Karol stares at her, tears running down his cheeks.

Red (Fraternity): Valentine, a young model in Geneva, knocks over a dog with her car. She takes the bitch in and goes in search for her owner, who turns out to be an embittered elderly retired Judge, living alone in neglect in a villa and eavesdropping on the telephone conversations of his neighbours. Initially indignant at what the man is doing, she is nevertheless drawn into a close friendship with him. The Judge begins to confide in Valentine, telling her of the cause of his disappointment (decades ago, when he was a student, a woman betrayed him). Finally, he anonymously denounces himself to the police for his eavesdropping and is condemned. The Judge is mysteriously aware that Valentine is a woman he should have met decades ago, and that there is, unaware to Valentine, a person living near her, Auguste, also a law student, who is the Judge's alter ego, and who will not repeat his deception, but will be happily united with Valentine. In the final scene, the Judge watches on TV the report on a ferry catastrophe near the Belgian coast, the sole survivors of which are the three couples from the *Colours* trilogy: Julie and Olivier, Karol reunited with his wife, Valentine and Auguste.

towards his reintegration, he later literally stages his own funeral, burying a bought Russian corpse; the Judge, this embittered lone observer, excludes himself from social life. Perhaps, *Red* takes this a step further than *Blue* and *White*.

In *Blue*, the sexual act during which Julie's Paulinian epiphany occurs is staged as her own solitary fantasy, a dream-like event not really involving contact with another person (this is the paradigm of a lot of sexual acts in Kieślowski, especially in *Véronique*: as if the woman experiences it alone in a dream).

In *White*, the reconciliation is externalised, staged as a successful 'getting even', which gives rise to the wife's renewed love. However, the couple remains separated, and, although the sign-language of her hands signals that she still loves him and will be ready to marry him again after serving her prison-time (a premonition confirmed by the final scene of *Red*), Karol's tears can also be read as part of a perverse strategy: first, you put your beloved in prison on a false conviction; then, you 'sincerely' pity her. Perhaps, then, *White* is Kieślowski's version of the Hollywood genre baptised by Stanley Cavell, 'comedies of remarriage': only the second marriage is the authentic symbolic act.

Actual reconciliation only occurs in *Red* – significantly, in the guise of the *silent* communication between the heroine and the paternal Judge, the ultimate embodiment of the pacifying figure of the father, the same father to whom Véronique returns at the end of *The Double Life of Véronique*, the same father to whom the daughter returns after the outburst of incestuous passion in *Decalogue 4*. This unique figure of the embittered Judge is, on the one hand, the last allegorical stand-in for Kieślowski himself, the master-puppeteer controlling the destinies of his creatures, and, on the other hand (and, perhaps, more importantly), the stand-in for the impotent Gnostic God who can only observe the corrupted ways of the world, unable to radically change the course of things. (The irony of the fact that he is a *lawyer* should also not escape us: the very personification of the Law is taught the hard lesson of learning the art of love beyond Law.)

The *Colours* trilogy can thus also be read with reference to the Hegelian triad of family, civil society and state: *Blue* accomplishes reconciliation at the intimate family level, in the guise of the immediacy of love; *White* brings about the only reconciliation that can occur in civil society, that of formal equality, of 'getting even'; in *Red*, we reach the highest reconciliation, that of the 'fraternity' of the community itself.

According to standard colour psychology, blue stands for autistic separation, for the coldness of introversion, of the withdrawal-into-self. Indeed, *Blue* is the story of a woman thrown into such a situation.[52] Her traumatic encounter with the Real dissolves symbolic links and exposes her to radical *freedom*. In such a state, one becomes much more susceptible to small 'contingent encounters' which we overlook when we are immersed in symbolic rituals. So, paradoxically, far from isolating us from reality, such a withdrawal from the socio-symbolic network opens us up to it, to its shocks. Only really lonely people are fully sensitive to the smallest signals from their environs; the self-immersed ones are not lonely, they live in their own world, lacking nothing, out of touch with the reality around themselves, like Julie's mother in *Blue* – she is not free, but precisely, as we usually put it, a prisoner of her memories.[53] The mother is thus unfree to the utmost, the opposite of Julie's 'abstract freedom' of a life in the total present, exposed to meaningless everyday contingencies.

In Kieślowski's opus, the precursor of *Blue* is *No End*: although *No End* and *Blue* are two very different films, they both tell the story of a woman who, after the death of her husband, desperately wants to break with her past and erase her memory. In both cases, the (husband's) past haunts her in the guise of his unfulfilled mission (the young dissident asking Urszula to take over his case in *No End*, Olivier asking Julie to finish the husband's composition). Likewise, *The End* leads us to believe that Urszula was the true thriving force behind the husband's professional success, in the same

No End (1984): The ghost of a young lawyer observes the world as it is after the imposition of martial law in Poland and appears to his widow. A worker accused of being an activist with the opposition and whom the dead lawyer was to defend, asks his widow for help; she only realises after her husband's death how much she loved him. After a series of desperate attempts to come to terms with his loss (casual sex with an American visitor who mistakes her for a prostitute, a visit to a hypnotist who tries to erase from her mind the memory of her husband), she finally accepts that there is no way out and commits suicide with the gas oven. In the final shot, they are seen as two ghosts happily walking together.

way that *Blue* hints that Julie was the truly creative spirit, if not the actual author, of her husband's music. In *No End*, the endeavour to erase the past even assumes almost comical proportions, when, in her effort to banish Antek's memory from her consciousness, i.e. to eliminate his spectral presence, Urszula seeks out a hypnotist. The attempt fails, Urszula realises that Antek's presence will haunt her for the rest of her life, so she commits suicide in order to join her husband in eternity. The denouement is thus the opposite of *Blue*: suicide instead of a successful reintegration into the social space – which means that *No End* and *Blue* are to be read together, as yet another example of alternative outcomes.

Is Julie's situation not that of a double loss? She not only loses her husband (and child), but, upon learning that her husband was in love with his mistress, who is pregnant, she loses the loss itself, the idealised image of her husband, as in the Roald Dahl short story filmed by Hitchcock, in which the young wife whose husband fell to his death on a Swiss glacier dedicates her life to his idealised memory; when, twenty years later, a thaw uncovers her husband's frozen body, the wife finds in his wallet the photo of another woman, his true love. There is a correct insight in this double twist of Dahl's story: when a person remains traumatically attached to a past relationship, idealising it, elevating it to a standard which all later relationships fail to meet, one can be absolutely certain that this excessive idealisation is there to obfuscate the fact that there was something terribly wrong with this relationship. The only reliable sign of a truly satisfying relationship is that, after the partner's decease, the survivor *is* ready to move along to a new partner. After her withdrawal, Julie's daily life is constantly threatened, haunted by the (primarily musical) intrusions of the past she wanted to erase. Her struggle against music is her struggle against the past; consequently, the main sign of her coming to terms with the past is that she finishes the deceased husband's composition, reinserting herself in the musical life-frame.

Julie's struggle against the musical past also accounts for the strange sudden black-outs in the middle of some scenes. When music intrudes, the screen blackens, there is a fade-out, as if Julie is undergoing a fading (*aphanisis*), losing consciousness for a couple of seconds. When she gathers herself again and successfully represses the insurgency of the musical past, the lights are turned on again, the previous scene continues. So what is the precise function of these intrusions from the past? Are they *symptoms* (returns of the repressed, of what Julie endeavours to erase) or, rather, *fetishes*? The fetish is effectively a kind of *envers* of the symptom. That is to say, symptom is the exception which disturbs the surface of false appearance, the point at which the repressed 'other scene' erupts, while fetish is the embodiment of the lie which enables us to sustain the unbearable truth. Let us take the case of the death of a beloved person: in the case of a symptom, I 'repress' this death, I try not to think about it, but the repressed trauma returns in the symptom; in the case of a fetish, on the contrary, I 'rationally' fully accept this death, and yet I cling to the fetish, to some feature that embodies for me the disavowal of this death. In this sense, a fetish can play a very constructive role in allowing us to cope with a harsh reality: fetishists are not dreamers lost in their private worlds, they are thorough 'realists', able to accept the way things are, since they have their fetish to which they can cling in order to cancel the full impact of reality. In Nevil Shute's melodramatic World War II novel *Requiem for a WREN*, the heroine survives her lover's death without any visible traumas; she goes on with her life and is even able rationally to talk about the lover's death, because she still has the dog who was the lover's favoured pet. When, some time after, the dog is accidentally run over by a truck, she totally collapses, her entire world disintegrates. In this precise sense, money is for Marx a fetish: I pretend to be a rational, utilitarian subject, well aware how things truly stand, but I embody my disavowed belief in the money-fetish. Sometimes, the line between the two is almost indiscernible: an object can function as a symptom (of a repressed desire) and almost simultaneously as a fetish (embodying the belief which we officially renounce). For example, a reminder of a dead person, a piece of his/her clothing, can function as a fetish (in it, the dead person magically continues to live) and as a symptom (the disturbing detail that brings to mind his/her death). Is this ambiguous tension not homologous to that between the phobic and the fetishist object? The structural role is in both cases the same: if this exceptional element is disturbed, the whole system collapses. Not only does the subject's false universe collapse if s/he is forced to confront the meaning of his or her symptom; the opposite also holds, i.e. the subject's 'rational' acceptance of the way things are dissolved when his or her fetish is taken away from him/her. Is this opposition also not sexed: feminine (hysterical) symptom versus male (perverse) fetish? So, back in *Blue*, are these intrusions of the musical past not in a way *both at the same time*, oscillating between symptom and fetish? They are returns of the repressed, yet they are also fetishistic details in which the dead husband magically survives.

In the middle of the film, during a visit to her late husband's house, Julie sees their old servant crying; when she asks her why, the servant answers, 'Because you are not crying!' This remark, far from being accusatory, demonstrates how the old faithful servant is fully aware of the depth of Julie's despair: her crying does *not* work as 'canned crying' (like the crying of the women hired by the deceased's relatives to mourn publicly on their behalf) – Julie is in such a state of shock and suspension that not only is she unable to cry, but even others cannot *cry for her*. *Blue* is thus not a film about mourning, but about creating the conditions for mourning: it is only in the film's last shot that Julie can *start* the work of mourning. It is like the common experience with small children: once they start to cry, one can be sure that the traumatic impact of the unpleasant shock that they have experienced is over, that they are returning to normal.

Previous to this ability to mourn, Julie finds herself 'between two deaths': dead while still alive. It is Peter Weir's underrated *Fearless* (1993) that provides the best exemplification of this notion: after miraculously surviving the plane crash, the hero (Jeff Bridges) is suspended, exempted from common mortal fate (he no longer fears death, no longer is allergic to strawberries ...). This topic of 'between two deaths' also echoes in Bruce Beresford's *Double Jeopardy* (1999), a structural inversion of Billy Wilder's *noir* classic *Double Indemnity* (1944): a wife (Ashley Judd) is imprisoned for allegedly killing her husband; when, in prison, she by chance discovers that her husband is alive, she learns about so-called 'double jeopardy' – you cannot be tried two times for the same crime, which means that she is now free to kill her husband with impunity. This situation displays the fantasmatic situation of finding oneself in an empty space in which an act becomes possible for which the subject bears no symbolic responsibility. The film repeatedly refers to this space 'between two deaths': when her husband gets hold of her, he locks her in a coffin in a New Orleans cemetery, so that now *she* finds herself in the position of the living dead. Furthermore, as a trap to catch the murderer, the heroine's benevolent protector, the parole officer (Tommy Lee Jones) threatens the husband that they will entrap him in the same way that he did her, making it appear that he killed her, while she will remain free, although officially dead. And, finally, does the appeal of Sebastian Junger's *The Perfect Storm*, the real-life story of the crew of a fishing ship who lost their lives in the storm of '91 south of Newfoundland, not reside in how it focuses on the very moment that precedes death: on the brief, but horrifying period when the crew members, while still alive, are certain that their death is imminent?

In Ivan Reitman's *Dave* (1993), this 'between two deaths' is nicely combined with the motif of the double: an ordinary guy who uncannily resembles the US President (Kevin Kline) is asked by the Secret Service to replace him at a public appearance; when, the same evening, the President suffers a stroke which reduces him to a permanent vegetable state, the manipulative Chief of Staff forces Kline to continue in the role of the President, so that he himself will be able to exert real control. The story then follows the predictable Capraesque line: Kline turns out to be the good common man who, once he discovers that he actually has the power to decide, imposes a series of progressive measures to fight the plight of the homeless and the unemployed; at the film's end, after thwarting the dark plot of the Chief of Staff, he executes his own disappearance (the real President's death is finally proclaimed, while Kline returns to his ordinary life, where the President's estranged wife, whose love he has earned, joins him). This serving as the President is thus located 'between two deaths': between the 'real' President's death (or, rather, its equivalent, total incapacitation) and his symbolic death (the public announcement of his death). In the triad of the 'real' President, his stand-in, and the Presidency as the symbolic *place*, which can be occupied by different actual individuals, the key image is that of the incapacitated 'real' President in a secret room beneath the White House, attached to a life-support machine – so, ultimately, the one who is 'between two deaths' is the 'real' President himself: he is still alive while socially already dead, reduced to a level of pure biological subsistence. And the theoretical conclusion to be drawn from this is that, far from being exceptional, such a constellation is the universal 'norm', whose genesis was narrated by Freud in his myth of the murder of the primordial father: in order for any human being to occupy the place of symbolic power, *there must be somewhere else, hidden beneath, a living corpse*, the corpse of the 'natural' bearer of power.

As we all know, Event Horizon is the region of space that surrounds a Black Hole: it's an invisible (but *real*) threshold – once you cross it, there is no way back, you are sucked into the Black Hole. If we conceive of the Lacanian Thing as the psychic equivalent of the Black Hole, then its Event Horizon is what Lacan, in his reading of *Antigone*, defines as the dimension of *ate*, of the horrifying space between two deaths. When Julie withdraws into the 'abstract freedom' of this space, the key detail is the mouse in a back room of her new apartment in the rue Mouffetard who gives birth to a large litter. The view of this thriving life disgusts her, since it stands for the Real of life in its thriving, humid vitality. Her stance of disgust is the one that, more than fifty years ago, was perfectly rendered by Sartre's early novel *Nausea* – a disgust at the inert presence of life. Nothing renders her subjective stance better at this moment than this aversion of hers, which bears witness to the lack of the fantasmatic frame that would mediate between her subjectivity and the raw Real of the life-substance: life becomes disgusting when the fantasy that mediates our access to it disintegrates, so that we are directly confronted with the Real, and what Julie succeeds in doing at the end of the film is precisely to restitute her fantasy frame.[54]

This restitution of the fantasy frame occurs in the film's final scene, in which the Paulinian *agape* is given its ultimate cinematic expression. While Julie sits in bed after making love, the camera covers four different scenes in one continuous long shot, slowly drifting from one to the other (accompanied by the choral rendition of the lines on love from Corinthians I); these scenes present the persons to whom Julie is intimately related: Antoine, the boy who witnessed the fatal car crash in which her husband and child died; Julie's mother, sitting silent in her room in an old people's home; Lucille, the young stripper friend of Julie, at work on the stage in a night-club; Sandrine, her dead husband's mistress, touching her naked belly in the last phase of pregnancy, bearing the unborn child of her deceased lover. The continuous drift from one set to the other (they are

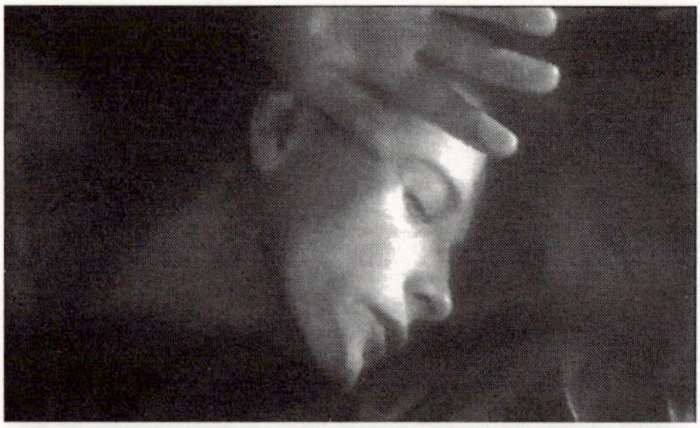

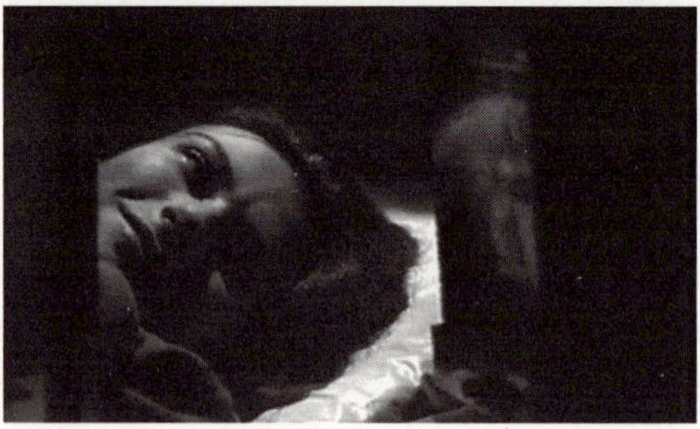

separated only by a blurred dark background across which the camera pans) creates the effect of mysterious synchronicity which somehow recalls the famous 360-degree shot in Hitchcock's *Vertigo*: after Judy is fully transformed into Madeleine, the couple passionately embraces; while the camera makes a full circle around them, the scene darkens, and the background which indicates the locale (Judy's hotel room) changes to the place of Scottie's last embrace of Madeleine (the barn of the San Juan Batista mission), and then again back to the hotel room, as if, in a continuous dream-like space, the camera passes from one to another stage within an indefinite dreamscape in which individual scenes emerge out of darkness.

How, then, are we to read this unique shot from *Blue*? The key to it is provided by the way this shot is related to another unique shot from the beginning of the film, when, after the crash, Julie is in the hospital bed, lying silent in an atavistic state of complete shock. In an extreme close-up, almost the entire frame is filled by her eye, and we see the objects in the hospital room reflected in this eye as derealised, spectral apparitions of partial objects – it seems as if this shot stages Hegel's famous passage about the 'night of the world':

> The human being is this night, this empty nothing, that contains everything in its simplicity – an unending wealth of many representations, images, of which none belongs to him – or which are not present. This night, the interior of nature, that exists here – pure self – in phantasmagorical representations, is night all around it, in which here shoots a bloody head – there another white ghastly apparition, suddenly here before it, and just so disappears. One catches sight of this night when one looks human beings in the eye – into a night that becomes awful.[55]

The parallel with *Vertigo* imposes itself again here: in the (deservedly) famous credits sequence, eerie graphic shapes which seem to announce the 'strange attractors' of chaos theory (developed decades after the film was shot) emerge out of the darkness of a woman's eye. The close-up of the eye in *Blue* stands for the symbolic death of Julie: not her real (biological) death, but the suspension of the links with her symbolic environment, while the final shot stands for the reassertion of life. The interconnection of the two shots is thus clear: they both render a scene which is fantasmatic – in both cases, we see partial objects floating against a dark background of the void (of the eye in the first case, of the screen's unspecified darkness in the second case). The tonality, however, is different: from the reduction of all reality to a spectral reflection in the eye we pass to the ethereal lightness of scenes whose reality (their embeddedness in particular life-situations) is also suspended, but in the direction of a pure synchronicity, of an almost mystical standstill, of a timeless 'now' in which these scenes, torn out of their particular contexts, vibrate in each other.

The two shots thus stage the two opposed aspects of *freedom*, the 'abstract' freedom of pure, self-relating negativity, withdrawal-into-self, cutting the links with reality, and the 'concrete' freedom of the loving acceptance of others, of experiencing oneself as free and finding full realisation in relating to others. To put it in Schelling's terms, the passage from the first to the second shot is the passage from extreme egotistic *contraction* to boundless *expansion*. So when, at the end of this scene, Julie cries (which, until this moment, she was not able to do), her work of mourning can finally begin, she is reconciled with the universe (Kieślowski's statement that he is afraid of real tears is of special significance here: we are dealing with a *fiction*!); her tears are not the tears of sadness and pain, but the tears of *agape*, of a Yes! to life in its mysterious synchronic multitude. If there ever was an attempt to render the experience of epiphany in cinema, this is it. This long panning shot thus directly renders Kieślowski's fundamental notion of the 'solidarity of sinners', of a community held together through the shared experience of guilt and suffering, through the loving acceptance of others in their very imperfection: 'That solidarity can have a Christian meaning, for it leads to the notion of a love that would embrace the whole man, with all his weaknesses, and even his crimes.'[56] Perhaps, Kieślowski's entire artistic development can be condensed in the formula 'from Solidarity to solidarity': from the political engagement epitomised by the 'Solidarnosc' movement to the more comprehensive depoliticised experience of the 'solidarity of sinners'. The crucial film is here *Blind Chance*, in which this very passage takes place: while the film is still full of direct actual political references, they are nonetheless clearly subordinated to the metaphysical-existential vision of the meaningless chance events which determine the outcome of our lives. (However, the point of the film is not simply how our life depends on pure chance: one should also bear in mind how, in all three alternative universes, Witek basically remains the same decent and considerate person who tries not to hurt others.)

There are nonetheless some features of this scene that, although usually overlooked, are crucial for its effect. Firstly, one should not forget the all too obvious fact that the synoptic panning shot which renders the mystery of *agape* occurs while Julie is in the middle of sexual intercourse. We are thus back again at the Lacanian notion that love supplements the inexistence of the sexual relationship. Usually, Freud's alleged 'pansexualism' is taken to mean that 'whatever we are doing and saying, we are ultimately always thinking about *that*' – the reference to the sexual act is the ultimate horizon of meaning.[57] Against this commonplace, one should assert that the Freudian revolution consists in exactly the *opposite* gesture: it was the *pre-modern* ideological universe which 'sexualised' the entire universe, conceiving of the very basic structure of the cosmos as the tension between the masculine and feminine 'principles' (Yin and Yang), the tension which repeats itself at different, ever higher levels (light and darkness, sky and earth), so that reality itself appears as the result of the cosmic 'copulation' of these two principles. What Freud accomplishes here is precisely the radical *desexualisation* of the universe: psychoanalysis draws the ultimate consequences from the modern 'disenchantment' of the universe, the notion of the universe as a meaningless, contingent multitude. The Freudian notion of fantasy points in exactly this direction: the problem is not what we are thinking when we do other, ordinary things, but what we are thinking (fantasising) when we *are* 'doing *that*' – the Lacanian notion that 'there is no sexual relationship' ultimately means that, while we are 'doing *that*', while we are engaged in the sexual act itself, we need some fantasmatic supplement, we *have to think (fantasise) about something else*. We cannot simply fully immerse ourselves into the immediate pleasure of what we are doing – if we do that, the pleasurable tension gets lost. This 'something else' that sustains the act itself is the stuff of fantasy – usually some 'perverse' detail (from some idiosyncratic feature of the lover's body or the peculiarity of the place in which we are doing 'it', to the imagined Gaze observing us).

In the summer of 2000, a disturbing advertising poster was displayed in all large German towns: it depicted a girl in her late teens in a sitting position, holding a TV remote control in her right hand, staring at the spectators with a resigned and, at the same time, provocative gaze; her skirt did not fully cover her slightly spread thighs, so that one could clearly perceive the dark patch between them. This large photo was accompanied by the words '*Kauf mich!*' ('Buy me!'). So what was this poster advertising? On closer inspection, it was clear that it had nothing whatsoever to do with sexuality: it endeavoured to solicit young people to play the stock market and buy shares. The *double entendre* on which its effect relied was that the first impression, according to which we, the spectators, were interpellated to buy the young girl herself (ostensibly for sexual favours), was supplanted by the 'true' message: *she* is the one who is doing the buying, not the one who is for sale. Of course, the efficiency of the poster relied on the initial sexual 'misunderstanding' which, although it was subsequently supplanted, continued to reverberate even when one discerned the 'true' meaning. *This* is sexuality in psychoanalysis: not the ultimate point of reference, but the detour of an initial misunderstanding which continues to reverberate even after we reach the 'true', asexual meaning.

One of the anti-antifeminist prejudices against Lacan concerns his alleged claim that, since desire and Law are two facets of one and same thing, so that the symbolic Law, far from preventing desire, is constitutive of it, only a man – being entirely integrated into the symbolic Law – can fully desire, while a woman is condemned to the hysterical 'desire to desire'. Such a reading misses Lacan's point: desire, at its most radical, *is* a reflexive 'desire to desire'. However, what one is tempted to do is to supplement this thesis with its quasi-symmetrical opposite concerning *fantasy*: only a woman can fully fantasise, while a man is condemned to the ultimately futile 'fantasising about fantasy'. Recall Stanley Kubrick's *Eyes Wide Shut* (1999): it is only Nicole Kidman's fantasy that truly is a fantasy, while Tom Cruise's fantasy is a reflexive fake, a desperate attempt to artificially recreate/reach the fantasy, a fantasising triggered by the traumatic encounter of the Other's fantasy, a desperate attempt to answer the enigma of the Other's fantasy: what was the fantasised scene/encounter that so deeply marked her? What Cruise does on his adventurous night is to go on a kind of window-shopping trip for fantasies: each situation in which he finds himself can be read as a realised fantasy – firstly the fantasy of being the object of the passionate love interest of his patient's daughter; then the fantasy of encountering a kind prostitute who doesn't even want money from him; then the encounter with the weird Serb (?) owner of the mask rental store who is also a pimp for his juvenile daughter; finally, the big orgy in the suburban villa. This accounts for the strangely subdued, statuesque, 'impotent' even, character of the scene of the orgy in which his adventure finds its culmination. What many a critic dismissed as the film's ridiculously aseptic and out-of-date depiction of the orgy works to its advantage, pointing towards the paralysis of the hero's 'capacity to fantasise'. This also accounts for the efficiency of the shot of Nicole Kidman sleeping, with the mask at her side, on her husband's pillow: in this version of 'death and the maiden', she effectively 'steals his dreams', being coupled with his mask, which stands for his fantasmatic spectral double. And, finally, this also fully vindicates the apparently vulgar conclusion of the film, when, after he confesses his nightly adventure to her, i.e. after they are both confronted with the excess of their fantasising, Kidman – upon ascertaining that now they are fully awakened, back into the day, and that, if not forever, at least for a long time, they will stay there, keeping the fantasy at bay – tells him that they must do something as soon as possible. 'What?' he asks, and her answer is: 'Fuck.' End of film, final credits. The nature of the *passage à l'acte* as the false exit, as the way to avoid confronting the horror of the fantasmatic netherworld, was never so abruptly stated in a film: far from providing them with a real-life bodily satisfaction that would render superfluous all empty fantasising, the passage to the act is rather presented as a stopgap, as a desperate preventive measure aimed at keeping at bay the spectral netherworld of fantasies. It is as if her message is: let's fuck as soon as possible *in order to* stifle the thriving fantasies, before they overwhelm us again. Lacan's quip about awakening into reality as an escape from the Real encountered in the dream holds more than anywhere apropos of the sexual act itself: we do not dream about fucking when we are not able to do it – rather, we fuck in order to escape and stifle the excess of the dream that would otherwise overwhelm us.

So, back to *Blue*, what we are getting here, in the final long scene, is fantasy at its purest, i.e. the reconstituted fantasy frame that enables Julie to sustain the impossible/Real of sex: with this panning shot, the circle is in a way closed, we are back at the beginning (after this long shot there is again the close-up of Julie's eye), with the crucial difference that, now, the eye is no longer the index of the 'night of the world', of the subject directly confronting the pre-fantasmatic Imaginary-Real of partial objects, but the locus of the reconstituted fantasy through which the subject regains access to reality. And, last but not least, what this repetition of the close-up of the eye signals is that the relationship between the 'abstract' freedom of absolute self-withdrawal, of the 'night of the world', and the 'concrete' freedom of love, of faith in others, of the acceptance of others, of the mystical communion with them, is not that of a simple choice: the ultimate lesson of the film is not only that, after the traumatic accident reduces Julie to the void of the 'night of the world', she has to traverse the painful road of loving reinsertion into the social universe, but that, in order for us to arrive at this mystical communion of *agape*, *we have first to pass through the zero-point of the 'night of the world'*. It is the accident at the beginning of the film that, by reducing Julie to the void of the pure Gaze, as it were cleans the slate for the emergence of the mystical communion: one must first lose all in order to regain it in the sublime mystical vision of *agape*. The link between sublimation and the death drive is thereby clearly asserted. One is thus tempted to describe the trajectory of *Blue* as the obverse of the psychoanalytic treatment: not as the traversing of fantasy, but as the gradual reconstitution of the fantasy that allows us access to reality.

After the accident and the ensuing loss, Julie is deprived of the fantasy's protective shield, which means that she is *directly confronted with the raw Real* – more precisely, with the *two* Reals. What accounts for Julie's stupor is the very fact that these two Reals are kept apart, that she is unable to mediate between them: the 'inner' Real of her 'psychic reality' (the spectral Real of her traumatic loss, which haunts her in the guise of hallucinatory musical fragments, whose sudden intrusion causes her momentary *aphanisis*, the disintegration of her subjective identity), and the 'external' Real of life in its nauseating cycle of generation and corruption. (We all know the relaxation training advice: in order to forget inner turmoil, focus on the outside, name voices and sounds, empty yourself. *This* is what Julie does – but what she gets from the outside are again messages about her inner trauma.) At the film's end, Julie reconstructs the fantasy frame which allows her to 'tame' this raw Real. The protective shield of this fantasy is neatly rendered by the window-pane through which we see her crying in the film's last shot. *Blue* is thus not a film about the slow process of regaining the ability to confront reality, to immerse oneself in social life, but rather a film about building a protective screen between the subject and the raw Real.

The weak point of *Blue*, the index of what is false about the film, is its musical score: the deceased husband had been commissioned to write a *Concerto for Europe* celebrating the unification of the continent, and this is the piece Julie finishes at the film's end. This hymn, devoid of any ironic distance, which underlies the final synchronic Paulinian vision of love, is composed in the New Age style of Gorecki's third symphony, inclusive of a funny reference to the non-existent seventeenth-century Dutch composer Budenmeyer. What if this apparent lapse in quality signals a structural flaw in the very foundation of Kieślowski's artistic universe? This ridiculous and flat political background of a unified Europe cannot be dismissed as a superficial compromise, of no importance in comparison to the intimate process of trauma and gradual recuperation of the heroine: the post-political notion of a unified Europe defines the only social co-ordinates within which the 'private' drama of the heroine can take place; it creates and sustains the space of such an 'intimate' experience. One is thus tempted to claim that the ideal public of *Blue* is the Brussels European Union *nomenklatura* – it is the ideal film to satisfy the needs of a Brussells bureaucrat who returns home in the evening after a day full of complex negotiations on tariff regulations.[58]

It is *White*, the next instalment of the *Colours* trilogy, the most 'political' of the three films, which seems to counteract this weakness by way of focusing on the plight of post-Communist Europe, East and West. The 'equality' of *White* is meant 'in the ironic sense of "getting even", or revenge':[59] Karol gets even with his wife who dropped him in a most humiliating way, i.e. the film is focused on *having*, on possession. Of course, the topic of possession is implicit already in *Decalogue* 6 (Tomek possesses Magda by observing her): it involves the position of an impotent observer who, precisely, cannot 'possess' the desired woman, and is thus reduced to the jealous Gaze observing the couple, i.e. his rival in contact with the desired object. Apart from *Decalogue 6*, this motif turns up in *Decalogue* 9 (the impotent husband), in *White* (Karol observing his ex-wife having sex with another man, hearing her making love) and in *Red*, in which Auguste observes his mistress with another man. In *White*, however, this topic is directly translated into the terms of the exchange economy of the market: becoming rich, buying, and then 'getting even'. In a stroke of genius, Kieślowski links this commodity possession (in the conditions of a return to capitalism in post-Communist Poland) to sexual possession/impotence.

In each instalment of the *Colours* trilogy, the final shot is that of the hero (Julie, Karol, the Judge) crying; this shot does not stage the re-entrance of the hero(ine) from isolation into contact with others, but, rather, the painful act of gaining the proper distance towards (social) reality after the shock which exposed her/him naked to reality's impact. They are able to cry because it is now *safe* to cry, one is able to relax enough to cry. In Veit Harlan's *Immensee*, the devoted husband to whom his wife remains faithful in spite of her passion for another man starts to cry upon learning that his wife has discovered her love for him; to her question 'Why are you cry-

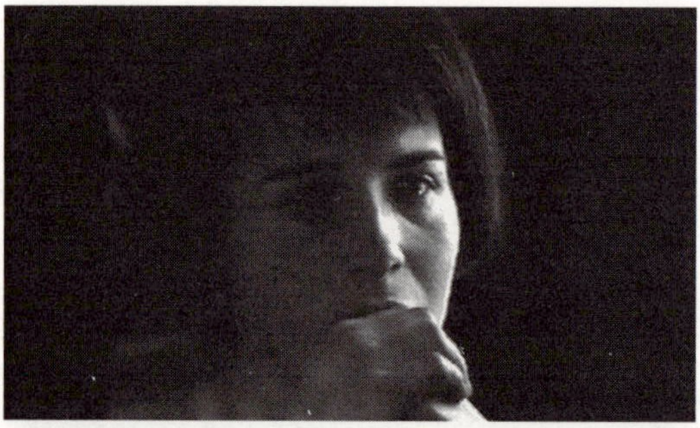

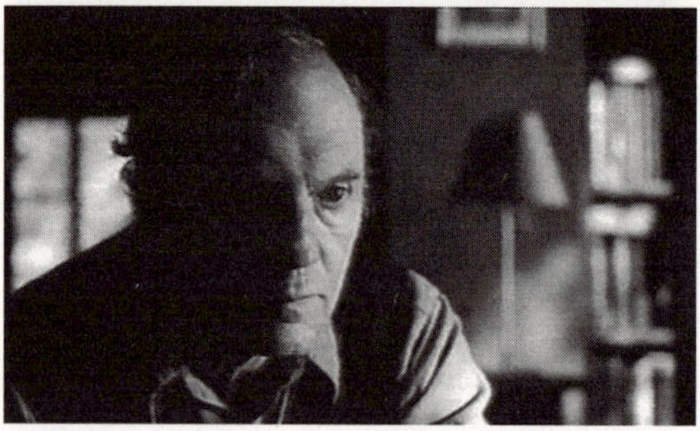

ing?', he answers, 'Happiness also has its tears.' Therein resides the basic lesson of melodramas, and to this narcissistic satisfaction in pain one should oppose the much more uncanny experience of the perverted laughter that can arise in situations of the utmost despair, from the concentration camps to mortal illness: 'Despair also has its laughter.'

It is thus quite appropriate that Kieślowski's opus, whose beginnings are marked with the fright of *real* tears, ends with the outburst of *fictional* tears. These tears are not the tears of breaking the protective wall and letting oneself go, expressing one's spontaneity of feeling, but theatrical, staged tears, the tears of regained distance, 'canned tears' (like the canned laughter of the TV set), or, to quote the ancient Roman poet, *lacrimae rerum*, tears shed in public for the big Other, precisely and even when we cared nothing for (or even hated) the deceased whom we are mourning. The regained distance concerns the gap between enunciation and statement: tears are a statement implying the opposite position of enunciation, one of happiness.

At the very end of *Red*, we have the duality of the framed subject and the fantasmatic interface-image: the Judge, framed by the window, cries,

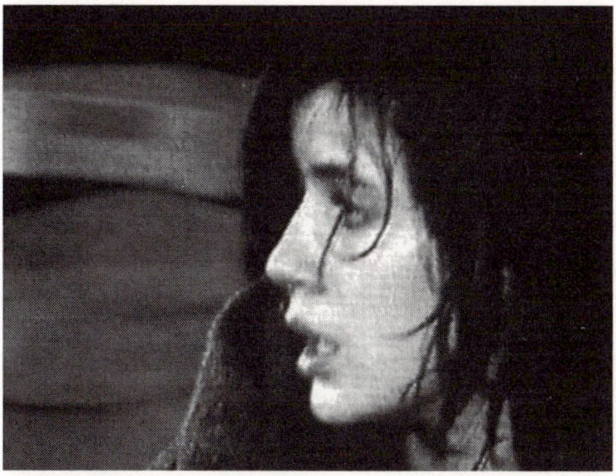

and this shot of him is followed by the very last shot of the film (and of Kieślowski's entire *œuvre*), the frozen profile of Valentine on the TV screen. Through the support of this frozen, spectral image, the Judge is 'renormalised'. Perhaps the mysterious effect of this shot resides in the fact that Valentine *is not dead*: in a standard narrative, such an image, signalling the woman's overwhelming spectral presence, should have followed her death, generating the message that, in her death, she is more powerful than in her life. However, Valentine is turned into a spectre *while she is still alive*. And, perhaps, this strange feature also accounts for the fact that, from this point-of-view shot of Valentine, we do *not* return to the objective shot of the Judge; the point-of-view shot of the frozen profile of Valentine on the TV screen rather persists indefinitely, exploding the frame of the point-of-view shot and thus acquiring a kind of autonomy of the fantasmatic image no longer rooted in a determinate subject's view of it – no longer the image of what someone sees, but rather the paradox of *a point-of-view shot 'in itself', mysteriously surviving also when it is deprived of the support of the subject's look*. This shot is, again, the interface which fills the gap of the failed suture: the very absence of a final suturing of the point-of-view shot of Valentine, i.e., of a supplementary shot that would re-anchor it in a diegetic personality, turns this shot into the properly metaphysical sublime object.

At the end of the long version of *Decalogue* 6 (*A Short Film About Love*), there is an exchange of shots which plays exactly the same role: the circle is closed when Magda enters Tomek's apartment and looks through the binoculars into her own apartment. She sees *herself* there in a previous time

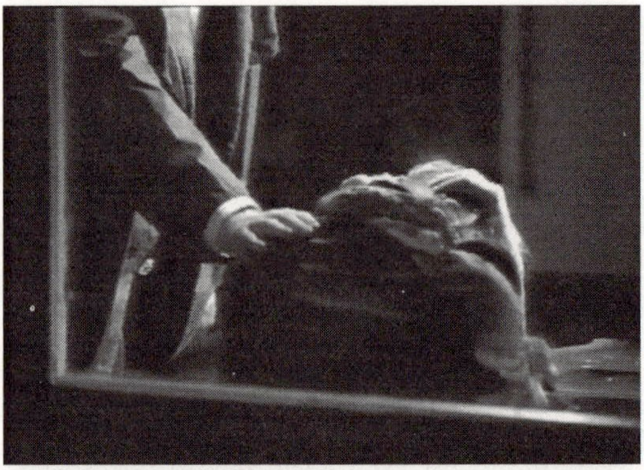

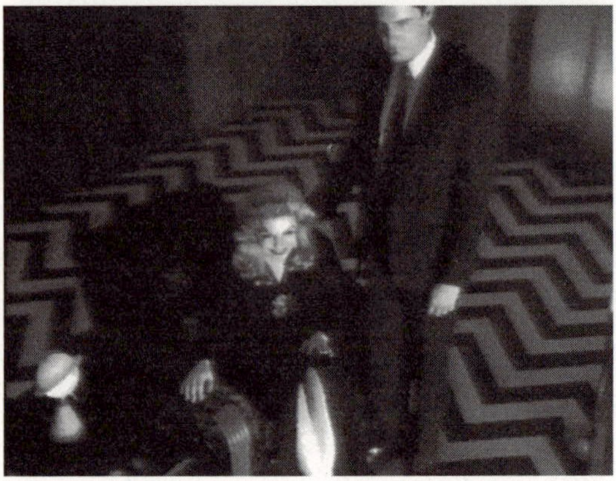

(as Tomek saw her), sitting at her kitchen table, alone and unhappy, spilling the bottle of milk on the table and then crying. Finally, she literally 'sees herself the way she truly is,' in her desperate solitude. However, this shot (still a kind of flashback) then grows into the *imagined* scene of Tomek entering her apartment and comforting her (standing at her side and putting his hand on her shoulder – exactly the same position as that of Agent Dale Cooper in the final dream scene of the redemption of the dead Laura Palmer at the very end of Lynch's *Fire Walk With Me*). This scene is presented in slow motion, derealised, as a kind of wish-fulfilment. (The fantasmatic nature of this last scene is clearly signalled by the fact that, after seeing herself alone crying at the table, Magda *closes her eyes* – only then, with her 'eyes wide shut', to quote Stanley Kubrick, is she able to perceive her fantasised supplement, i.e. Tomek's soothing appearance.) Compare this to the end of the short version of *Decalogue 6*: unable to find

Tomek in his apartment, Magda goes to the post office, where she confronts him with an expectant smile, only to be rebuffed by his cold answer: 'Now I no longer observe you.' According to Kieślowski, it was the actress herself (Grażyna Szapołowska) who suggested the more upbeat ending of the long version; Kieślowski comment's on it was: 'Possibilities are open, in the cinema version. The ending is such that everything is still possible, although we already know that nothing is possible.'[60] Is this not the most concise version of the ultimate paradox of the Kieślowskian multiple universe? And is Kieślowski's ultimate choice (which is a non-choice) not the one between the two versions of *A Short Film About Love* – resignation at the missed encounter which asserts the gap, or the closed loop of fantasy which fills this gap?[61]

Notes

Introduction

1 David Bordwell and Noel Carroll, 'Introduction', in Bordwell and Carroll (eds), *Post-Theory* (Madison: The University of Wisconsin Press, 1996), p. xvi.

2 Stephen Prince, 'Psychoanalytic Film Theory and the Problem of the Missing Spectator', in *Post-Theory*, pp. 71–86.

3 Alan Sokal and Jean Brichmont, *Impostures intellectuelles* (Paris: Odile Jacob, 1997).

4 There is, of course, a homologous temptation at work in the counterpart of Theory, in *poetry*: if Theory can 'regress' into talk 'about' its topic (instead of practising it), poetry can 'regress' into a kind of mental laziness, when, instead of enduring the effort to formulate a thought, we concede defeat by escaping into poetic pseudo-depth, into a bundle of metaphoric descriptions of what is otherwise a commonplace. A parallel to Freud's 'dream-work' might be of some help here: in the same way as the true desire of the dream does not reside in the latent dream-thought, but is articulated in the very work of translating/displacing the dream-thought into the manifest dream-text, a poem's true 'message' is not some meaning 'expressed' in the metaphoric poetic language, but resides in the very 'poetic' displacement of this meaning.

Part One

1 Ben Brewster's *Theatre to Cinema*, co-written with Lea Jacobs (Oxford: Oxford University Press, 1997), is the definitive account of the topic its title refers to.

2 David Bordwell and Noel Carroll (eds), *Post-Theory* (Madison: The University of Wisconsin Press, 1996), pp. 56–7.

3 See Jerrold Levinson, 'Film Music and Narrative Agency', in *Post-Theory*, pp. 248–82.

4 See David Bordwell, 'Convention, Construction, and Cinematic Vision', in *Post-Theory*, pp. 87–107.

5 David Bordwell, *On the History of Film Style* (Cambridge, Mass.: Harvard University Press, 1997), p. 155.

6 Does David Lynch's *Dune* also not practise a kind of return to early, pre-narrative cinema, in the sense that it does not function as a standard cinema version of the novel, rendering its entire narrative line, but rather as a series of *tableaux* of the most memorable scenes from the novel, which presupposes that the viewer knows the novel (like the early silent versions of the great literary masterpieces)?

7 See Chapter 6 of David Bordwell, *On the History of Film Style*.

8 See André Bazin, *Orson Welles: A Critical View* (New York: Harper and Row, 1978), pp. 72–3.

9 V. F. Perkins, *The Magnificent Ambersons* (London: BFI Film Classics, 1999), p. 12.

10 See, again, Bordwell, 'Convention, Construction, and Cinematic Vision'.

11 There is a codified exception to this rule: the rescuers can arrive too late, but this can happen only if we are dealing with a well-known historical battle, in which the very defeat serves the 'higher' purpose of military self-sacrifice (like the battle at Little Big Horn, with the Cavalry arriving just after General Custer and his men were slaughtered).

12 The last point to be noted is that *Intolerance* was not, for Griffith, a way to exculpate himself for the aggressive racist message of *The Birth of a Nation*; quite the contrary: he was smarting from what he considered 'intolerance' on the part of groups that attempted to have *The Birth of a Nation* banned on account of its anti-black thrust. In short, when Griffith complains about 'intolerance', he is much closer to today's fundamentalists decrying the 'politically correct' defence of universal rights of women etc. as 'intolerant' towards their specific way of life, than to today's multiculturalist assertion of differences. This paradoxical fact that the greatest plea for tolerance in the history of cinema was made in a defence against the 'intolerant' attacks on the celebrator of the Ku Klux Klan tells us a lot about the extent to which the signifier 'tolerance' is very much a 'floating' one, to use today's terms.

13 See Jacques Derrida, *Glas* (Paris: Editions Galilée, 1974).

14 Another version of this paradox occurs apropos of globalisation: when one speaks about globalisation, about the immaterial 'Global Village' of the World Wide Web, or the global financial markets in which transactions are accomplished in seconds in cyberspace, etc., one should never forget that this globalisation itself has a *material* existence in (particular) institutions and practices that serve as its support, a more and more important species of what Althusser called 'Ideological State Apparatuses'. There are 'centres' in which the global dimension 'as such' is embodied: Wall Street, the London Stock Exchange and other financial centres; or, in art, cities which organise global 'biennales', from Venice to Kassel.

15 Bordwell, *On the History of Film Style*, pp. 121–2 and 131–2.

16 Ernesto Laclau, *Ideology and Politics in Marxist Theory* (London: Verso, 1975).

17 Francois Regnault, *Conférences d'esthétique lacanienne* (Paris: Agalma, 1997), p. 6.

18 See George Lakoff, *Women, Fire and Dangerous Things: What Categories Reveal About the Mind* (Chicago: University of Chicago Press, 1990).

19 See Steven Pinker, *Words and Rules* (New York: Perseus, 1999).

20 See Jacques-Alain Miller, 'Suture. Elements pour une logique du signifiant', in *Cahiers pour l'analyse* no. 1, 1966, pp. 37–49; English translation 'Suture (Elements of the Logic of the Signifier)', *Screen* vol. 18 no. 4, 1977–8.

21 Jean-Pierre Oudart, 'La Suture', I and II, *Cahiers du Cinéma* nos 211 and 212, April and May 1969.

22 I rely here on the standard exposition in Daniel Dayan, 'The Tutor-Code of Classical Cinema', in Gerald Mast et al. (eds), *Film Theory and Criticism* (Oxford: Oxford University Press, 1992).

23 See Stephen Heath, 'Notes on Suture', *Screen* vol. 18 no. 2, 1977–8; and Kaja Silverman, 'On Suture', in Mast et al. (eds), *Film Theory and Criticism*.

24 See William Rothmann, 'Against the System of the Suture', in Mast et al. (eds), *Film Theory and Criticism*.

25 See Michel Chion, *The Voice in Cinema* (New York: Columbia University Press, 1999), pp. 17–29.

26 See Chapter IX in Jacques Lacan, *The Four Fundamental Concepts of Psycho-Analysis* (New York: Norton, 1979).

27 Jacques Lacan, *The Seminar, Book I: Freud's Papers on Technique* (New York: Norton, 1988), p. 215. I rely here on Miran Bozovic, 'The Man Behind His Own Retina', in Slavoj Žižek (ed.), *Everything You Always Wanted to Know About Lacan (But Were Afraid to Ask Hitchcock)* (London: Verso, 1992).

28 See Chapter III in Raymond Bellour, *The Analysis of Film* (Bloomington: Indiana University Press, 2000).

29 See Annette Insdorf, *Double Lives, Second Chances. The Cinema of Krzysztof Kieślowski* (New York: Miramax Books, 1999), p. 54.

30 It was Gilberto Perez who drew my attention to this scene from Antonioni; see also the discussion of other similar cases in his outstanding *The Material Ghost* (Baltimore: Johns Hopkins University Press, 1998).

31 See Lacan, *The Four Fundamental Concepts of Psycho-Analysis*, p. 63.

32 For a closer analysis of these shots, see Chapter 4 of Slavoj Žižek, *Tarrying with the Negative* (Durham: Duke University Press, 1993).

33 Chion, *The Voice in Cinema*, p. 161.

34 In the final minutes of *Parsifal*, within a single long shot, the camera gradually withdraws from the stage of action to the crane on a sand beach within which the action is revealed to take place, then from the crane to the Bayreuth theatre building, and, finally, from the Bayreuth theatre building to Edith Clever's (Kundry's) hair which is revealed to encompass (the model of) the theatre building. Within one and the same shot, the scene is thus three times reframed and thus resutured.

35 Chion, *The Voice in Cinema*, p. 161.

36 See Kaja Silverman, *The Acoustic Mirror: The Female Voice in Psychoanalysis and Cinema* (Bloomington: Indiana University Press, 1988).

37 *Rembrandt* (1936), *Letter to Three Wives*, *Rebecca* (1940): in these three films, the Fatal Woman is absent, not shown on screen, replaced by a faithful-modest wife – as if her traumatic status is inscribed in the very form of the film, in the guise of her *invisibility* to the camera.

38 See Veit Harlan, *Im Schatten meiner Filme* (Guetersloh: Sigbert Mohn Verlag, 1966), pp. 158–65.

39 See Rudolf G. Binding, 'Der Opfergang', in *Die Geige. Vier Novellen* (Potsdam: Rütten und Löning Verlag, 1925), pp. 127–83.

40 Ibid., p. 183.

41 At this climactic point, when, during the summer holidays, the composer

tries to seduce the heroine, the film almost becomes truly subversive – for a moment, it looks as if she will succumb to his seduction. In this case (and with the remainder of the story unchanged), we would have a truly Lacanian ethical position of fidelity – what counts is not fidelity while the partner is still alive, but the fidelity to the *dead* partner, when there is no external pressure or moral obstacle to rejoining the lover.

42 Another noteworthy moment in the film occurs in a dialogue between the heroine and the composer during his visit to her, after her marriage, during the summer holidays: they are alone on a boat in the middle of a small lake, staring at each other, with the tension rising, their passion threatening to explode, when she says to him: 'Say something. Silence can be dangerous.' In their situation, silence itself is pregnant with ominous potential, making palpable their shared repressed passion. The only way to ease the tension is to distract attention by way of engaging in a superfluous exchange.

43 I owe this point to a conversation with Frank Born, Essen.

44 Chion, *The Voice in Cinema*, p. 37.

45 I owe this example to the late Elizabeth Wright, Cambridge – in the spirit of true friendship, the present book is dedicated to her.

46 See Gilles Deleuze, *The Fold* (Minneapolis: Minnesota University Press, 1993).

47 One can also put it in the terms of the opposition of desire and drive: *the* standard suture procedure follows the logic of desire, while the closure of interface, its condensation of shot and reverse-shot within the same shot, follows the self-affecting logic of drive – as in the example of the lips kissing themselves, in the interface shot-within-a-shot a shot is 'embracing itself.'

48 What is fundamental fantasy? In a French film from the 60s, a secret state agency wants to get a hold on a top scientist in order to make him work for them: through analysing his private papers and belongings, they establish that the scientist is homosexual, although he doesn't admit this to himself. The agency then sets up a young agent to seduce the scientist; the seduction succeeds, but the scientist finds it unbearable to act out his innermost fantasy, so he immediately kills himself.

49 For a more detailed analysis of *The Lost Highway*, see Slavoj Žižek, *The Art of the Ridiculous Sublime* (Seattle: Washington University Press, 2000).

50 This procedure was not limited to horror movies – like the famous scene of

the murder of the little girl in *The Leopard Man* (1943) – but also worked in Westerns: in his last production, *Apache Drums* (1951), Indians lay siege to a group of white people entrapped in a church. We never see the scene from the outside, the action takes place inside. Only occasionally do we catch a glimpse of an Indian through a narrow window, otherwise we only hear the raiders shouting and shooting.

51 See Étienne Balibar, *Écrits pour Althusser* (Paris: La Découverte, 1991).

52 See Phil Powrie, *French Cinema in the 1980s* (Oxford: Clarendon Press, 1997), pp. 50–61.

53 The effect of naming is here even more mysterious; I clearly remember how I reacted when, for the first time, I tasted *zuppa inglese* ('English soup') Italian ice-cream: although I had no idea whatsoever of how 'English soup' should taste, the effect of recognition was instant and spontaneous – I immediately 'knew' that what I was licking tasted like *zuppa inglese*.

54 John Searle, *The Rediscovery of Mind* (Cambridge, Mass.: MIT Press, 1992), p. 228.

55 For a closer reading of these three films, see Part II of Slavoj Žižek, *Looking Awry* (Cambridge, Mass.: MIT Press, 1991).

56 There is a male chauvinist phrase which, along the same lines, renders perfectly the distinction between imaginary semblance and the symbolic redoubled semblance: there are women about whom one says 'She looks like a woman of thirty-five who looks as if she is only twenty-five.' So the point is not that she simply looks only twenty-five: we *do* notice that she is thirty-five, but at the same time she radiates such a freshness that she looks – *not* twenty-five – but someone of thirty-five who *looks like* someone of twenty-five.

57 Is not a similar reflexivity discernible in *American Beauty* (1999)? The film clearly displays its ideological limit when, after the hero (Kevin Spacey) successfully seduces his daughter's friend whom he (mis)perceives as sexually active, and learns to his surprise that she is still a virgin, he does not consummate the act, but withdraws out of respect. Superficially, this may appear to be the gesture of decency: upon establishing that the love-object doesn't fit his fantasy, upon becoming aware of her tender fragility and inexperience, he restrains from intruding. However, this, precisely, is a clear 'sexist' act, since it relies on the opposition virgin/whore, on the notion of

woman as a fragile being, a potential victim of men. As Fredric Jameson remarked (in a private conservation), we have here a clear case of non-contemporaneity: as to its topic (middle-aged father's sexual crisis, etc.), *American Beauty* is effectively a film from the 50s strangely misplaced into the late 90s – the reversal of the 'nostalgia for the present' films which transpose our present into the mythic *noir* universe of the 30s or 40s.

58 See James Harvey, *Romantic Comedy in Hollywood* (New York: Alfred A. Knopf, 1987), pp. 161–6.

59 Therein resides Capra's proto-Fascism: in his rendering of 'ordinary people' as *already* naive and good, not as struggling towards this goal, in the same way the Stalinist films presented the Soviet citizens as *already* good – in a kind of Kantian paralogism, 'goodness' becomes a direct, positive quality, not an elusive feature that only briefly appears in magic moments.

60 See her unpublished paper, 'Antigone, the Guardian of Criminal Being'.

61 *Krzysztof Kieślowski. Textes réunis et présentés par Vincent Amiel* (Paris: Positif, 1997), p. 147.

Part Two

1 Although, from *No End* onwards, the scenarios of all Kieślowski's films were co-written by Krzysztof Piesiewicz, a Catholic lawyer whom Kieślowski met while working on a documentary about the trials against Solidarity members during the martial law period (and a lot of leftist critics tend to blame Piesiewicz for the alleged religious-apolitical turn of Kieślowski's late work), one should insist on the thematic unity of Kieślowski's opus – if there ever was an *auteur*, it is Kieślowski.

2 Danusia Stok (ed.), *Kieślowski on Kieślowski* (London: Faber and Faber, 1993), pp. 54–5.

3 *Kieślowski on Kieślowski*, p. 86.

4 For a detailed analysis of the notion of interpassivity, see Chapter III in Slavoj Žižek, *The Plague of Fantasies* (London: Verso, 1997). In this account of shame in terms of interpassivity, I rely on a conversation with Mladen Dolar.

5 One can also see where Hans Christian Andersen, in his 'The Emperor's New Clothes', got it wrong: far from providing a sigh of relief, the child's statement of the obvious (that there are no clothes, that the emperor is

naked) activates shame and embarrassment in others who until now have been politely playing the game of pretending. From this point on, they can no longer pretend that they do not perceive the emperor's nakedness.

6 On this notion, see Philippe Lacoue-Labarthe, *Musica ficta* (Stanford: Stanford University Press, 1994).

7 Theodor W. Adorno, *Quasi una fantasia* (London: Verso, 1992), p. 243.

8 Along the same lines, melancholy itself is redoubled today: it is no longer primarily a melancholy triggered by the loss of images which Old Testament iconoclasm entails, but a melancholy concerning the loss of the purity of Word itself in today's plague of simulated images. This reversal is discernible even in particular political phenomena: is not *Ostalgie* (the nostalgia for the defunct GDR) also a nostalgia for the Word, since the defeat of the GDR and its integration into the FRG was also a shift from words to (Western consumerist) images?

9 A further point to be made here is that iconoclasm does not necessarily exclude painting: is not abstract painting (in whose invention Jewish artists, from Kandinsky to the American Abstract Expressionists, played a key role) precisely a form of painting which endeavours to respect the prohibition on making images *within the medium of painting itself*?

10 A variation of the same reflexivity is operative when a big star with a well-defined screen persona plays a role: Sharon Stone does not simply play a role – she rather *plays herself (her screen persona) playing that role*.

11 Paul Coates, 'Introduction', in Coates (ed.), *Lucid Dreams: The Films of Krzysztof Kieślowski* (Trowbridge: Flicks Books, 1999), p. 11.

12 What one should also be attentive to here are the *two* meanings of the globalisation of discourse: there is no limit as to what one can say, everything can be publicly confessed, *and* there is nothing *outside* discourse, no objective reality, everything appears as the effect of discursive mechanisms. These two meanings are interdependent: external and internal limits ultimately *coincide*, i.e. the moment one can 'say everything', the moment there is no inherent prohibition to what we can say, the external limit that separates 'words' from 'things' also falls and everything becomes a discourse-effect.

13 Paul Coates, 'Kieślowski and the crisis of the documentary', in Coates (ed.), *Lucid Dreams*, p. 48.

14 Do we not find a similar triad in the life of Vladimir Mayakovsky, *the* poet of the October Revolution? Crucial in his development is the shift from his early poetry to his later ruthless renunciation of poetry as an end in itself, his conscious self-instrumentalisation as the poet of and for the Revolution (as he himself put it, he 'mercilessly stepped on the throat of his Muse'). Since Mayakovsky – in contrast to Kieślowski – could not even imagine 'life' outside the revolutionary mission, for him, the third stage was not the retreat into 'just living', but, logically, his suicide in 1930 – the only calm was the calm of death itself.

15 For a more detailed exploration of this phenomenon, see Slavoj Žižek, *The Art of the Ridiculous Sublime* (Seattle: Washington University Press, 2000).

16 Stephen Jay Gould, 'Time Scales and the Year 2000', in Gould et al., *Conversations About the End of Time* (Harmondsworth: Penguin Books, 2000), p. 41.

17 One should be careful when interpreting such tapestry-narratives in which the multitude of parallel lines interact: the easy-going deployment of rhizomatic plurality is deceptive; its relaxed unfolding conceals an extreme underlying tension which finally explodes in a violent *passage à l'acte*. In Robert Altman's *Short Cuts*, for example, the key person is Jennifer Jason Leigh's husband, a working-class fellow cleaning swimming pools in rich homes, who is unable to tolerate the thoroughly phlegmatic way his wife engages in hardcore phone talk on 'hot lines' (in order to earn additional income) while doing her housework – say, while changing her baby's diapers, she talks into the phone 'Yeah, I feel your hard cock in my mouth, mmhm, how good it tastes!' ... His repressed frustration finally explodes in an act of murderous violence, displaced onto another woman: on a Sunday trip with his friends, he brutally beats to death an innocent passer-by. (Incidentally, Altman's *Nashville* [1975] also culminates in a similar act of a woman's 'irrational' murder – at the film's end, the young silent man from out of town shoots the main country music star at the concert.) Based on this and other similar cases, one is tempted to claim that tapestry-narratives ultimately deploy different variations of the impossibility of the sexual relationship.

18 See Janet Murray, *Hamlet on the Holodeck* (Cambridge, Mass.: MIT Press, 1997), pp. 37–8.

19 Of Alain Masson, in *Krzysztof Kieślowski. Textes réunis et présentés par Vincent Amiel* (Paris: Positif, 1997), p. 57.

20 One of the indications of this reflexive stance is that, at the airport at the end of the film, we see a female airline attendant from the first version carrying documents for the Communist Party delegation which is also travelling abroad, as well as Stefan, a figure from the second version – the flight at the end of the film is thus the same flight Witek was supposed (but failed) to take in the previous two versions.

21 *Lola* is thus unexpectedly similar to the underlying fantasmatic structure of Hitchcock's *Notorious* (1946), in which, also, each of the two main characters has to undergo a fantasmatic death in alternative reality in order for the happy ending to take place (for a closer reading of *Notorious*, see Chapter IV of Slavoj Žižek, *The Plague of Fantasies*).

22 It is nonetheless interesting to know that, in Italy in the autumn of 2000, Tom Tykwer was making *Heaven*, a film based on the scenario co-written by Kieślowski and Piesiewicz, the first part of the planned trilogy *Heaven, Hell, Purgatory* – so there *is* some affinity between the two directors.

23 See Annette Insdorf, *Double Lives, Second Chances. The Cinema of Krzysztof Kieślowski* (New York: Miramax Books, 1999), p.175: Insdorf claims that in this conversation Kieślowski directly referred to Kierkegaard's *Repetition*.

24 Paul Coates, 'The curse of the law: *The Decalogue*', in *Lucid Dreams*, p. 103.

25 Sergio Leone's *Once Upon a Time in America* (1983) goes even further in staging a unique double frame for the flashback; that is to say, at the film's end, it remains thoroughly ambiguous from which point in time the narrative is rendered: is the main part of the film a flashback from the standpoint of old Noodles returning to New York in 1968, thirty-five years after the main events, or is the 'real' anchor of the narrative the opium den, with Noodles desperately sucking the pipe (the very last shot of the film), so that all that takes place 'later' is just Noodles's opium-induced vision, his escape into an alternative future through which he endeavours to wash himself of the guilt of betraying his best friend Max (by fantasising that Max himself in fact betrayed him, masterminding his own faked death and substituting another burned body for himself)?

26 See Gary Zukav, *The Dancing Wu Li Masters. An Overview of the New Physics* (London: Fontana, 1979), pp. 237–8.

27 Vincent Amiel, *Kieślowski* (Paris: Rivages, 1995), pp. 42–4.

28 More precisely, the displacement of this impossibility is triple: Charlotte loves Humbert Humbert who loves Lolita, who loves Quilty, who doesn't love anyone.

29 What, perhaps, accounts for this bleak vision is the fact that la Bute is a practising Mormon – and are Mormons not the closest one can get to the realisation of the archetypal notion, from science-fiction films of the early 50s, of the aliens invading the US? They look like us, act like us, but there is something monstrous, totally alien, about them, some 'human touch' missing in their behaviour. So, perhaps, it is this alien gaze that allows la Bute to perceive our daily sexual interactions in all their hypocrisy and automaton-like meaninglessness.

30 The heroine of O. Henry's 'Memento' is a dancing girl who ends her show by throwing her silk garter into the applauding audience; disgusted by her life in cheap night clubs, she leaves Broadway and moves to a small Long Island town where she again assumes her true name and falls in love with the local priest, who tells her in confidence that, in his past, there was an unfulfilled passionate love – he never actually met the girl in person; all that he has is a memento he keeps in a small box. When alone in his apartment, the girl finds this box, opens it up and, horrified, immediately leaves the town: in the box was one of her own silver garters. It is all too simple to reduce this denouement either to another version of what Stanley Cavell called the 'melodrama of the unknown woman' (the priest didn't even recognise her as the same woman), or to the girl's disappointment (after escaping the big city's filth and taking refuge in a small town, she discovers there the same secret, filthy fantasies). The point is rather that she *doesn't want to be loved for herself*: the fact that the true love of her fiancé was 'the other woman' fits her perfectly – once she learns that she herself is included in that fantasmatic support, she loses the distance that provided her a breathing space. This short-circuit is homologous to Hitchcock's *Vertigo*, only with the reverse effect: in contrast to Judy (who only gradually and out of her love for Scottie concedes to transform herself into Madeleine, her own previous identity), O. Henry's heroine does *not* want to be loved for herself. And one is tempted to add that O. Henry was right: his heroine's desire is much closer to the feminine stance.

31 See Joan Copjec, 'Introduction', in Copjec (ed.), *Shades of Noir* (London: Verso, 1993).

32 In delicate negotiations, the same role is played by the proverbial translator who intentionally 'embellishes' the message to be translated – say, when he translates 'No way, what you're saying is a cheap trick!' as 'The gentleman is saying that, although he basically agrees with you, he thinks some details should be discussed further.'

33 On to these 'formulae of sexuation', see Jacques Lacan, *Encore* (New York: Norton, 1998).

34 This, of course, in no way entails that appearances do not matter. In order to feel the power of appearance, imagine the following mental experiment: let us take a married couple where the wife and husband deeply love each other, and another marriage with no love, in which the wife only clings to the public appearance of the happy family, regularly staging the appropriate social spectacles (visiting relatives, etc.). If the husband decides to leave the wife, the divorce would be much more traumatic for the wife in the *second* case: precisely because there is no love between them, her whole identity clings all the more to the mere appearance of marriage, so that, if this appearance is taken from her, there is *nothing* that remains to her.

35 See Insdorf, *Double Lives, Second Chances*, p. 165.

36 *Kieślowski on Kieślowski*, p. 161.

37 Charles Eidsvik, '*Decalogues* 5 and 6 and the two *Short Films*', in Coates (ed.), *Lucid Dreams*, p. 85.

38 Ibid.

39 See Amiel, *Kieślowski*, pp. 64 and 70.

40 *Alien Resurrection* emphasises the dark, fantasmatic support of 'post-modern' subjectivity. The line is blurred between the human individual and three other forms of life: its clones, the artificially produced androids and the undead alien. So we have four humanoid – 'thinking', intentional-stance – entities. In a series of ironic twists and reversals, clones and androids are depicted as more human than humans themselves: they are the only ones who display a minimum of freedom, i.e. who have a free choice. On the other hand, *Alien Resurrection* clearly links these uncanny phenomena to the mysterious Corporation, which attempts to breed the alien monsters in order to exploit them for its profitable purposes. In a further analysis, one should

emphasise the film's ambiguous sexual background: is Ripley a woman confronted with a phallic monster, or a man (a masculinised/desexualised being) confronting a primordial horrible (M)Other?

41 And the ultimate irony is that this same point holds for Schelling's writing itself, for the very text(s) in which he deployed this pre-ontological dimension of proto-reality, his *Weltalter* fragment: there are three consecutive drafts, as if we have three alternative-reality versions of the same text. See Chapter I of Slavoj Žižek, *The Indivisible Remainder: An Essay on Schelling and Related Matters* (London: Verso, 1996).

42 Another aspect of this life-intensity is the Wellesian life-asserting generosity which has to meet its downfall – recall, in *Wild at Heart*, the figure of Bobby Peru (played by Willem Dafoe). The Wellesian larger-than-life hero and Bobby Peru both give body to the excessive nature of drive (signalled in Welles by his oft-repeated story of the scorpion who bites the frog which is carrying it over water, although it knows this will also mean its own death – it cannot but follow its drive; signalled in Lynch by Peru's assertion of life in the very act of self-annihilation). In both cases, this excess is rendered by a series of features which bear witness to their 'autonomy', their independence from the petty considerations of profit and other narrow human concerns: after firing his closest collaborator and almost-friend, Leland, for writing a bad review of Susan's operatic debut, Kane nonetheless finishes this review in the disparaging tone of Leland; after extorting from Laura Dern her consent to the sexual act, Bobby Peru does not act on it but, in a supreme sovereign gesture, lets her go.

43 On the very first page of John Irving's *A Widow for One Year*, Ruth, an eight-year-old girl, surprises her mother Marion in bed with her young lover Johnnie. The words used by Marion in order to calm her down ('Don't cry, Ruth. It's just me and Johnnie!') are repeated verbatim more than thirty years later, when Johnnie and Marion, reunited after not seeing each other for all this time, visit the surprised Ruth, who again starts crying. This phrase is a kind of *sinthom* that insists and waits to be repeated – the subtitle of *A Widow for One Year* could have been 'the story of how a certain phrase, pronounced by Miss Marion in an embarrassing situation, had to wait for thirty years in order to be repeated in front of the same persons in more respectable circumstances'.

44 See Jean-Claude Milner, *L'oeuvre claire* (Paris: Seuil, 1995).

45 Insofar as love involves this effect of 'always-already' (i.e. it is as if everything were predestined, the entire lives of me and my partner were directed towards the magic moment of our encounter), it is quite justified, within this fantasmatic illusion, to be jealous of the past affairs of my partner, before we even got to know each other – the partner betrayed the destiny that was always-already his or hers.

46 Another purely formal feature which disqualifies the scientific credibility of New Age wisdom is that its acquisition involves a narrative about the overcoming of an Other who cheats (in Redfield's case, no lesser agents than the CIA and the Catholic Church joined forces to prevent the discovery of the message): wisdom is a secret to be uncovered by combatting forces which want to prevent it from being disclosed, a journey of discovery in which the path is as important as the result.

47 For a closer analysis of Tarkovsky, see Slavoj Žižek, 'The Thing From Inner Space', in *Sexuation* (SIC 3), ed. by Renata Salecl, (Durham: Duke University Press, 2000).

48 See Antoine de Vaecque, *Andrei Tarkovski*, (Paris: Cahiers du Cinéma, 1989), pp. 81–114. Among recent English writers, Ruth Rendell did the same for the decaying London suburbs, discerning the poetic potential of abandoned backyards full of debris and half-reclaimed by nature.

49 Christopher Isherwood, *A Single Man* (New York: The Noonday Press, 1964), pp. 90–91.

50 I rely here on Michel Chion, *Le Son* (Paris: Editions Nathan, 1998), p. 191.

Part Three

1 Among the other conjectures about the relationship between the series of Ten Commandments and the instalments of Kieślowski's *Decalogue*, the most convincing is the claim that Kieślowski jumped over the second Commandment which prohibits images (perhaps, in an ironic reflexive nod to the fact that *Decalogue* itself is composed of moving *images*), and split the last Commandment into two: do not covet thy neighbour's wife (*Decalogue* 9) and his material goods ('Do not covet thy neighbour's stamps' in *Decalogue* 10). In this reading (developed in Véronique Campan, *Dix brèves histoires d'image* [Paris: Presses de la Sorbonne Nouvelle, 1993]), *Decalogue*

1 stages the first Commandment, 'Thou shalt have none other Gods but me': the father is punished because he celebrates the false god of science and technology. What gets lost in this reading is the paradoxical 'infinite judgment' which arises if we read *Decalogue* 10 as the staging of the *first* Commandment: the equation of God (the highest Being) with stamps, the arbitrary material object elevated to the dignity of the Thing.

2 What would have been the Hegelian 'infinite judgment' in music? Perhaps the Australian 'queen of yodelling' Mary Schneider comes closest to it in her recent CD *Yodelling the Classics* (Koch Classics, 1999), the unique exercise in the high art of tastelessness, where we get yodelling versions of Rossini's 'Wilhelm Tell' overture, Brahms's 'Hungarian Dances', even Beethoven's 'Minuet'. The tension between form and content is absolute here, so that the listener can only oscillate between laughter and utter disgust.

3 Paul Coates, 'The curse of the law: *The Decalogue*', in Coates (ed.), *Lucid Dreams: The Films of Krzysztof Kieślowski* (Trowbridge: Flicks Books, 1999), p. 105.

4 Kenneth Burke, *Language As Symbolic Action* (Berkeley: University of California Press, 1966), p. 431.

5 Alain Masson, in *Krzysztof Kieślowski. Textes réunis et présentés par Vincent Amiel* (Paris: Positif, 1997), p. 92.

6 However, as if in a counter-movement to this suspension, *Decalogue* 10 ends with fulfilled paternal identification: the two sons are on the way to becoming stamp collectors themselves, thus assuming the paternal mandate, i.e. following the path of their deceased father.

7 One is tempted to mention here Claude Lanzman's *Shoah* – is *Shoah* (1985) not a kind of cinematic equivalent to the superego? The film was in a way *made not to be seen*: its prohibitive length guarantees that most of the spectators (*including* those who praise it) did not and will not ever see it in its entirety, so that they will forever feel guilty for it, and this guilt for not seeing it all clearly serves as the equivalent of our guilt at not being able to see the entire horror of the Holocaust. Furthermore, this extraordinary length is to be read together with the fact that *Shoah* explicitly presents itself as the ultimate, unsurpassed and unsurpassable film about the Holocaust, making us guilty and implicitly accusing us of no less than disrespect for the victims if we enjoy other films about the Holocaust, the ones which stage it

within the frame of standard narrative fiction (recall Lanzman's notorious aggressive disdain for Spielberg's *Schindler's List* [1993] – worthy of the reaction of the Old Testament jealous God). Is it not that Shoah, this paradox of a documentary with the self-imposed limitation of not using any documentary footage, thus enacts all the paradoxes of the iconoclastic prohibition constitutive of Judaism? 'Thou shalt not make to thyself any graven image . . . For I the Lord thy God am a jealous God' – thou shalt not shoot and/or view any narrative fiction or use any documentary footage about the Holocaust, for I, Lanzmann, am a jealous Author. And is this pretension not undermined by the common, but undeniable, fact that a Hollywood product like the 70s TV mini-series *The Holocaust* (with Meryl Streep), although a commercial, melodramatic product (and, perhaps, for that very reason), undoubtedly did more to raise awareness of the Holocaust among different strata of the population, especially in Germany itself, than *Shoah*? (A closer analysis of *Shoah* would have to mention the significant fact that, in spite of the film's extraordinary length, most of the interpreters focus on a couple of scenes, like the interview with the old Poles from the site of the Auschwitz camp who even today flaunt their anti-Semitic attitudes. The underlying premise of this interview, which makes it deeply problematic, is that the causes which brought about the Holocaust are still alive today. But does this premise not court the danger of equalising widespread popular anti-Semitic *ressentiment* with the incomparably more horrifying systematic state-organised Nazi 'final solution'?) It is thus as if the untouchable character of the Holocaust as the ultimate crime is displaced onto Lanzman's film itself: there is an unwritten rule enforced in most of today's academia, at least, that one is not allowed to discuss *Shoah* normally and criticise it – one is only permitted to admire it.

8 Krzysztof Kieślowski and Krzysztof Piesiewicz, *Decalogue. The Ten Commandments* (London: Faber and Faber, 1991), p. 45.

9 Coates, 'The curse of the law', in Coates (ed.), *Lucid Dreams*, p. 100.

10 See Vincent Amiel, *Kieślowski* (Paris: Rivages, 1995), p. 77. Perhaps, there is a parallel with Hitchcock's *Psycho* here, in which also the true trauma is the *second* murder, staged with a cold, God's-view distance.

11 Otto Weininger, *Sex and Character. Authorized translation from the sixth*

German edition (London: William Heinemann; New York: G. P. Putnam and Sons, n.d), p. 249.

12 Jacques Lacan, *The Four Fundamental Concepts of Psycho-Analysis* (New York: Norton, 1979), p. 264.

13 Pascal Pernod, in *Krzysztof Kieślowski. Textes réunis et presentes par Vincent Amiel*, p. 75.

14 Is this not precisely the solution of *Casablanca*? Rick overcomes his covetousness towards Elsa, his neighbour's (Viktor Laszlo's) wife, by deciding for the larger historical cause of the anti-Fascist struggle. At work here, of course, is the intricate logic of the forced choice: it is only if one demonstrates to the beloved woman that one is not slavishly dependent on her, but strong enough to forsake her for the higher cause, that one will retain her love. If one chooses the woman directly, one loses her (respect and love); only if one chooses duty, does one retain whatever remains of her love.

15 For a more detailed reading of *Decalogue* 6, see Slavoj Žižek, 'There Is No Sexual Relationship', in Renata Salecl and Slavoj Žižek (eds), *Gaze and Voice as Love Objects* (SIC 1) (Durham: Duke University Press, 1996).

16 P. T. Anderson's *Magnolia* (1999) is perhaps as close as Hollywood can get to Kieślowski. Everything is there, from the idea of the 'network' of the multitude of parallel narrative lines which interconnect in contingent encounters, generating the effect of uncanny coincidences and leaving the spectator to oscillate between the effect of pure meaningless contingency and the notion that the hand of some hidden fate is running our lives, to the idea of the Judgment Day, of the final catastrophe in which each individual is compelled to settle his/her accounts (instead of
Kieślowski's catastrophes like the ferry sinking at the end of *Red*, or the planned explosion which ruins the entire building in *Decalogue*, *Magnolia* opts for a more bizarre version: in a torrential rainstorm, thousands of frogs start to fall from the sky). There is an even more refined parallel between *Decalogue* and *Magnolia*: in both cases, it seems as if we dwell in a closed universe in which a limited set of people interact. We never get to know the wider social environs, as if we are contained in a closed social space in which an unknown social experiment is staged for an external observer, who can be

simply the spectators (as in the recent *Big Brother* shows), or, ultimately, God Himself.

17 Available in Kieślowski and Piesiewicz, *Decalogue*.

18 It would be interesting to systematise and analyse the subversive potential of this strange genre-unto-itself, the great Hollywood failure, i.e. the expensive blockbuster which flops: Sergio Leone's *Once Upon a Time in America*, Michael Cimino's *Heaven's Gate*, David Lynch's *Dune*, the two Costner films (*Waterworld* [1995] and *The Postman*) – they often contain an unexpected ideologico-critical dimension.

19 See Berel Lang, *Heidegger's Silence* (Ithaca: Cornell University Press, 1996).

20 Quoted in ibid., p. 21.

21 Or is he silent because his wartime experience – as a Resistance fighter falsely suspected of being a Gestapo collaborator – was simply too traumatic to be symbolised?

22 Martin Heidegger, 'Language in the Poem', *On the Way to Language* (New York: Harper & Row, 1982), pp. 170–71 (translation modified).

23 Ibid., p. 191.

24 When Lacan says that 'woman doesn't exist', and explains it in the terms of the missing signifier of a woman, one is almost tempted to read this statement against the background of the well-known eighteenth century anecdote of a wife who, when her husband unexpectedly returns home and surprises her with a lover, calmly retorts: 'No, I am *not* unfaithful to you! Now you can prove your love for me: if you really love me, you will believe my words, not your eyes!' Along the same lines, a Lacanian would answer the naive counter-argument 'But there are women, I see them all around me!' with 'Whom do you believe, your eyes or my words?'

25 Heidegger, 'Language in the Poem', p. 174

26 Ibid., p. 179.

27 English translation: Michel Houellebecq, *Atomised* (London: Heinemann, 2000).

28 Available on CD in ECM: New Series 1656, 1999.

29 This cause need not be in itself 'dignified': in an inversion of Véronique's situation, Anna Moffo, the beautiful soprano famous in the 60s, cut short her career when forced to choose between opera singing and intense promiscuity inclusive of fellatio (her doctors informed her that swallowing

semen would destroy her voice). According to tenacious rumours, Moffo chose fellatio and accepted the ruin of her voice – *se non e vero, e ben trovato*. Due to its excessive 'irrational' character, this anti-cause, anti-Véronique choice *also* is an ethical choice.

30 Alain Masson, in *Krzysztof Kieślowski. Textes reunis et présentés par Vincent Amiel*, p. 108.

31 Significantly, we find among Coelho's admirers Bill Clinton, Jacques Chirac and Boris Yeltsin!

32 Is there not also a homology with Ruth Rendell's *A Dark-Adapted Eye*, with its incestuously close relationship between the two sisters, although, in this novel, Vera, the 'normal' sister, ends up killing the 'fatal' Eden?

33 As Elisabeth Cowie emphasised in '*Film noir* and Women', in Joan Copjec (ed.), *Shades of Noir* (London: Verso, 1993).

34 G. K. Chesterton, 'A Defence of Detective Stories', in H. Haycraft (ed.), *The Art of the Mystery Story* (New York: The Universal Library, 1946), p. 6.

35 See Richard Maltby, ' "A Brief Romantic Interlude": Dick and Jane go to 3½ Seconds of Classic Hollywood Cinema', in David Bordwell and Noel Carroll (eds), *Post-Theory* (Madison: The University of Wisconsin Press, 1996).

36 Do we not have here a reversal similar to that of Marx's development of the commodity form? Firstly, the official story is supplemented by the series of fantasised transgressive readings/equivalents; then enters the reversal to the universal equivalent, i.e. it turns out that all these multiple fantasised alternatives circulate around one, the fundamental fantasy.

37 There is, however, in van Sant's *Psycho*, another added shot which is arguably the single greatest achievement of the film: the shot behind the final credits, which follow the shot that ends Hitchcock's film and goes on for a number of minutes, a continuous crane shot showing what goes on around the car being dragged out of the swamp, the bored policemen around the towing truck, all this accompanied by a soft guitar repeating in an improvised way the main motif of Herrmann's score. This feature supplements the film with the unique touch of the 90s. *This* move from the original *Psycho* stands for post-modernism at its best.

38 Recall also Albert Brooks's comedy *Defending Your Life* (1991): after his premature death in a car accident, the hero finds himself in the divine court (which looks suspiciously like a wealthy tourist resort); everybody's life is

judged there – if you have led a courageous ethical life, you progress to a higher level of being; if you fail the test, then you are condemned to be born again as an ordinary human being. Towards the film's end, the hero fails his test and is sent back to earth; from the bus that drives him to the site from which he will be sent back to earth, he perceives in another bus that is running parallel to his his great love whom he met while undergoing the ordeal. She means to him 'more than life itself', so he jumps from his bus to the adjacent bus to be reunited with her, although this involves great risk and terrible pain. However, at this point, we are shown how the judges have been observing this event through hidden cameras – *this* was the true trial, and he had passed it . . . The actual test is not where we think it is: it is the choice we have to make *after* the apparent trial, when we think we have nothing more to lose or gain, that we undergo the *true* test.

39 'The deed, once accomplished, sinks immediately into the unfathomable depth, thereby acquiring its lasting character. It is the same with the will, which, once posited at the beginning and led into the outside, immediately has to sink into the unconscious. This is the only way the beginning, the beginning that does not cease to be one, the truly eternal beginning, is possible. For here also it holds that the beginning should not know itself. Once done, the deed is eternally done. The decision that is in any way the true beginning should not appear before consciousness, it should not be recalled to mind, since this, precisely, would amount to its recall. He who, apropos of a decision, reserves for himself the right to drag it again to light, will never accomplish the beginning.' (F. W. J. von Schelling, *Ages of the World* [Ann Arbor: The University of Michigan Press, 1997], pp. 181–8.) For a more detailed analysis of this notion of *Ent-Scheidung*, see Chapter 1 of Slavoj Žižek, *The Indivisible Remainder* (London: Verso, 1997).

40 Reprinted in vol. 5 of *Heinrich von Kleist. dtv Gesamtausgabe*, (Munich: dtv, 1969).

41 Immanuel Kant, *Critique of Practical Reason* (New York: Macmillan, 1956), pp. 152–3.

42 I rely here on an unpublished paper by Julia Reinhard Lupton and Kenneth Reinhard, 'The Subject of Religion: Lacan and the Ten Commandments'. For a further elaboration of this topic, see also Slavoj Žižek, *The Fragile Absolute* (London: Verso, 2000).

43 Actually, there are *seven* survivors, and one is tempted to claim that the additional anonymous survivor is no other than the mysterious Christ-like bearded homeless stranger who appears in most of the instalments of the *Decalogue*.

44 See Alicja Helman, 'Women in Kieślowski's late films', in Coates (ed.), *Lucid Dreams*.

45 Ibid., p. 120.

46 Ibid., p. 126.

47 Ibid., p. 127.

48 In spite of its apparent banality, there are (at least) three features which distinguish *Die Legende*: 1) the active role of women in seduction: it is men who are reduced to the 'objects of desiring gaze'; 2) the uncannily dark finale: after the apparent happy ending (Paula reunited with Paul and expecting a child), she walks along a street and steps down into a subway entrance, disappearing in its darkness, while the anonymous narrator's voice informs us that, soon thereafter, she died at childbirth; 3) the scene of the final reconciliation of Paula and Paul is staged as a shared *collective* experience: when Paul wants to break down the door of Paula's apartment, a willing neighbour lends him an axe; Paul then enters the apartment with a dozen of the neighbours, who all approvingly observe the breakdown of Paula's sulking resistance and their passionate embrace. No matter how manipulative such scenes can be in commercial films (recall, also, the final scene at the subway station of *Crocodile Dundee* [1986], and the restroom reconciliation between Cameron Diaz and Julia Roberts in *My Best Friend's Wedding* [1997]), there always remains a minimal utopian emancipatory potential in them.

49 Christa Wolf, *The Quest for Christa T.* (New York: Farrar, Straus & Giroux, 1970), p. 55.

50 This is the reason why *Christa T.* is Wolf's key novel: it abandons the full acceptance of reality of the *Ankunftsroman*, but also avoids the easy way out into the eco-feminist ideology characteristic of Wolf's later work.

51 See Claude Lévi-Strauss, 'The Symbolic Efficiency', in *Structural Anthropology* (New York: Basic Books, 2000).

52 The visual motif of a woman swimming alone in a blue pool at night as the 'objective correlative' of her solitude and proto-psychotic exclusion from

society is also used in Randa Haines's *Children of a Lesser God*, to emphasise the (self-) exclusion of the embittered deaf-mute heroine.

53 Generally, the lonely figures in Kieślowski (the doctor in *Decalogue* 2, the mistress in *Decalogue* 3, the ethics professor and the tailor in *Decalogue* 8) are haunted by some past trauma.

54 Although it is easy to discern the class element in this nausea (Julie leaves it to her lower-class neighbours to take care of the mice, as if the lower classes are somehow closer to the generation and corruption of life), one should not succumb to 'class reductionism' and conceive of this nausea itself as a displaced form of the disgust triggered by the encounter with lower-class individuals, as if this general nausea 'really means' nausea against lower classes: the experience of nausea with regard to life as such is a primordial ontological experience, and its displacement on to the 'lower classes' is ultimately a kind of defensive measure, the way to gain distance towards the object by interpolating 'lower classes' between us and life.

55 G. W. F. Hegel, 'Jenaer Realphilosophie', in *Frühe politische Systeme* (Frankfurt: Ullstein, 1974), p. 204; for a closer reading of this passage, see Chapter 1 of Slavoj Žižek, *The Ticklish Subject* (London: Verso, 1999).

56 Tadeusz Sobolewski, 'Ultimate concerns', in *Lucid Dreams*, p. 28.

57 Insofar as one accepts this notion of sexual relationship as the ultimate reference, one is tempted to rewrite the entire history of modern philosophy in its terms: Descartes: 'I fuck, therefore I am,' i.e. only in the intense sexual activity do I experience the fulness of my being. (Lacan's 'decentring' answer to this would have been: 'I fuck where I am not, and I am not where I fuck,' i.e. it is not me who is fucking, but 'it fucks' in me). Spinoza: within the Absolute as Fuck (*coitus sive natura*), one should distinguish, along the lines of the distinction between *natura naturans* and *natura naturata*, between the active fucking penetration and the object being fucked – there are those who fuck and those who get fucked. Hume introduces here the empiricist doubt: how do we know that fuck as a relationship exists at all? There are just objects whose movements appear co-ordinated. The Kantian answer to this crisis: 'the conditions of possibility of fucking are at the same time the conditions of possibility of the objects [of] fucking'. Fichte then radicalises this Kantian revolution: fucking is a self-positing unconditional activity which divides itself into fucker and the fucked object, i.e. it is fucking itself which

posits its object, the fuckee. Hegel: it is crucial to conceive Fucking not only as Substance (the substantial drive overwhelming us), but also as Subject (as a reflective activity embedded in the context of spiritual meaning). Marx: one should return to real fucking against idealist masturbatory philosophising, i.e., as he literally put it in *The German Ideology*, real, actual life is to philosophy as real sex is to masturbation. Nietzsche: the Will is, at its most radical, the Will to Fuck, which culminates in the Eternal Return of 'I want more', of a fuck going on forever. Heidegger: in the same way as the essence of technology is nothing 'technological', the essence of fucking has nothing to do with fuck as a simple ontic activity; rather, 'the essence of fucking is the fucking of the essence itself', i.e. it is not only we, humans, that fuck up our understanding of essence, it is the essence which is already in itself fucked up (inconsistent, withdrawing itself, erring). And, finally, this insight into how the essence itself is fucked up, brings us to Lacan's 'there is no such thing as a sexual relationship'.

58 In a similar way, the unexpected economico-political background of Wagner's *Tristan* turns out to be a kind of peasants' socialist self-management. That is to say, at the beginning of Act III, when Kurwenal describes to Tristan the socio-political situation in his land during his absence as the errant knight, we get a strange lesson in self-management political economy: Tristan's peasant serfs were running the business so well in his absence that Tristan simply ceded his right over his land to them, rendering them fully autonomous: 'Yours is the house, the court and castle! The people, true to their dear lord, have tended as best they could his house and court that my hero once bequeathed to his serfs and vassals for their own as heritage, when he left all behind to go to a foreign land.' Is, then, this socialist self-management as the ultimate feudal-socialist dream not the only possible economic background for Tristan's wandering around?

59 Annette Insdorf, *Double Lives, Second Chances. The Cinema of Krzysztof Kieślowski* (New York: Miramax Books, 1999), p. 153.

60 Danusia Stok (ed.), *Kieślowski on Kieślowski* (London: Faber and Faber, 1993), p. 170.

61 The mechanism of this loop and choice is somewhat similar to Somerset Maugham's short story 'The Colonel's Lady' (in *Collected Short Stories 2*, Harmondsworth: Penguin Books, 1972) and the change of its original

ending in the omnibus-film version. In the story, an old gentleman learns from the slim volume of poetry published by his wife that she, whom he considered the model silent housewife, had recently had a passionate love affair with a younger man. His best friend, to whom he complains about it in the club, tells him that he can do nothing but pass over it in silence. In the cinema version, he confronts his wife, who explains him that the young lover is really he, the husband himself, the way she remembers him for ever from their love passion in their youth, and they are happily reconciled. See also Maugham's 'The Kite' (*Collected Short Stories 4*, Harmondsworth: Penguin Books, 1972): the husband who left his wife and child because she wasn't able to tolerate his passion for flying kites persists in this attitude even when he is sent to prison – in no way is he ready to renounce his cause on behalf of the family life. The cinema version finds a way out: the wife joins him in kite-flying, learning to share his passion, so they are happily reunited.

List of Illustrations

d director

pr co production company

Index

Note: works of literature are entered under the names of their authors. Illustrations are not included in the index.

DATE DUE		
Aug. 31/09		